Fundamental?

— What is nature

p. 150

Holiness is harder today

sense individual responsibility is greater

p. 3 42
344

Bob
Francoeur

11ᵉ Nov. 19th.

CONTRACEPTION AND HOLINESS

CONTRACEPTION AND HOLINESS

The Catholic Predicament

Introduced by
✠ THOMAS D. ROBERTS S.J.

HERDER AND HERDER

1964
HERDER AND HERDER NEW YORK
232 Madison Avenue, New York 16, N. Y.

Library of Congress Catalog Card Number: 64–8201
© 1964 by Herder and Herder, Incorporated
Printed in the United States of America

Contents

CONTRACEPTION AND HOLINESS

INTRODUCTION

✠ THOMAS D. ROBERTS, S.J.

No issue in recent years has so rent the Catholic community and so awakened the interest of non-Catholics in the
effectiveness of Pope John's up-dating of Catholic thought
as has the question of contraception. I have discussed this
question openly during the past years, and I have never
hesitated to say that the reasons given by Catholic moralists for its condemnation have never been clear to me. It
was, indeed, my public observations to that effect that
elicited from the English bishops their statement that contraception is unchangeably against the law of God. However, if it is the law of God, that is, if it is part of the
natural law, then it would seem that it ought to be tenable
on rational grounds. Thus far I have not been persuaded by
any of the natural-law arguments against contraception.
They do not seem to me to be conclusive, and if I were not
a Catholic, I probably would feel obligated on the grounds
of my own rational examination of the question to accept
the viewpoint of the Lambeth Conference and of the large
body of non-Catholic theologians and philosophers. For it
seems to me, that on the grounds of reason alone, one can
conceive of many cases in which a husband and wife might,

after having examined their consciences, decide that contraception was the only means for preserving the health of one or the other spouse, or for preserving the marriage itself. If that is so, then, with the most spiritual of motives such a husband and wife might be convinced that contraception was necessary for the growth in holiness which is the aim of the sacrament of matrimony. Now it is not apparent how on the basis of reason alone, one could condemn the decision of such a married couple.

Most non-Catholic observers of the present crisis over birth control within the Catholic community have great difficulty understanding the Catholic position precisely because it is based on the natural law; if that position were based on the teaching of the Church only, then submission to it would be understandable as an act of religion. Such non-Catholic observers must wonder what kind of a natural law it is that is discernible only by Roman Catholics, and if that is so, what there is about this kind of law that can properly be called "natural." The non-Catholic is, for what seem to him good reasons, offended by this Catholic assumption of a higher wisdom than the rest of humanity is privy to, and he is even more offended by the implication of Catholic teaching that a marital practice which is approved by most Christian churches should be described by Roman Catholics as "intrinsically immoral and unnatural." Not only are non-Catholics insulted by this position, but by extension so also must be a large portion of the non-Christian world; for "natural law" is not merely something that is known by Catholics and Protestants only; it is known and binding among all peoples everywhere.

Obviously, then, the Catholic view on birth control is

fraught with unexpected consequences that are both political and religious. With regard to the first, one may consider the example of India, whose government in effect must be told by the Church that it is engaged in fostering unnatural and immoral practices among its people by the advocacy of various contraceptive techniques. With regard to the second of these unexpected consequences, I have already referred above to the sentiment of other Christians when they are faced with such Catholic epithets as "immoral" and "unnatural" for actions they believe entirely in accord with their natural and religious duties. Of course, the political or ecumenical consequences of the present Catholic attitude to birth control are of much less importance than are the personal moral agonies it raises and the confusion it causes among all people of good will.

I have never hesitated to say that the reasons thus far supplied by Catholic theologians in condemnation of contraception do not strike me as cogent; it may be that I am less endowed with the powers of logical analysis than are these theologians; if so, this is a deficiency I share with great numbers of other Catholics, Protestants, and non-Christians; and one *does* wonder about a rational faculty that seems to have been ordained for the exclusive use of theological thinkers of a certain persuasion. For this reason I can accept the present teaching only on the basis of the Church's authority. Unfortunately this reliance on ecclesiastical authority is equally ambiguous and contradictory because it is precisely the authority of the Church which maintains that this *is* a question of natural law that can be resolved purely through the powers of reason. As an English Catholic I cannot but recall a similar dilemma of conscience which faced my ancestors when Pope Pius V, after glorifying the secular power as of truly divine origin, went on to depose Queen Elizabeth and to free her subjects from all allegiance to her. It is to be feared that there is a comparable danger on the part of ecclesiastical authorities today of enthroning human reason in theory and of deposing it in practice. Certainly one would think that any argument based on human reason could be sustained on the grounds of reason. It is not here a question of the Church supplying an auxiliary light to that of reason. It is a question, so the non-Catholic would maintain, of reason throwing no light on this subject at all. It is little wonder then that the non-Catholic is tempted to believe that what Catholics call the light of reason, at least with regard to this question, is really the light of faith.

Theology is an ancient science and history is a new one, but neither can afford to neglect the other. And history teaches us that where religious and moral questions are concerned there is little certainty that formulations and solutions from the past will remain permanently immutable. For example, the attitude of any modern theologian to what used to be called usury is completely different from that of his predecessors six hundred years ago; no modern theologian condemns lending money at interest, though the theologians were unanimous in launching such condemnations in the past. Economists have taught us that interest-bearing notes are almost essential to the good of the community, that is, to commerical, industrial and consequently social progress. In like manner contemporary theologians give an entirely different meaning to the word "Church" from the one which was prevalent in the sixteenth century;

even as, one suspects, theologians of the future will give a
different definition to the word "nature" and to the term
"laws of nature" than is now being supplied. A few centuries ago the word "Church" meant to theologians the
Roman Catholic communion, so that the maxim "no salvation out of the Church" virtually precluded all non-
Catholics from being saved; today, the word "Church" is
understood with much more elasticity to include in effect
all theists of good will. Thus the authoritative teaching
four centuries ago concerning salvation outside the Church
can be recognized as radically different from the position
of the bishops of the Second Vatican Council. In like
manner the statements on freedom of conscience which
have been proposed for acceptance by the Second Vatican
Council are patently impossible to reconcile with the statements of Pope Pius IX on this same question only a century ago. There are many other examples of radical changes
in the position taken by authority at various times during
history, all of which would confirm what Cardinal Newman said concerning the proclamation of papal infallibility:
"What one Pope can do another can undo." And it is a
truism of modern Catholic thought that the Church must
live in and be responsive to the various currents of history;
only in that manner can she be faithful to her mission of
incarnating Christ in the real world.

There is no need to catalogue all of these reversals, but
one is particularly relevant to the matter of contraception
because it is still used by Catholic theologians to illustrate
the proper use of the sexual organs. Following Aristotle and
St. Augustine up to about the fourteenth century the Catholic teaching on lying was that any disagreement between

speech and thought was always wrong on the ground that the tongue was given to man only for the expression of truth. St. Augustine used the example of an innocent man fleeing from his assailants and taking refuge in a private home. If the assailants came to this home the master of the house could not say something like: "The man you are seeking is not here, but if you hurry in that direction you will find him." This would be a lie, and rather than commit it both the master of the house and the refugee must be willing to face death. For St. Augustine it is never lawful to tell a lie, and his view was for centuries traditional in Catholic moral theology. Its two sources were Holy Scripture, reputed to condemn lying as absolutely and unreservedly as murder and fornication, and the natural law. The tongue being an organ clearly designed to convey truth, any disaccord between thought and word was a monstrosity in nature, a thing intrinsically evil, and always inexcusable.

The difficulty of reconciling that principle with the rival claims of preserving life, reputation, property, and social relations of every kind caused one of the biggest controversies of all time. In the course of it the division emerged between Catholics pledged to the absolute immorality thesis, and between most Protestants who admitted the "lie of necessity" as moral, moral because the tongue is directed by a human brain and heart to attain the whole purpose of human nature in its full complexity. Truth, on this supposition, being sincerity with discretion. But Catholics had a more difficult job; one may read any history of mental reservation or equivocation, and learn to what depths casuistry can fall under the pressure of the

will to preserve at all costs an abstract principle of natural
law governing every separate movement of the tongue.

The bearing of this example on the question of contraception is evident from its appearance in the recent widely
used theological treatise, *Medical Ethics*, by Charles J.
McFadden O.S.A., Ph.D. (fifth ed. Philadelphia 1961).
The author writes: "Just as the gift of speech has been
given to man for the social purpose of communicating
his thoughts to fellow men, so has the power of reproduction been given to man for the social objective of
procreating the race" (77). And he goes on to observe that
to lie is to use speech "not in a natural, but in an unnatural
manner." But it is apparent, from the fact that not even
this author would require the refugee and his guardian in
the above example to die rather than equivocate, that we
are faced with two different interpretations of the word
"natural." And that with regard to disclosing the truth
what was "unnatural" for St. Augustine is quite "natural"
for Father McFadden and other Catholic theologians of
today.

Now on purely rational grounds it is difficult to determine why one could not apply the same flexible concept
of "natural" to the question of contraception as to that of
lying. Indeed most Catholics agree with non-Catholics on
what is natural in the use of speech, but non-Catholics cannot understand why this same principle cannot be used
with regard to the organ of sex. They would argue that St.
Augustine's narrow definition of what is natural and therefore allowable did not take into account the whole purpose
of nature in endowing man with speech, and that the
present Catholic view on sexuality is still in an "Augustin-

ian" stage because it does not take into account the whole
purpose of nature in giving man the power of sexual union.
The whole purpose of human sexuality is not to produce as
many children as possible; it is to produce as many children
as it is possible to cherish and educate in a family union
where love—and this includes the sexual love of husband
and wife—is the informing principle.

Since the Catholic position is supposed to be a position
universally binding on all men, any such arguments as
those above must be answered entirely on the ground of
what all men have in common, that is on the ground of
reason. To take a concrete example, from a situation which
is only too well known to me, consider the following. An
Indian lives in a mud hut with his wife and several children, too poor to be able to afford any light or recreation
and forced to find the expression of devotion to his wife
as well as the most effective release from the strain of an
impoverished existence in sexual union. The Catholic missionary tells him that it is absolutely wrong for him to em-
ploy any means to avoid children except complete abstinence or the use of the "safe period." On the other hand,
the nurse or doctor at the local clinic tells him that the
government has spent great sums of money on various
rhythm methods only to be convinced that they are not
entirely trustworthy. The doctor or nurse will offer him free
sterilization because another pregnancy will either leave
his six children motherless or, if mother and child survive,
add another stomach to eight already swollen with hunger.
Similarly the Protestant missionary will tell him that nature
did not endow him with sexual organs only for the production of more and more unwanted offspring; the Protestant

missionary will tell him that the function of sex is also, and independently of any reproductive intent, to provide him with a means for expressing his love for his wife. As the lesser misfortune, the missionary will provide him with contraceptives in order that he may not be driven to accept sterilization, abortion, or the death of his wife and the dissolution of his family. Now it is all of this which Catholic theologians condemn as "unnatural and intrinsically immoral." Very few other Christians, or pagans either for that matter, would be able to follow the "reasoning" behind such a condemnation.

What seems to me, therefore, most urgent is that the council should re-examine this entire question of the relation of natural law to contraception. It is necessary that the Church should offer convincing reasons for its position, as Ronald Fletcher, author of the Penguin book on marriage declared, for it is precisely the Church that insists on reason as the basis of its condemnation. As I have already said, it is not of much value to anyone to argue on the grounds of a natural law that only Catholics are able to recognize as natural: a natural law by definition ought to be a law natural to every creature endowed with human nature—what else could the term mean? If it does not mean this, then it is certain that the entire effort of Catholics during recent years to revive the natural-law concept as an antidote to positivism is doomed to failure. It would be preposterous to expect to persuade others of the merits of the natural law concept on grounds that are not logically demonstratable. As M. H. Penty, Secretary of the Newman Association Studies Group, wrote in the *Tablet* for May 16, 1964:

As lawyers see it, the question is: "Is the natural law something that can be established to exist independently of revelation?" It would appear that an affirmative answer is a *sine qua non* if there is to be any hope of gaining acceptance for natural law in this country as a foundation for, and philosophy with which to test, positive law.

At the recent university extension course, the consensus of opinion reached can be expressed by saying that there should be no appeal to natural law principles in circumstances where the only forum capable of having jurisdiction in the event of its contravention is the forum of conscience. If, on the other hand, this should not be so and natural law is only after all an adjunct of moral philosophy, then are we lawyers just wasting our time?

What I plead for, then, is clarification. And the only way this clarification can come about is if all the people directly involved—married couples, psychologists, social workers, doctors, pastors, theologians—should be consulted and allowed to express their opinions freely. Just as war is too important a matter to be left to the generals, this is too important a matter to be left to the theologians. In order to abet this general process of clarification I have drawn up a number of questions that I would like to submit to any other Catholic's correction and that ultimately I would like to see discussed by the Vatican Council. The basic question is: *"Is a non-Catholic presently living under a vow of virginity, and seeking to enter the Catholic Church with the purpose finally of joining a religious order, to be refused admission because his informed conscience cannot accept the condemnation of contraception by natural law?"*

Before broaching the second question I would like to set it in the context of problems facing India, because it is in this country that birth control is a matter of national urgency if poverty and misery are to be alleviated. For

India, the limitation of births is the most pressing of all its needs, and it is almost impossible for someone who has not lived there to really understand both its complexity and its tragic character. A visitor, for instance, to Surat, renowned in the history of the British East India Company, may read on the tombstones in the old cemetery there a story of scores of young husbands and wives who died and were buried with whole families of children. Millions of other burial places particularly throughout the non-western world tell the same story of the devastation caused by plague or famine in a country where the population has far outstripped its material resources. It is a sad paradox that it is largely the devotion and medical skill of Christian missionaries, who have introduced systematic campaigns against contagious diseases, that are largely responsible for the population explosion in these lands.

But the difficulties facing India are even more complicated than in other underdeveloped nations because nowhere is the sexual act more profoundly bound up with religion. So fundamental is the religious belief of husband and wife as "two in one flesh" that the orthodox tradition of Suttee required the widow to burn herself alive on her husband's funeral pyre. However barbaric this custom may seem to western eyes, it was simply an expression of the same instinctive drives which, for example, animated the pagan fertility cults or which are expressed in the Old Testament in the marital bond between God and his chosen people. Because of this religious element, there is no exaggeration in saying that the Indian woman has little to live for if her husband denies her the expression of this unity of flesh and spirit. It is not surprising, then, that although the Indian government has made a broadscale effort to foster the rhythm method, this method has not enjoyed any success, and this both for the religious reasons I have mentioned and also because of widespread illiteracy, barriers to communication, shortage of clinicians, etc. The one method that has proved effective, though not favored by large numbers of the population, is voluntary sterilization, which is offered to those who have three children and whose economic or medical condition would render any additional offspring an almost insupportable burden. For the most part the various Protestant missionaries, as well as non-denominational social workers, have agreed with the Indian government's policy and are helping to carry it out. The question, therefore, that an Indian Catholic might put to the Fathers of the Vatican Council is as follows: "*Is it a mortal sin for me to ask the medical authorities for temporary sterilization if the doctor tells me that another pregnancy will leave my children motherless?*" And this question would have as a corollary: "*How is it wrong for the state to grant me for the good of my family what, according to many Catholic theologians, the state could impose forcibly on me as a punishment if I committed a crime?*"

These questions must be faced by the council if it is to be truly ecumenical. A gathering of 2500 Roman Catholic bishops can be called ecumenical only if it concerns itself with problems that are of universal import, that are of concern not only to the Roman Catholic Church but to all the Christian world, and even to the world which has never known Christianity. The council was envisioned by Pope John as opening the door of Catholicism to those of

other faiths; it is obvious therefore that any issues that tend
to keep the doors closed must be examined; anything that
interferes with a meaningful dialogue among the Churches
and even among the non-Christian religions must be removed. There is no doubt that most non-Catholics today
would view the whole question of contraception as a serious
bulwark against any cordiality among the churches; it is
not just the theoretical difference of opinion, or that Roman Catholics are enjoined to regard their non-Catholic
brothers as engaging in systematic immorality and unnatural practices by the acceptance of birth control; it is also
that as mixed marriages continue to multiply, a greater and
greater tension, and possibly a needless friction, is engen-
dered by this radically sharp difference of outlook concerning
the role of sexuality in marriage. This tension will undoubtedly be exaggerated as more and more mixed marriages are
entered into due to the growing cohesiveness of our present-
day life; the former barriers which kept religious adherents
of differing views apart have now been removed; no longer
do people of one region marry only among their near
neighbors, no longer can regional and local affiliations be
regarded as an important factor in choosing a marriage
partner. There is no doubt that mixed marriages are going
to increase on all levels including intermarriage of people
from other races and religious traditions. How will a Catholic doctrine which derides contraception as intrinsically
immoral be accepted in these changed national and global
circumstances?

One of the teachings that has been reaffirmed by the
Second Vatican Council is that of collegiality, and there is
certainly no area where a true understanding of this teach-

ing is as necessary as in the discernment of the relationship
of contraception and the natural law. In its deepest meaning collegiality is merely an acknowledgement of the unity
of the Church and the unity of the entire human race
which the Church is destined to sanctify. This more profound notion of collegiality would require that the council
should examine every cultural and spiritual tradition, that
it should call upon all the resources of all the specialized
sciences before attempting to determine the relationship of
natural law to contraception. It is above all necessary that
non-western attitudes, customs, and traditions, as well as
those of the rest of the Christian world, should be allowed
to supply evidence in support of their particular notions of
what is "intrinsically unnatural and immoral."

The present book is an important step in this direction,
since it draws upon the resources of bishop, priest, and laity
in a forthright but reverent examination of the entire question from the vantage of theology, philosophy, law, sociology, and biology.

Conscience and Contraception

Stanley E. Kutz, C.S.B.

Public Opinion in the Church

The following words of an eminent theologian offer the best explanation of why an article such as this can be written by a priest of the Catholic Church; they perhaps even explain why it must be written:[1]

Are we really allowing the formation of that public opinion in the Church which Pius XII declared was an unconditional necessity for her? Is it clear to everybody that if such a thing is to be formed, the Church, even in her public life, is going to have to be tolerant and patient in letting individuals speak out, even if the immediate effect is that the chorus of voices is no

[1] Karl Rahner, S.J., *The Christian Commitment*, New York 1963, 111. I should add that although this essay is written by a priest-theologian, it is not the type of theological treatise in which a mass of evidence is brought to bear upon a carefully delineated problem for the purpose of arriving at a conclusion. Rather, it seeks to register the personal convictions of the author with respect to a problem which is of such urgency and complexity that the voices of as many consciences as possible must be heard if it is to be resolved in a manner consonant with Christian responsibility. Finally, it is written in a spirit of service to the Church, and dedicated to those Catholic couples whose burdens I may have increased by my own confusion and lack of clarity about this subject in the past. I hope that they will read these pages and understand.

longer harmonious? Or are we always scared that any difference
of opinion in the life of the Church is automatically a sign of
weakness and damaging "disunity"? Or, again, are we always
afraid of "giving scandal" by letting people see (as the "others"
have known for a long time, anyway) that even the Church does
not have a ready-made store of the best prescriptions for all concrete problems, and that therefore we have to argue with each
other and thus slowly reach agreement, not just *any* agreement
but as good a practical decision as we can manage?

The Church can well be described as a network of gifts.
For before one speaks of Church as society and as institution, one must speak of the Church as the gift of God, the
extension in time and space of God's redeeming love made
visible and available to men in the incarnation, death,
resurrection and glorification of Christ. The salvation accomplished in Christ is communicated to men through the
gift of the indwelling Spirit of adoption, who apportions
his gifts not in some uniform and univocal manner, but in
variety and multiplicity, so that the Church is made up not
simply of many individuals cast in a single mold, but of
many persons, each of whom is called by name to incarnate
in his life in a unique way the redeeming love which all have
received from the same Spirit. The distinction between
Christians is qualitative, rather than numerical. Taken collectively, Christians do not make up simply a multitude,
but a body in which each part must first be *itself* before it
can be of service to the whole organism. "If all were a
single organ, where would the body be?" (1 Cor 12:19).
In the light of modern physiology, we can carry St. Paul's
argument one step further: it is precisely when one type of
cell begins to be multiplied in a purely quantitative fash-

ion, without qualitative distinction (as happens in cancer) that the whole body is in the gravest danger.

Now in this one body of Christ, unified by the one Spirit of love, God "has appointed first apostles, second prophets, third teachers, then workers of miracles, then healers, helpers, administrators, speakers in various kinds of tongues" (1 Cor 12:28). St. Paul felt at home in a Church constructed out of a diversity of gifts. He expected to find spontaneity and variety in the churches, because he knew that the Spirit breathes where he will, and cannot be constrained by the small-minded plans of men. We may even postulate that he would have been surprised to find a church in which all was in a state of quiet, where a very few spoke and none responded, for he believed that "the spirits of prophets are subject to prophets" (1 Cor 14:32). He would have been surprised at a church in which nothing was tested, for he believed that everything must be tested. "Do not quench the Spirit, do not despise prophesying, but test everything; hold fast what is good, abstain from every form of evil" (1 Th 5:19-22).

Paul placed only one condition on the manner in which the gifts of the Spirit were to be manifested: "That all things be done decently and in order" (1 Cor 14:40), "for God is not a God of confusion, but of peace" (*ibid.* v. 35). And the one test by which the various manifestations of the Spirit were to be judged was simply this: do they contribute to the "edification"—i.e. to the building up— of the whole body? Now this is a very delicate point. We are always tempted to reject out of hand that which is new or unusual, that which challenges traditional convictions or customs. We tend to look no further than the immediately disquieting effect which a new attitude may have on customary ways of thinking and acting, and to assume that this new approach is therefore destructive of the unity of the Church. But is this not to take too narrow a view of life? Very often that which is initially disturbing and strange may ultimately have a very salutary effect. Unity is never something given, whole and complete; rather, it is always something being sought, something being realized anew. And if the unity of the Church is to have always that dynamic, expanding quality which is synonymous with life, then it will only be because there is room also for diversity, for the free expression of the manifestations of the Spirit of life.

Unity must never be confused with that type of acquiescent uniformity which is satisfied so long as all the voices are chorusing the same refrain, even though there be no unity of conviction. Such uniformity may satisfy the needs of a totalitarian state, but it has nothing to do with the unity of the children of God, whose submission is meaningless unless it is *free*. The canticle of the sons of God must be a harmony of many parts, not a loud and brassy monotone. It must be of such a range that even discordant voices are gathered together into a transcendent theme. If such a harmony is to be realized, we must have the patience and humility to wait and see whether the discordant notes can be reconciled into a new theme. We cannot afford to reject them out of hand, simply because we do not at first see where they might fit. If we were to judge too hastily, we might find ourselves rejecting the voice of the Holy Spirit from the very choir which claims to be singing his praises. We can always afford to take seriously the admonition of Gamaliel to the Sanhedrin.

Men of Israel, take care what you do with these men . . . for if this plan or this undertaking is of men, it will fail; but if it is of God, you will not be able to overthrow them. You might even be found opposing God!" (Acts 5:35-39).

This is surely the attitude which corresponds to St. Paul's advice to the young churches: do not snuff out the Spirit, but test everything, holding fast to that which is good— i.e. to that which proves itself of value for the building up of the Church.

Now it is of Catholic faith that it pertains to the office of the bishops, in communion with the pope who is the sign of their collegial unity, to make the final determination of what is and what is not an authentic manifestation of the Spirit, of what does or does not contribute to the building up of that community of faith and love which is Christ's body. What is often not sufficiently stressed, however, is the manner in which the bishops, with the pope, arrive at these judgments. There is a temptation to think of them as *sources* of Catholic faith and practice, as persons who no longer have to listen for the voice of the Spirit in the Church. In fact, of course, the very opposite is true. It is the Father who, through the communication of the Spirit, draws all men to Christ, who is the only *source* of faith. And it is for this reason that bishops, even more than other Christians, must first of all be listeners. It is they who have received a special charism, and with it the corresponding obligation, to discern the voice of the Spirit of the Church—the Spirit who is given to all of Christ's faithful,

Role of Bishops

who breathes when and where and how he will, and who wishes to lead Christians to an ever-deeper understanding of the meaning for them of God's love in Christ. The teaching authority of bishops should always be seen first as a gift of God for the service of the people of God, and only thereafter as a right pertaining to an office. Let it be noted that this way of considering the Church gives rise to no title by which Christians might justify disrespect or disobedience to their bishops. Rather, it says something about the obligation of bishops to listen everywhere, attentively, patiently, and with humility (recognizing that no one is exempt from the dangers of self-delusion) to the voice of the Holy Spirit, who is the only final source and guarantor of the unity of the Church.

What we have said of the teaching office of bishops (i.e. that it is primarily a gift and a service, and only derivatively a "right") must also be said of the "witnessing office" of all Christians. Those who begin by ostentatiously "claiming their rights" succeed only in provoking others to claim contrary rights: and that which should have been a dialogue of love issuing in understanding becomes a strident chorus of conflicting monologues in which brute force is the victor (even "moral" force can be brutal), and truth is the loser. This is to act "after the manner of the Gentiles," forgetting that with us it must be otherwise (see Mk 10:35ff). The Christian who has learned how to listen to the voice of the Spirit in his heart, who has learned that what is noble and generous and expansive in himself is not of his own doing, but is the gift of the Spirit of love who is given to him: such a Christian will know how to witness to his experience of God's love without threatening or reviling those who disagree with him. He will not be anxious about what he ought to say, he will not need to store up angry words in his heart, for the Holy Spirit will teach him, at the right time, what he must say (see Lk 12:11-12). And such witness will be received in the spirit in which it is offered—as a gift and a service, not as a threat.

The Church, so long as she is a pilgrim awaiting the final coming of her Lord, will never attain to that state of peace in which the relations of all her various members to one another are governed by perfect love. Just as truly as the gift of the Spirit is diffused in the hearts of all, so also is the malice of selfish and arbitrary whim. There will always be members of the flock who will noisily claim their "rights," forgetting that they have nothing to boast of except the Lord (see 2 Cor 10:17); and there will always be shepherds who, with a myopic view of what edifies the Church, will be more inclined to tyrannize over those in their charge than to become true models to their flocks (see 1 Pt 5:3). These failures of individuals will not be decisive, so long as we recognize them as failures. The matter would only become tragic if, in our search for the easy, one-answer solution, we were to deny the very right to existence of one of the poles of this dynamic tension: if the flock were to imagine it had no need of shepherds who exercise true authority, or if the shepherds were to imagine that the flock had no further purpose for existing than to be ruled over.

The Church has not entirely escaped the effects of that functionalization which has tended to depersonalize so much of contemporary existence. There is the temptation to define ourselves and others in terms of our functions

within a given structure, rather than in terms of the persons
that we are. This has led to a way of thinking which would
see some members exclusively as teachers in the Church,
and the rest as listeners or learners. What must be said,
without equivocation, is that every Christian (and those in
authority all the more so precisely because they are in
authority) is first of all a listener, one who is open to the
voice of the Spirit wherever it may be heard; and every
Christian is a teacher, a witness to the meaning of the love
which has been poured out in his heart. The fact that it is
given to bishops to discern and to judge with authority
among the manifestations of the Spirit will not lead other
Christians to imagine themselves absolved from the obligation of witnessing to their convictions; much less will it
lead bishops to think it dangerous for that witness to be
heard. For Christians believe that it is the *truth* that will
make them free (see Jn 8:32), and they have no fear of
the outcome of the search for truth because they know that
their Redeemer lives (see Job 19:25).

So sacred is the Christian's respect for the truth of the
faith that he may be required to witness to it in embarrassing and painful circumstances—namely by public protest
against his fellow Christians and even against prelates.
When St. Thomas treats of the question of fraternal correction, he points out that there may be instances where a
subject would be obliged, in humility and reverence, to re-
buke an ecclesiastical superior. Because of the respect due
to the office of the superior, this will always be done pri-
vately, except in the case where there is danger to the
faith itself. In that instance, says St. Thomas, prelates
should be corrected even publicly, as was the case when

Paul confronted Peter at Antioch.[2] One does not expect that such a situation will arise so long as subjects have confidence in the guidance which the Holy Spirit exercises in and through their pastors, and pastors are attentive to the voice of the Spirit as it may be manifested in the sincere convictions of those who are in their charge.

The Role of the Theologian

Among the multitude of voices which, throughout the whole Church, bear joyous witness to the meaning of the love which God has shown for man in Christ, the voice of the theologian surely enjoys a special status. Like every other Christian, his first testimony is one of gratitude for the redemption which he has received. But beyond that, he has devoted his life in a special way to the effort of discerning and interpreting for others the direction in which the Holy Spirit is leading the whole of the convenanted people. For the Church is historical not only inasmuch as she takes her origin in an historical event, but also inasmuch as she is a pilgrim Church, *still on the way* to final consummation with her Lord. As such, she is subject to the laws of growth and organic development; and like any conscious organism, she must seek to understand the meaning of her past so that she may play a relevant and vital role in the present, and prepare at least the next step into the future. It pertains to the theologian to serve the Church in this task of discovering and elaborating her true nature. In fulfilling this role, he is not so much one who hands on "timeless truths," nor one who "proves" something about

[2] ST II-II, 34, 4, ad 2.

God and man; rather, realizing with what difficulty and after how much conflict of opposing convictions man actually comes to a limited insight into the truth, he seeks to discover the point at which many probabilities (no one of which is probative if taken singly) converge in such a way as to elicit an assent that is in keeping with the mystery of man's freedom. From this vantage point, the theologian is in a position to interpret to his fellow Christians the possible significance of the present moment of grace, and to indicate the options which open out into the future.

To accomplish so delicate a task, it is necessary that the theologian be a man who possesses the courage of his beliefs, and that he be as free as is possible in our human condition from external constraint. The confidence which the Christian people place in him would be betrayed if it became apparent that he was afraid to speak the truth as he has been given to see it in the light of his faith and study, or if he were seen to be merely a functionary who repeats without conviction someone else's understanding of the truth. And, as Daniel Callahan has pointed out, the hierarchy must, precisely in order to ensure the authenticity of its own teaching, allow freedom of expression to the theologian. "Otherwise, it could never have confidence that he was not simply fawning on authority or that a purported theological consensus was the real one." [3] We do not trust a man who makes a point of saying only the things we expect him to say.

All of the preceding has been preamble to the following section on the meaning of conscience. And that in turn will

[3] "Authority and the Theologian," *The Commonweal*, June 5, 1964, 322.

be preamble to our main concern: conscience and contraception. This development should not surprise the reader, for what is at issue here is much more than an isolated ethical problem. To quote again from the essay of Callahan cited above: "The birth control question is, above all, a test case of the Church's understanding of itself and especially of its understanding of the development of doctrine." We concur in this judgment, and it is for this reason that it is necessary to treat of many other issues before coming to the main question.

The Meaning of Conscience

It may be safely asserted that conscience is, if not a new word in the vocabulary of Catholics, at least a new dimension in their existential wrestling with ethical problems. As Bishop John J. Wright has pointed out: "Conscience is one of those words which everyone uses readily enough and which most think of as not only basic but also very simple, though an invitation to define it usually reveals confusion and embarrassment." [4] And it seems that no one is exempt from the danger of this confusion. In the second session of Vatican II, when Bishop de Smedt presented the schema on religious liberty (which is but one aspect of the problem of conscience), he thought it not superfluous to warn even the council Fathers against four possible misinterpretations of this very carefully prepared document.[5]

To speak of conscience is to speak of that mysterious

[4] "Reflections on Authority and Conscience," *The Critic*, April/May 1964.
[5] *Council Speeches of Vatican II*, New York 1964, 237-253.

reality which every person experiences at the innermost core of his self-awareness, at the center of his being where he is most himself. Pope Pius XII bore eloquent witness to the profundity and inviolability of this mystery in a radio broadcast on March 23, 1952. He spoke of conscience as "the innermost and most secret nucleus in man. It is there that he takes refuge with his spiritual faculties in absolute solitude: alone with himself, or rather alone with God—whose voice sounds in conscience—and with himself. . . . [Conscience] is a sanctuary on the threshold of which all must halt, even, in the case of a child, his father and mother . . ." [6]

The dimensions of conscience are thus proportioned to the dimensions of man himself. Respecting the complexity and sacred character of this mystery, we do not expect in these few pages to solve or prove anything about conscience, but only to reflect on some of its manifold aspects. In attempting to articulate our own insights, we hope to stimulate others to make their contribution to the dialogue on this subject.

We think it is futile to begin speaking of conscience unless we possess a fundamental intuition of what it means to exist as a *person*. We use the word "intuition" advisedly, because it seems to us that we are here in the realm of "total knowing" where the truth must impress itself on the mind in a direct encounter with concrete reality (with the "other"), rather than be deduced from some prior principle.

The problem is complicated by the fact that so much of our understanding of the meaning of personhood is still in

[6] AAS 44, 1952, 270.

an emerging state. Whereas in the past man was studied primarily as part of a whole (the universe, the Church, the state, the family, etc.), with a consequent emphasis on what is common and general to all men, today the primary emphasis falls on man as we actually encounter him in the concrete, as a unique person, an individual, a subject of rights, a source of creative initiative and energy; in short, an image of that God who is pre-eminently person, pre-eminently creator, pre-eminently free. Instead of under-standing himself as deriving his meaning simply from the fact that he is a single unit in a larger structure, man now sees himself as responsible for the shape and direction of the evolving structures and patterns of his existence. Need-less to say, this does not imply a denial of his social nature, or of the need for structure and pattern in his life; it rather means that community will attain its fully human signifi-cance only when it is a community of *free persons*.

I believe that these reflections help us to understand the insights to which Pope John gave expression in *Pacem in terris*. What is original in this encyclical is not that it in-troduces some entirely new value or concept, but rather that it orders and relates traditional values and concepts in a new way. Whereas it had been customary for Catholic theology to speak first of nature, and only derivatively of person, first of duties and then of rights, Pope John chooses to invert this order and to treat of persons and rights as the more immediate and evident realities. He speaks of natu-ral law as do his predecessors, but it is a natural law that reveals itself to the conscience of a free person; it is an order that unfolds itself in the course of existential en-counter with persons and events.

This is an approach to order in human affairs which is quite different from the one which (rightly or wrongly) is commonly attributed to Catholics—i.e. an order that is deduced with inexorable logic from a few abstract principles about the nature of man. The universal acclaim with which *Pacem in terris* was received by men of the most divergent convictions is incomprehensible unless we appreciate how profoundly Pope John responded to the emerging sense of personhood which characterizes the best philosophical and theological thought of our day.

Creative Responsibility

For many people conscience seems to be simply a reminder of laws to be kept, or worse, some kind of casuistical gymnastic whereby one minimalizes his obligations when the demands of law are not clear. It should be apparent that these misconceptions have nothing in common with the doctrine of conscience implied in *Pacem in terris*, where the role of conscience is as positive and as comprehensive as the consequences of existence as an "image of God." The term "creative responsibility" perhaps best sums up the implications of Pope John's thought.

Now when we speak of responsibility we must not think of it in narrowly moralistic terms, as though responsibility meant no more than imputability. "Responsibility" is derived from "response"; it implies the process of a subject opening himself to reality, perceiving reality as offering itself to him, and responding in gratitude and joy to the mystery of existence of which he finds himself a beneficiary. To describe this response as creative is equivalent to saying that it is personal—i.e. that it proceeds from a subject who exists once for all, who will never be repeated, who is called by a name that is his and his alone. He is called to actualize the implications of his unique existence, in a certain sense to create his own personhood, by making a response to reality which no one else can make for him. If he does not make it, it will never be made, and all of reality will be poorer because a center of freedom, a source of creative love, a person who might have been, has failed to flower. In this sense, every person is a creator; he fashions meaning and beauty where, but for the response by which he affirms and augments his personhood, there would be only silence and void. And it is conscience which sums up and gives urgency to this invitation to creative responsibility.

The dynamics of conscience can thus be described in terms of a dialogue between man's spirit and the whole of reality which somehow presents itself to him as a "thou," as a partner who helps to reveal to man the depths of his own creative potential and the expanding meaning of his own existence. And for the Christian, this becomes a fully personal dialogue between his own spirit and the Holy Spirit, the Spirit of adoption, who is poured forth in his heart to interpret for him the meaning and the personal consequences of the love which the Father has shown for him in the death and resurrection of the Son.

It will be evident from the foregoing that to follow conscience is in no sense the same as following one's arbitrary and self-seeking whims. Our God is not a God of confusion, but of peace, and his Spirit is poured out upon all flesh for the very purpose of leading us out of the isolation and al-

ienation of self-gratification into that community of love
which is the Church. By the very excess of God's love
which is implied in the gift of his own Spirit, we are im-
pelled toward unity and communion, the very opposite of
arbitrary whim. Thus, when one asserts the doctrine of
liberty of conscience, one asserts human autonomy from
external coercion, but not from the internal consequences
of the love of which a person knows himself to be the
recipient. In this context, we can do no better than to
quote from Bishop de Smedt (*loc. cit.*):

> The human person endowed with conscious and free activity,
> since he can fulfill the will of God only as the divine law is per-
> ceived through the dictate of conscience, can obtain his ultimate
> end only by prudently forming the judgment of conscience and
> by faithfully carrying out its dictate.
> From the nature of things, in forming this judgment, whereby
> man tries freely to conform to the absolute demands of God's
> rights, neither any other man nor any human institution can
> take the place of the free judgment of man's conscience. There-
> fore, the man who sincerely obeys his own conscience intends to
> obey God himself, although at times confusedly and unknow-
> ingly, and is to be considered worthy of esteem.
> . . . The greatest injury is to prevent a man from worshiping
> God and obeying God according to the dictates of his own con-
> science.

Conscience and the Magisterium

It seems to us that much conflict between conscience
and the authoritative teaching of the Church arises from a
misconception of the nature of that teaching. Many people
speak as though this conflict were practically inevitable,
for the voice of conscience arises in the innermost spirit of

I disagree if he thinks this is not the case

the believing Christian, whereas the official teaching is presumed to originate with "them"—i.e. popes, bishops, theologians. "They" are rarely thought of as believers, and it is presumed that they obtain the content of their teaching from some esoteric source or other—in any case, not from the witness of the conscience of simple, down-to-earth people like "us." (This misconception is of course particularly pernicious when it is applied to the problems of conjugal morality, where "they," by definition, have no direct experience.)

Such a view completely misconstrues the teaching function of the Church. The magisterium does not produce truth; rather, it delineates the degree of certainty which a particular expression of the truth has attained in the consciousness of God's people. The Church teaches infallibly what the Church already believes. And this belief is the gift of the Holy Spirit, who recalls to the minds of all the faithful the things that Christ taught and guides them into all truth (see Jn 14:26). This action of the Spirit on the conscience of the faithful, guiding them into an ever more profound understanding of the implications for them of the death and resurrection of Jesus, finds its fullest expression in the celebration of the liturgy, where all listen to the Word, proclaimed with authority, and respond to it in a manner that is at once personal and communal (see *The Constitution on the Sacred Liturgy*, §33). We may well hope that a revitalized liturgical practice will diminish the area of conflict between conscience (still conceived too individualistically) and authority (still conceived too impersonally).

God's people or the theolog[y]

When the teachings of the Church are thus understood

True but is this reality as it is?

as authoritative declarations of those insights into the divine mysteries which the Spirit has already produced in the Church through his action on the consciences of all believers, and when it is realized that these declarations are always capable of being more adequately formulated in proportion as the Spirit leads the covenanted people to a new and deeper understanding, then the whole problem of conscience v. authority will be seen in a different perspective. Conscience will realize that it needs the guidance of authoritative teaching, for without it there could be no growth or progress in understanding, but only an endless agonizing over first questions. And authority will discover that it can only be true to itself as Christian authority by a scrupulous respect for the existence and freedom of conscience. If God governs his free creatures in a way that always respects their freedom (and surely religion has no meaning in any other context), then those who govern in God's name—even when they are absolutely certain that they act with his authority—can do no less. Dostoyevsky's Grand Inquisitor thought that he was able to "correct" the work of Christ by replacing man's free response to the Gospel with a sterile conformity to a system of ecclesiastical rules. We may hope that he speaks for no contemporary Churchman.

If our reflections on the nature of conscience are valid, it will mean that we have to make room in our understanding of Christian existence for an element of tension, and even of uncertainty. The individual conscience may often find itself one step ahead of (or one step behind) that conscious articulation of the faith which the whole Church has attained at a particular moment in her history. The tension which results does not exist for its own sake, but only as a step toward a new harmony, a new synthesis, a new *consensus fidelium* which will be richer and more dynamic as a result of the tension out of which it grew.

In this dynamic interplay of tension and harmony, we must leave room for the free exercise of even those consciences which we must regard as erroneous—provided always that the genuine demands of the common good, particularly the integrity and liberty of the consciences of others, be respected. Cardinal Newman, on the basis of his own experience, always insisted that habitual obedience to a sincere conscience (even when it was erroneous) would ultimately lead to objective truth. The man who adheres to a sincere conscience intends to obey God himself, and all others must have the wisdom and patience to let God bring him to the fullness of truth in his own good time.

From time to time issues will arise over which the conscience of the whole Church is seriously divided. There are many indications that such a state of divided conscience exists today in regard to some aspects of conjugal morality, particularly that of contraception. Because these are issues which affect the majority of Christians in such an intimate way, it is all the more necessary that the witness of as many consciences as possible should be heard before any new attempt is made to formulate an authoritative statement of Christian conviction. In this regard, we can take heart from the informal remarks of Pope Paul to a group of cardinals on June 23, 1964. He took note of the many areas of competence which must be heard from in any study of birth control; in the forefront of these is the "competence of married people, that of their freedom, of their conscience, of their love, of their duty." The Church exercises her own area of competence—that of proclaiming and interpreting God's law. But "the Church will have to proclaim this law of God in the light of scientific, social and psychological truths which in these times have undergone new and very ample study and documentation." It is in the hope of furthering this complex task that the following pages are written.

Christian Morality in the Light of Conscience

Before we may speak of the manner in which an adequate doctrine of conscience might help Christian couples to approach the problems peculiar to their state, we must try to understand the implications of conscience for the total challenge of Christian living. For certain basic attitudes are proper and necessary to every Christian existence, regardless of the state of life in which they achieve their final "incarnation."

There has been an unfortunate tendency in the tradition of the recent past to speak of the Christian life in a very fragmented and disjointed fashion. A great many "commandments" or obligations were acknowledged, and the impression was given that they could be fulfilled in isolation from one another, or from any context that would confer on them a vital unity and coherence. The emphasis was placed on the morality of individual acts, and they were analyzed and judged in apparent isolation from the person who was the living source of their meaning and of their relationship to each other. The Christian may have appeared as a man who was busy about many things, forgetting that one thing is necessary (see Lk 10:38ff).

The moral life, viewed in such a perspective, would hardly deserve the name of "life" at all, for high among the attributes of life rank the qualities of continuity and coherence. And when the life in question is that of a reflecting subject, a person conscious of his own existence and freedom, of his duration and creative self-possession (in short, a person with a conscience), then these qualities assume an absolutely central significance.

In point of fact, men do not live their lives in a disjointed and fragmented manner. (Those who do, we recognize as mentally ill; when the fragmentation is total, so that their actions possess no coherence, and hence no predictability, we consign them to an institution, both for their own safety and for that of others.) On the contrary, men recognize that in every normal life there is an inner direction, a unity of purpose, a "project of existence," and that individual actions are only more or less adequate manifestations of this inner direction. Individual actions are manifestations of a *person*, of a subject, rather than entities in their own right, and moral imputability would seem to attach primarily to the person, to what is in his "heart"—i.e. to that which is most truly and centrally his "self"—and only derivatively to what he does.

This way of thinking is confirmed in our everyday judgments. We expect to discover a consistency and a direction in the lives of people. When a person whom we know well acts in a way that is totally untypical of him, we say: "He is not himself today." Or we say that a person who acts in

a fragmented and incoherent manner is "not all *there*"—
i.e. not truly, personally *present* to his action. When a person whom we know to be generous, just, and noble acts in
a reprehensible way, we are surprised and disappointed, and
we will search for an excusing circumstance, because we
feel that "he just could not have done that." On the other
hand, if a person who is basically selfish and dishonest
suddenly acts generously, we instinctively search for some
"ulterior" motive which might explain this uncharacter-
istic action. When we speak of a sinner, we ordinarily do
not mean the man who has failed in a single instance, even
though seriously and consciously, but rather the man whose
whole attitude toward life is characterized by pride and
arbitrary self-indulgence. Very often we think we can spot
such a man simply from his words and appearance, even
though we have not observed him in any sinful action.

We do not need to construct our case simply on our
everyday manner of thinking and judging. The biblical view
of man confirms these reflections. It is true, of course, that
the ten commandments prescribe and proscribe certain
specific actions. But even they are promulgated in the context of a covenant of love, and are intended to indicate
what should be the minimum attitude of response of a
people which knows itself to have been redeemed gratuitously from a life of slavery, a people whose whole "heart"
is therefore "toward the Lord." And when we appreciate
the spirit in which the psalms and the prophetic writings
were composed, we realize that it is always the conversion
of the heart, the turning of the whole person toward God
that is desired.

Basically, only two options are open to man: to accept God's gift of life and merciful salvation, and live out his life in grateful love, or to become an egocentric doer of "works" by which he comes to imagine himself as God's creditor. The drama of this twofold choice reaches its climax in the words of Christ, who comes to announce to the "poor in spirit" that his Father is their Father, and in the writings of St. Paul, with his insistence on justification by faith—i.e. justification through the grateful acceptance of the *gift* of justice which God offers to man in the death and resurrection of Jesus. For the Christian, the "one thing necessary" is the loving relationship in Christ to the Father through the power of the Spirit of adoption. This relationship is pure gift from the divine Persons, and it achieves its full meaning only when it elicits a fully personal response of love in its human recipient, a response that is individual, unique, creative—in a word, subjective.

This response of the Christian to the love which has been poured out in his heart takes place at the very center of his freedom, in the depths of his spirit where he is mystery even unto himself, where "we do not know how to pray as we ought," where "the Spirit himself intercedes for us with sighs too deep for words . . . according to the mind of God" (see Rom 8:26). Both the biblical testimony and our common experience tell us that it is at this level, a level not fully transparent to our conscious analysis, that the decisive choice for or against salvation is made: the choice of faith, whereby we accept in gratitude the gift of the spirit of adoption, or the choice of self-sufficiency, whereby we make ourselves the center of reality around which all else must orbit. In this general context, the reader is referred to chapter two of *Existence and the Existent*, by Jacques Maritain, Garden City 1957, 56-69.

This fundamental option will of course work outward from the center of freedom where it is made, and manifest itself, incarnate itself, in individual choices and actions which are subject to our own conscious analysis and, to some degree, subject to the judgment of others. More than that: individual choices and actions not only *manifest* the direction of our fundamental option, they also *modify* it, strengthening or diminishing its thrust. To a limited degree, individual choices can be said to "create" the fundamental option, for the "self" is not a "finished product," a static entity given once for all. Rather, we are continually in the process of creating our personhood, and our individual choices are not only information about who we now are, but are also *effective* of who we will be. We become by doing. In this sense, our individual choices do possess a moral value or disvalue of their own, and rightly become the object of moral concern and moral judgment.

Nevertheless, the Christian who knows what it is to be a person, what it is to possess a conscience, will realize that moral quality attaches only derivatively to these individual choices, whereas it attaches primarily to the fundamental option, which is always more than an amalgam of individual choices. Because we are *incarnate* spirits, our person, our "self" is but rarely so fully *present* to any of its individual choices that it is totally engaged, totally committed to a new direction. Even when it is a question of a whole series of choices of a particular type—a series which we might have to characterize as a disvalue if we were considering it in isolation—we should hesitate to say that the moral quality of the person, the direction of his "project of existence," can be "read off" from this series of actions alone. Rather, we should have to seek verification for our judgment in the whole tenor of the person's life, and not base that judgment exclusively on a particular series of acts. For it is entirely possible that the person is merely confused or mistaken in this one area, rather than sinfully self-seeking, and it is only by considering the whole that we should be able adequately to discern whether this one part is truly a manifestation of malice, or merely of confusion and weakness.

This does not mean that one would deny the possibility of a person ever being fully "present" to an individual choice, either for good or ill. On the positive side, one thinks of such items as the choice of a religious vocation, or the life-long commitment to marriage; on the negative side, a true sin of despair, or the radical rejection of the responsibilities of one's state in life. It will be noted that these are usually choices which are made only after a long period of reflection and preparation; one does not expect them to emerge full-blown and instantaneously.

Ultimately, the question of how we understand the relationship of God and man comes down to the image which we form of God. The parable of the prodigal son is instructive in this regard. Here we have clear instances of a turning away from the father, and a turning back. And it is these changes of heart which are decisive—not the squandering of money, nor the loose living. The sin of the prodigal lay primarily in his desire to be self-sufficient, to possess his life and his wealth independently of the father who was their living source. And his salvation lay precisely in his turning back. Naturally, we do not expect the prodigal to repeat his infidelity the next day. But on the other hand, we do not expect him to become at once the perfect model of sonship either. It will take him time to discover the full significance of the love which his father bears him. (The very fact that he could imagine his father accepting him in the status of a servant shows how little he really understands of love.) What is important is that he is on the way. He has "turned," he has taken a new direction. It may require years for him to learn how to respond adequately to the love he has received—or he may never succeed in doing so. What matters is that he is once again his father's son; he was dead, and now he lives. And this would seem to correspond to the basic Christian experience of the redeeming love of God in Christ.

The parable of the prodigal encourages us to see man's relationship to God his Father as analogous to (though obviously of a different order from human filiation and friendship. We know that it is possible for us to be disappointed, saddened, and even angered by the thoughtlessness and disloyalty of a friend. But we do not for that reason assume that the friendship has been destroyed. On the contrary, if our friendship is profound, we realize that it entails accepting the other precisely *as other*—i.e. as he really is, including those qualities which we might prefer to see him abandon. We may well hope that our love will eventually lead the friend to such a degree of sensitivity to our person and our preferences that he will *wish* to abandon those ways of acting which are offensive to us. But our love, if it is at all genuine, does not depend on this, least of all on its being accomplished at once. What counts is whether the friend respects and needs us as a *person*. Only when he rejects our very person, when he "no longer has time for us"—a remarkably apt phrase—is the friendship terminated: and even then only on his side. It is he who has excluded himself from our friendship, not so much by some particular stupidity or infidelity, as by choosing simply to go another way, to turn his back on us, to cut us out of his sphere of interest. In effect, he dies to us.

If this is our experience of friendship in human terms, what must divine friendship be like? The Christian who knows that his God is not a distant God, but God-with-us and God-within-us; who knows that he is no longer called a servant, but a friend; who has read in the written Word that God's people are as dear to their Lord as bride is to husband; who has heard from the lips of the Incarnate Word that the Father of mercies is his own Father: such a Christian will know how to understand the meaning of God's love for him, will know what it requires of him in return, and will know when he has rejected that love.

Conscience and Marriage

When a priest begins to speak of how the conscience of married people might function with respect to problems peculiar to their state of life, he begins to overstep the bounds of his competence. It should be noted that what follows is presented not as the fruit of celibate speculation, but as a synthesis, in the author's own words, of the convictions which many married people have shared with him over a period of several years.

Marriage has been well described as a vocation to the service of life. Of course, this would be a good description of any Christian vocation, and when we apply it to marriage, it must be with the awareness that with marriage there is given a distinctive way of serving life, namely procreation. But perhaps that is the special advantage of this description: it forces us to turn our attention first to the *manifold* human and Christian considerations implied by "service of life"; it locates procreation in a context which prevents it from being reduced to a mere biological function.

If marriage is a vocation to the service of life, it would seem obvious that the life of the spouses must receive our first attention. Their first challenge, and the one which endures throughout their lives, before their children are born and after their children are grown to maturity, or even if they cannot or may not have children, is the challenge of promoting the full human and Christian life of each other. And it is only on the condition that they joyously and courageously affirm this task by a daily rededication of their love for each other that they have any right to think of bringing children into the world. Creation is a gift of God's love; procreation, if it is to be a true act of cooperation with God's love, must be the fruit of a gift of human love. The giving of life can never be separated from the giving of love.

So the first obligation of the married state is to be a school of love, a school of Christian perfection, as the fathers of the Church did not hesitate to call it. It is here that husband and wife may learn what it truly means to serve and to obey, to love one's neighbor as oneself. When such a commitment to life and to love has incarnated itself in the new life of the child to be born, one will truly be able to speak of an act of *procreation*, and not merely of an act of *reproduction*. The child who is the fruit of such love will experience, from the very beginning of his existence, what it is to be loved. And he will learn, as his life is nourished on the love and respect which his mother and father bear for one another, that he has another mother (in the community of those who have accepted the gift of God's love in Christ), and another father (who is in heaven); and that between this Mother and Father there also exists an inseparable bond of love and respect, out of which he is nourished with eternal life.

This is the ideal. This needs to be said, and said often, to Christian married people. But we do not wish to fall prey to that temptation which especially threatens the celibate: of romanticizing the glories of married love, at the cost of overlooking some of its harsher realities. Obviously, the mutual devotedness of husband and wife does not spring forth, full-blown, with the pronouncing of the marriage vows. The honeymoon is to be the beginning, not the end of love. Before the end is reached, there will be many a painful "eye-opening."

Love always involves a moment of risk, and those who are excessively fearful are in no better condition than the irresponsible. On the one hand, one does not expect married people to wait until they are absolutely "sure" of each other before they accept the challenge of procreation. On the other hand, one does not expect them either to "have a child" in the vague hope that this will be the "salvation" of a love that appears to be disintegrating. There must be an appraisal of their mutual commitment that is at once courageous and realistic. Christ spoke no beatitude for the consolation of either the fearful or the blind.

Love of any kind, and perhaps especially married love, is a process of growth. Only the love of eternity will be *tota, simul et perfecta,* as the theologians say. Here on earth, it is always a groping thing, often awkward and ill-expressed, sometimes hurting where it means to console. Like all our attempts to reveal in action the mystery of freedom which is our person, it is more in the order of gesture or promise than of fulfillment. And those who would love must learn that patience and that sensitivity which discover love even in the unsatisfactory gesture.

We might go even further. Is it not our experience that failure can in a certain sense be *necessary* for growth in love? The bland and unruffled friendship, either in marriage or elsewhere, rarely possesses real depth and authenticity. By way of example: the wife who would pander to every whim of an egoistic husband would hardly be showing him real love. She knows that if her own love were more refined, she would be able to discover a fully adequate way of bringing him to himself. But she cannot wait until she is perfected in virtue before she speaks. She must act *now,* do the best she can, and be prepared to accept the pain of her own inadequacy, of her own lack of perfect love. Love that is real needs to be humble about its own imperfection, and forgiving of the imperfections of the partner. It needs a sense of humor. Without these qualities, there is no love, no concern for the growth in life of the other, but only a pharisaical gloating over one's own (supposed) perfection.

It will be apparent that every friendship, and especially every marriage is a *new creation*, a new and unrepeatable search for meaning and beauty. If this search is to be successful, there must be room for expansion and experiment. Each partner must become what he is—an image of him who is Person, Freedom, Creativity—and each marriage must become what it is—an image of the absolutely unique love between Christ and his Church. If this is to happen, we should not attempt to measure each marriage simply by its conformity to an abstract ideal or rigid rule, but must rather allow generous scope for the exercise of that freedom of the sons of God which will indeed bring us to a common goal, though perhaps by diverse and unexpected paths. When we teach about marriage, our attention should be focused on *values*, and we should leave the concrete realization of these values more and more to the creative responsibility of the couples themselves. For values will be realized, precisely *as values*, only if they are realized in freedom of conscience.

Now this growth in mutual devotedness, this manifold service of life, this imaginative and creative search in each marriage for a new and distinctive "incarnation" of the love between Christ and his Church, will learn to express itself in a multitude of ways short of sexual intercourse. But what must be said is that the *normal, typical*, and by all counts most *complete* and *intense* embodiment of all these gestures of love will be found in that two-in-oneness which, by no accident, we have come to designate simply as "*the* marriage act."

We have learned, in sacramental theology, that we cannot discover the proper meaning of a sacrament by starting with an analysis of the bare minimum required for validity and treating all the rest as mere "ceremony." The minimal case is always the exceptional case, never the norm by which we judge other cases. And even when the full liturgical celebration is for some reason impossible, we try to approximate it as closely as we can, never being satisfied with the absolute minimum. Now marriage is a sacrament not only at the moment of its celebration; rather, it is meant to be a *continuing sign* in the world of the love between Christ and his Church. Consequently, our analysis of the meaning of marriage must always take as its norm the full and distinctive expression of marital love, not merely the essential minimum (i.e. the mutual consent of the partners to an indissoluble union). If it should then happen in a particular case that illness or enforced separation or some other factor renders the typical expression of love impossible, we shall still be able to show that this remains a true marriage. But we shall not take this limiting case as the norm by which we judge other marriages. On the contrary, we shall perhaps discover a way of affirming that in situations where the fullest expression of marital love—i.e. one which would look forward to a child being conceived—cannot be responsibly undertaken, the closest and most meaningful approximation to it that is acceptable to the spouses may and ought to be sought.

Conscience and Contraception

If our reflections on personhood, on conscience, on the basic structure of Christian existence, and on the fundamental values of marriage are valid, what consequences might follow for the problem of contraception? How might a Christian whose conscience has been formed through a free acceptance of God's personal love view this very complex question? We might begin by making the following observations.

No one will wish to propose that contraception in any form (including the systematic practice of rhythm) is an absolute good. The bond between love and life is so strong and so spontaneous that any *arbitrary* separation of one from the other would surely seem to be "unnatural." While we have seen that the service of life includes much more than merely bringing new life into existence, it must still be affirmed that any use of marriage which, *as a matter of principle, or for totally selfish ends,* rejected even this one dimension of the service of life would in fact be a negation of the whole gift-vocation to life and love. Such a choice would be no more than mutual egoism, and this must be emphatically disavowed. We believe that this indestructibility of the bond between love and life is the unchanging value which the Catholic teaching on the ends of marriage has sought to preserve and affirm, even if the ways in which this teaching was proposed have not always been the most adequate.

By way of corollary, it may be suggested that every sexual expression of marital love which is so planned or executed as to deliberately exclude the possibility of procreation will be experienced by the Christian married couple as a gesture of love which is less adequate than, *ideally and in the abstract,* they would wish it to be. It is obvious that the use of contraception can be, and perhaps often is, motivated by considerations that are almost exclusively selfish and hedonistic. The inclination to egoism is, after all, rooted deep in the hearts of all of us, and none of us has any absolute guarantee against its becoming the dominant option of our lives, corrupting all that we are and do. But if the foregoing observations had to be made, they may not be allowed to stand alone, for in each case, they express only a part of the truth. They need to be balanced and completed in somewhat the following manner.

If it is true that every arbitrary interference with the bond between love and life must be rejected, it is likewise true that there are a great many factors which would remove the option for contraception from the realm of the arbitrary, and could even make it, in the concrete, an expression of virtue. These factors are well enough known, and have often been listed, even in papal documents, as justifying causes for the use of rhythm. In addition to the factors traditionally listed (financial, physical, eugenic, sociological), one might wish to emphasize that of psychic health and balance, for the discoveries of depth psychology have made us keenly aware of the damage that can be done to a child by an emotionally disturbed parent.

If every deliberate interference with the gift to procreate is sensed by the Christian conscience to be less than an ideal expression of love, it must be added that we never live our lives in the realm of the ideal. The human condition as we know it is a limited and imperfect condition, in which fulfillment always falls short of promise, and the gesture is never a fully adequate revelation of the person who makes it. We are, to our dying breath, men on the way, not men already arrived. The person who can never do anything that is less than perfect is the one who rarely does anything at all. We are constantly faced with the dilemma of responding to many invitations at once; we are never granted the luxury of confronting our problems one by one, in isolation from the total context of our lives. The best we can ever do is to attempt to strike a balance, in humility and prudence, between the many obligations which confront us simultaneously. In this context, it seems entirely possible that a couple who would reject every form of contraception if that were the only choice they had to make might, in perfectly good conscience, choose some form of contraception in preference to total or lengthy abstinence, so that at least that limited service of life which is realistically open to them, here and now, might be affirmed. And this choice, which when viewed in the abstract might be repugnant to them, could in the concrete be taken in humble joy.

When we say that contraception can be an expression of hedonistic selfishness, we must also say that the same can be true of a biologically "correct" use of marriage, even when it issues in a large family. There are some people who reject contraception not from any motives which Christians could approve, but because they do not wish to sacrifice the smallest part of the "pleasure" which seems to be the be-all and end-all of their marriage. They either obviate the possibility of children by some more drastic means (abortion or sterilization), or they irresponsibly burden society with children whom they have no intention of caring for —and what is infinitely worse, burden their children with a life in which there is no love.

What these observations would seem to add up to is this: the real religious and moral challenge of procreation in

Christian marriage, the point at which essential values must be discovered and affirmed, cannot be identified simply with the question of the licitness of various means of contraception. The decisive choice which confronts the Christian, in marriage or elsewhere, is the choice between accepting and returning love on the one hand, and loveless egoism on the other. And neither of these options may be equated simply with a particular mode of external conduct, for they belong to the order of ends rather than of means. Unless we are to equate morality with biology, we must look beyond the physical integrity of the act of marital intercourse to the *meaning* which it has in the total human and Christian context of a given marriage.

An objection immediately arises; it is serious, and must be faced squarely. Does not this way of thinking lead to the complete relativism of "situation ethics"? We think not. In the first place, there is a very great deal of truth in "situation ethics," and this fact has always been acknowledged in the Catholic teaching on the significance of the circumstances which enter into a human act, and in our insistence that the *subjective* morality of an act derives finally from the intention, or the conscience, of the person acting. But more to the point: what is rightly to be rejected in situation ethics is its denial that there are *any* standards or values which are truly normative for human conduct, and its exclusive emphasis on the "fulfillment" of the individual who is acting. What we have been trying to establish in this essay is that there is indeed a decisive norm that is valid for all human conduct—the norm of open and generous love. And precisely because the norm is one of love, of real concern for the *other*, it can never be reduced to what the individual might find "fulfilling." He who loves is no longer his own master, but finds himself "determined" by the real needs of the loved one. There is an "objectivity" about love: not the kind of objectivity that can be discovered and imposed *a priori* from an abstract analysis of a given kind of act, but an objectivity that can be discovered in the results and consequences of a way of acting. Those ways of acting which truly edify, i.e. which truly build up human community, be it familial or societal, can be called the ways of love; and those which destroy, which produce discord and alienation between persons, cannot. We must have the patience to allow people to discover what is love and what is delusion. What is even more necessary: *we must have the courage to believe that they want to.* A lack of complete conformity of moral practice may not be a desirable thing in itself, but it is surely not too high a price to pay for the free submission to God of men who act from conviction rather than fear, of men who know that their Redeemer lives.

Conclusion

Our reflections have taken us far afield. We have touched on many facets of an exceedingly complex mystery, without having done justice to any one of them. We can only hope that the other essays in this book, together with the background which our readers bring to it, will provide a context in which our remarks will assume a greater coherence and intelligibility. The basic intent of this essay has been to record the personal convictions of the author. It has sought to raise questions rather than to supply conclusive answers.

Only the witness of the whole Church can lead us in the direction of a solution. With this realization in mind, we should like to conclude by addressing the following questions to those men who give authoritative expression to the witness of faith of the Catholic Church, the bishops deliberating at Vatican II.

May we not hope that this council will take a searching look at the manner in which Christian moral values are communicated, and will seek for an expression of these values which will be more in keeping with our present understanding of the mystery of human personhood or (what comes to the same thing) of personal conscience? May we not hope that, while affirming the permanent values of Christian marriage, the council will discover a way of stating that these values can be realized even through actions which, if viewed in isolation might be objectionable, but which, in the total context of a given marriage, may be constructive and holy? Must we continue to exclude from the sacraments of reconciliation and unity those Christians who, after serious thought and prayer, have come to the clear conviction of conscience that they *must* practice contraception if they are to make the best of a life that will never be perfect in this world?

Procreation and the Person

Kieran Conley, O.S.B.

Other contributors to this book will discuss the moral
implications of anovulants, the validity of the distinction
between rhythm and other contraceptive methods, the importance of the second term in the traditional phrase concerning the "procreation and education" of children; I
would like to concern myself here with a rather different
approach to the problem of birth control by focusing on certain consequences of the concept of morality as the response
to the call of another person. The very word "responsibility"
carries an etymology which suggests that to be responsible
means precisely to respond and to respond implies person
as correlative.

Whether or not the modern emphasis upon moral action
as a meeting of obligation, coupled in a Catholic context
with a rather mechanistic conception of nature, even human nature, is traceable simply to the Kantian ethic is a
question beyond our discussion here. I do think, however,
it would be extremely revealing to have St. Paul return to
the contemporary Christian scene—one thinks immediately of Dostoyevsky's Grand Inquisitor meeting Christ.
With St. Paul's emphasis upon freedom, as expressed in

both Romans and Galatians, he might find it rather difficult to see in our elaborate code of discipline and our ordinary legalistic approach to moral living an adequately
Christian response to the person of Christ. Are we not
overly concerned with law and obligation and perhaps too
unaware that "owe no man anything except to love" means
precisely that.

But whatever St. Paul would say in viewing contemporary Catholic moral thought and action, there are those of
a deeply personalist bent who are severe in their criticisms.
Where indeed is the I-Thou relationship to God in most of
our moral decisions? Where is the recognition that persons
are the only absolutes, created images of *the* Absolute?
How often do we hear morality discussed merely in terms
of abstract nature without consideration of personal call
and loving response. That is why the work of a moral theologian such as that of Bernard Häring has received such a
sympathetic response. For he shows himself to be deeply
aware of person and love and above all of that Person and
that Love which is Christ.

There is a place of course for attention to objective nature, but never without Christianity's concern for person, a
concern which touches more deeply the human reality.
Besides, our experience of man as fallen and redeemed
hardly offers a clear picture of human nature to unaided
reason in the first place. Such an essentialist conception of
man must always be, in Karl Rahner's phrase, a "remain-
der-concept," that is, a kind of residual notion left after
abstracting from man existentially involved in sin and its
consequences. This realization lies behind the contemporary criticism of traditional natural-law theory, even among

certain Catholic theologians. Man is never merely an object or a thing, and to discuss morality only in such terms seems to falsify the issues of human moral life.

The free response of a person in a moral situation must become more consciously a matter of encounter and dialogue with the divine persons who call us in and through the needs of created persons. This is not to be taken in a Platonic sense, viewing other persons as mere means to one's dialogue with God; nor in a pantheistic sense which would identify the created absolutes with the uncreated Absolute. But there is a kind of simultaneity or immediacy in this response to person: as I respond to any "other" I respond to Christ who has told us, "Whatever you do to the least of these, you do to me." In loving others we love the God who in his gracious gift of the incarnation has chosen to identify himself with men.

But what can all this really mean for Christian morality? Basically, that every moral decision must be seen as a response to the call of a loving God who speaks to us in the needs of his created images, ourselves and others. The Christian must be forever open to the needs of persons in his family, among his friends, in the political or religious community—to the needs of all those with whom and for whom he lives. "Owe no man anything except to love."

The problem of moral decision thus becomes a matter of determining where and to what is God truly asking for my response. Baptized into Christ, the sacrament of God's love, must purpose all my actions to be identified with the redeeming purpose of the incarnation—to give to Christ my hands and feet, my mind and heart, with which he may accomplish his saving work. My task in this com-

plex world of interpersonal relationships is to discover
among the many possible calls, which one is truly God's,
at this moment, in this place. This does not imply a situation ethics; it does, however, preclude that type of moral
universalism so comfortable for the univocal mind, where
human life is seen only in the sharp lines of black and
white; the grays are lost to eyes undimmed by the blinding
light of the mystery we call person.

As I do attempt to discover God's call, it may frequently
seem that I must exclude him calling me in one area to answer him in another. For example, it is Sunday morning
and time for Mass. Because I am a Catholic parent, God
calls me through the legislation of the Church and in the
persons of my parish community to celebrate the Christ-
event in the eucharistic liturgy. My ordinary response is a
freely chosen sharing in the community worship. My child,
however, is sick and God seems to call me also in the need
of that child. I must decide which is truly God's call but it
may seem phenomenologically that God's call is excluded in
one area to be answered in another.

A second example. A person giving evidence regarding
someone's character or action seems called on the one hand
by the need of that someone to remain silent and, on the
other, by the need of society to speak. The decision to speak
the truth in love represents a choice between alternate
calls of person or persons, and what would otherwise be
detraction becomes an act of love. God's apparent call in
the individual person is disregarded in favor of his more
imperative call through the persons of society.

A third example. Lying in itself suggests a deliberate
refusal to respond to the call of a person. And yet where

other persons are concerned, even the traditional moralists are conceding in certain circumstances the right to lie. It may be to protect another's good name; it may be to prevent a serious quarrel; it may even be to save someone's life. In any case, an exclusion of call in one direction makes possible a response to call in another.

All this is not merely a morality of commitment versus a morality of code. It is indeed a morality of commitment —to person—but one freed from an over-simplified conformity to impersonal and objectively abstract nature as well as from a dangerously pharisaical following of mere law or code. This does not make morality easier but indeed at a deeper level far more difficult. Based in the Christian revelation of human dignity, in full recognition that human life must be a continual response out of love to call of person, such a moral vision sees the Christian in his only true guise: as identified by selflessness with Christ who came "not to be served but to serve." Here the selfishness that characterizes all sin is overcome by a generous openness to the "other," the only ultimate criterion of morality and virtue.

But now this more immediately personalist view of moral life must be applied to the question under discussion. In what way does this emphasis upon response to call of person provide a solution to the problem of birth control?

Every responsible human act is truly responsive, conceived in love, nurtured by respect, and given birth in surrender to another and in that "other" to God. This is especially true of the act *par excellence* of conjugal love. Like the eucharistic sacrament of Christ's love, the marital act is both the sign and the cause of the couple's being at one with each other. This is true of course only if the marriage is open to life in a spirit of generous fecundity. Without such openness the marriage would be a travesty.

But given such openness, is the morality of sex in marriage really a matter of an individual act or rather of a fundamental option, in this case, the option for life and responsible parenthood? Father Schillebeeckx and others have suggested that "all human significance of the marriage need not be realized in every separate act." It is a truism to point out that sexuality in human beings is not merely procreative in a biological sense. The reproductive cycle itself and the absence of simple estrous in women adequately attests to this. Abstracting from this line of reasoning, however, while admitting its importance, there is much that can be said simply within the framework of the moral act viewed as response to call of person.

Imagine the couple who, for whatever reasons, are faced with the real necessity of avoiding pro-creation at this time. It is true that physiologically for about forty-eight hours a month God seems to be calling the couple to pro-creation. But Christian reason indicates that in the total situation he really is not calling them to procreation. Can we say therefore he is not calling them to engage in the sign and cause of their unity? With the continual need for this expression of their love and the means for its deepening, cannot the couple respond to God in the call of each other, in the needs of the children already born, in the needs of the society of persons beyond the family, using whatever may be necessary to preclude the procreation to which God is not calling them in the first place? It might be consid-

ered as excluding God at one level in order to answer him
at another. This seems to be already implied in the
Church's acceptance of periodic continence. And any consideration of the merely biological structure of the act
seems in the totality of interpersonal communication to
be splitting hairs. As Canon Janssens has indicated, in
the fullness of the positive human act what is really the
difference between temporal and spatial obstruction of the
physiological possibility of procreation? In this particular human act—i.e. intercourse during a non-fertile period
by a couple practicing rhythm—the element of time enters
as a positive determinant and not merely negatively.

We are faced then with a situation wherein the end of
procreation is no longer, as judged by Christian reason,
really part of God's will here and now. Yet, while procreation may be outside God's intention for the couple in
the present situation, the other ends of marriage, growth in
mutual love and sexual fulfillment, remain and must be
recognized as true ends. Must the judgment of Christian
reason in such a case heed the merely physiological when
God indicates in the genuine need of persons another finality? Can we legitimately disregard this multiple call of persons which may well reveal the call of divine person more
imperatively than the simple biological datum of cyclic
fertility?

Sexuality and all that it implies is rooted naturally in the
need for procreation but the totality of its meaning is not
to be found exclusively there. The recognition of this by
the Church has prompted recent developments regarding
responsible parenthood as the ideal, as well as the acceptance of rhythm as a method of birth control. But is this

method really the natural as well as the truly personal solution to the problem?

It belongs to man by nature to use physical or chemical means to attain the legitimate ends he sets for himself. He is an animal that lives by reason and art rather than by mere instinct. In the light of this, the simple avoidance of dependence upon what may be artificial in seeking the end of personal growth in marriage hardly renders such activity more natural. If rhythm really is an acceptable contraceptive means, to term any other method unnatural and therefore sinful seems to overlook the very naturalness of man's artificial activity. And is it not possible that nature always remains relative to personal good? If so, then the principle, *the end does not justify the means,* applies only to means which are in themselves destructive of personal good. Any other means becomes something man uses for the end of person and is therefore good precisely because of that end.

If a marriage is truly lived according to the principle of responsible parenthood, therefore, must it be forever subordinated to the simple physiology of procreative function? Is it necessarily an immoral intervention in nature when; in response to the good of persons, a couple judges that here and now physiological procreation may be prescinded from? In proposing how such procreation might be prescinded from I hesitate to use the word "contraception" because this word has been given—justly or unjustly as the case may be—too many overtones of selfishness. Obviously, whenever there is real selfishness there is immorality. And this is equally true in the case of rhythm. But when an act is indeed selfless as a loving response to the call of person, and when responsible reason enters to exercise the dominion over merely physical nature given to it by God, it seems extremely unfair to label such an action as necessarily sinful.

Much more should be said and no doubt has been said by others more competent than I. But in leaving this discussion of morality as response to person, may I suggest what I believe to be three particularly fruitful lines of inquiry.

First of all, in the context of a deeply personalist morality what is the importance of the moral principle of totality? Is it really possible to judge a human act by abstracting from the phenomenological involvement of the persons whose call and response form the pattern of the act itself? Moreover, is it enough to apply totality only to the individual person? What might be said regarding the totality of the couple, that new and wondrous totality whose principle is the sacramental bond? What might be said regarding the totality of the family or that of the community as well?

Secondly, and this suggestion follows upon what has just been said, what does it mean to say that the end does not justify the means? I have already indicated the possibility that anything truly impersonal is always relative to the good of persons. Even for St. Thomas, the very nature of the means is taken from the end (*ratio eorum quae sunt ad finem sumitur ex fine*). It may be that something merely natural becomes good or evil only in reference to person as end. The moral question then would be: is it or is it not for the good of person or persons? Moreover, in many cases —the present problem is especially pertinent—there seems to be a kind of telescoping of means and end. In certain circumstances to speak truly the language of love and surrender may require in itself the exclusion of pro-creative possibility.

Thirdly, the traditional language used to define—perhaps canonically and not theologically—the act of love should be carefully restudied. The expression "an act in itself apt for generation" (*actus per se aptus ad generationem*), seems impoverished in the light of the educational demands of the primary end of marriage as well as the need to foster mutual love and personal growth. Would it not be better expressed as an act apt or designed for the nurturing and development of all the persons involved in the total marriage picture, that is, the marriage partner and the children already born, as well as the possible child? One might add also, the persons of society whose good is served by a healthy, responsible family unit. In any case, the usual definition seems seriously lacking in regard to the complex integrity of purpose proper to the sexual act in marriage.

What has been said here is offered to those concerned about the Catholic position on birth control. Perhaps the Catholic stance has not been catholic enough in the sense of embracing the *whole* reality of sex in marriage. In the world of today the Church must show herself, in imitation of her Servant Lord, deeply concerned with the suffering and hardship in the lives of many of her people. She cannot simply take refuge in solutions of the past which may well depend more upon a syncretic dualism than upon the revelation of person and love found in the New Testament.

This is the revelation that must become ever more evident in the teachings of Christian morality.

With the hope of moving in this direction, the ideas here presented are one man's attempt to suggest lines of reflection on an awesome topic. I know that arguments can be mustered from traditional natural law sources to show a distinction between rhythm and other contraceptive methods. It may be ignorance on my part—I hope it is not obstinacy—but such arguments do not seem to embrace the total human act of married persons and their articulation of the language of love. They emphasize the category of nature rather than that of person and are thus guided more by the insights of Aristotle than by those of St. Paul. Until these attempts to solve the problems of morality include more obviously an awareness of persons as the only absolutes, they will remain incomplete and ineffective.

Family morality, like Christian morality in any area of human life, is measured by selfless response to God who calls us in and through the persons we confront. Such a response in marriage, in order to be Christian, must always breathe the spirit of generous fecundity and responsible parenthood. Only then can marital love reflect the concern for person and responsibility so evident in the relation of Christ and his Church. As we discuss therefore the moral problems in marriage, may we overcome that not uncommon temptation to view morality without the dimension of person and love. For—to paraphrase Newman—in the evening of life we shall encounter a Person and we shall be judged on love.

Birth Control and the Ideals of Marital Sexuality

Rosemary Ruether

The present controversy in the Catholic Church over the licitness or illicitness of various methods of birth control is so heated and fraught with polemic that it seems increasingly difficult to think through the whole issue in a simple and sane fashion, and yet such simple and sane thinking is desperately needed on this issue, now more than ever. The Church can scarcely afford to perpetuate the present muddle much longer without the gravest danger to the consciences of thousands of sincere persons within the Church as well as the general disrespect and contempt which the situation is engendering among non-Catholics both Christian and non-Christian.

Much of the difficulty which impedes clear thinking on this issue is a frightful semantic muddle. Words used by one person to mean one thing are used by another school of thought to mean another. Thus the present author wrote in the *Saturday Evening Post* (April 10, 1964) that the Church should clearly recognize that the relational aspect of the marital act is a genuine value and purpose in itself, and cannot just be subsumed as a means to the end of procreation. The critics immediately replied that this meant promiscuity and extra-marital intercourse, since, for some strange reason, procreation in their minds necessarily implied marriage whereas the relational aspect of the marital act did not seem to imply any permanent bond between two human beings. Now obviously one can have babies outside of marriage just as well as one can have sexual relationships outside of marriage. If we are to have any intelligent discussion of this problem at all, we must be convinced that we are talking about *marriage* and not promiscuity. Within this context we must then make clear that the procreational and the relational aspects of the sexual act are two semi-independent and interrelated purposes which both are brought together in their meaning and value within the total marriage project, although it is not only unnecessary but even biologically impossible that both purposes be present in every act.

Another semantic muddle exists in regard to the term "procreation" or, more specifically "procreativeness." The present proponents of the rhythm method have redefined procreativeness until it simply means a kind of formal structure of the sexual act, irrespective of whether that act can procreate or not. Thus, since rhythm doesn't interfere with this formal procreative structure, it is licit, while mechanical contraceptives, which supposedly interfere with this procreative structure, are illicit. Now it is very strange that procreativeness should be defined only in terms of the operation of the sperm as it travels into the uterus, but the presence or absence of the ovum is deemed irrelevant to the definition of procreativeness. One almost suspects some hangover of the medieval notion that the sperm alone was the generative agent, the existence of the ovum being then unknown. In any case it is obvious that procreative means nothing less than the actual possibility of the act procreating, although this may not always occur, and this capacity to procreate entails the presence of ovum just as much as the viability of the sperm. Hence, sexual acts which are calculated to function only during times of sterility are sterilizing the act just as much as any other means of rendering the act infertile. It is difficult to see why there should be such an absolute moral difference between creating a spatial barrier to procreation and creating a temporal barrier to procreation.

In any case it is necessary to clear away these semantic squabbles and rethink clearly and succinctly the various values that are at stake in the birth control controversy, and how these various values ought to be related to each other within an understanding of the total nature of the marital relationship; then, in terms of this evaluation of the nature of the marital relationship, to consider the various methods of birth control and how they may be conducive to or destructive of these values.

First, let us think about marital morality in terms of the full expression of its ideal nature. The sexual act exists on several levels of meaning and purpose. First of all, it is a biological act whose purposive goal is the generation of a new human being. Secondly, it is an act of love in which the married couple express their union with each other. In this union they both express their union and make this union; that is, the sexual act does not merely express the union of their persons, but in this expression it also makes this union, and so it is the cement that holds together the relationship, and not only of the couple to each other, but also as the parents of their children. This union does not just exist on a physiological level, but it expresses the mutuality of their union on all levels of their being, their total I and Thou with each other.

The sexual act would be expressed ideally when all these purposes and meanings could be present in a total and harmonious whole. This would mean that the couple truly give themselves to each other in deep devotion and love; that from this act of love a child should actually spring, as its natural fruition, and that the act of love and the biological cause and effect that produce the child be no mere chance coincidence, but, in loving each other, the couple should also choose to create a child as an authentic act of will. For man is not just an animal, and should not just procreate as an animal does as the servant of biological chance, but he should choose his own existence, and the effects of his own acts in an authentically human way.

This, then, would be the nature of the sexual act under ideal circumstances. This is, perhaps, the way it might have been before the fall of Adam, when nature was as God intended it to be before it became disordered and its existence as a created image of God was blurred. However, in actual reality, under our present situation, this complete unification of all the goals of marriage in a single and harmonious act can only occasionally occur at best. First of all, man never knows when his sexual acts will actually procreate, so that he cannot will a sexual act to be an act of procreation and know that he has actually effected this end. In the order of fallen nature, the sexual act is used many hundreds of times and only procreative occasionally. Sec-

ondly, the limitations of man's social life, particularly in
the modern world, are such that man feels less and less free
to procreate. The psychological demands of living within
a sexual union impel a relatively frequent use of the sexual
act, and yet man, particularly in our urban society, only
feels really free to allow himself, perhaps, between two and
five children. Many couples may have more than that, and
society today will make these couples feel (and with some
reason since we cannot ignore the realities of economic
and social life) that they have produced more children
than is in the common good. Thus we see that the actual
use of the sexual act and the number of children that can
be positively desired are radically out of tune with each
other.

We have discussed the sexual act from the point of view
of its ideal completion in procreation and shown how the
limitations imposed upon man, both from biological nature
and the social structure, create a radical and inevitable falling away from the ideal in practice. Let us now consider
the marital act from the point of view of its expression of
the person to person relationship of the couple. This purpose of the sexual act also has its inner laws of perfection.
Above all an authentic act of love should be given freely,
without external force. The couple should not feel forced
to love when they are not genuinely drawn together, or
forced not to love for reasons external to their personal
well being. Above all it should be an act arising from the
total communion of the couple, without calculation, so
that, for example, a conversation in the evening which
brings with it a deepened sense of person to person understanding might lead on into the expression of their relation-

ship in physical union. All traces of lust should be expelled, so that one partner never approaches the other as a mere thing to be used for his own gratification, but the pleasure of the sexual act should arise as a by-product of their mutual self-giving to each other.

However, in actual practice, the limitations of a man's lack of charity, preoccupation with selfish concerns or mere day to day business create a falling away from this ideal. Most couples do not express the full mutuality of their persons in the sexual act for the simple reason that they have not achieved such mutuality, because their understanding of each other is distorted and fraught with petty tensions and dislikes. A thousand concerns press upon them and fragment the wholeness of their persons and thus impede their communion. The sexual act, in practice, may seldom be an expression of deeper commingling, but may be a casual thing, or even forced upon the one partner by the desires of the other. Seldom are the moments when the two turn equally to each other in full openness to the spirit of each other. The sexual natures themselves of man and woman make union difficult, for the two are not temperamentally compatible, but the man's sexual desires are more constant, while the woman's are more variable, and the two have different cycles of crescendo in the act itself. Thus many factors, both in the biological nature and in the social nature of the relationship, tend toward a falling away from the ideal of full mutuality.

Having accepted the fact that, in actual life, the achievement of the ideal nature of the sexual act at all times is impossible, because man can neither desire nor have a child with each sexual act, nor can he give himself to his partner as lovingly as he ought, what should be our guidelines in coming as close as possible to the various ideals and purposes of marital sexuality? When we spoke of the perfection of the procreative nature of the sexual act, it was clear that this purpose of the act is best expressed when man does choose to procreate as an authentic act of desire. But man, as we have seen, can only desire perhaps three, four or five children (and there is no point telling people they ought to have more children when the circumstances of their life mitigate against it). The second best expression of the ideal would then be that those children which are born are genuinely desired and authentically chosen; that is, at the time they are begotten, the couple is actually making use of the sexual act with a desire to procreate. Now we come to the ironic fact that in our present situation man is only able fully to say "yes" to procreation if he is also able to say "no." If, on the other hand, he has at his disposal only an ineffective method of birth control which does not give him the freedom to say "no," then he will not really have the freedom to say "yes" either, because his efforts will be expended on trying to prevent the birth of more children than he feels he can provide for, and to space those children with an insecure method; and so the children that he does have tend to be "accidents" rather than products of authentic human will. Only when he can be confident that the "accident" will not occur is he then able to feel free to stop holding his procreative powers in abeyance at appropriate intervals and to make love with the full intention of creating a child, although, of course, he can never be absolutely sure when or if a child will be conceived. Therefore, we arrive at the paradox that, in man's present situation, his ability to approach the ideal of marital sexuality, where all the purposes of the sexual act can be present harmoniously, is dependent on his ability to hold his procreative powers in abeyance at other times.

Having shown that man's ability to choose procreation authentically is dependent on his ability not to choose it at other times, let us look at the various methods for holding the procreative powers in abeyance, to see which are suited to the best ordering of the primary and auxiliary purposes of the marital act. Looking at the question from one point of view we might be inclined to feel that man should only make love when he can really desire a child, and when he does not so desire, he should dispense with the sexual act altogether. This might be the ideal situation from the standpoint of radical morality, but in actual practice it is both impossible and inadvisable for most couples. As we have seen, man's sexual desires and his desire for procreation are not actually in tune, and this is a fact of his nature which he cannot well overcome. The demands of living in the sexual union are real and meaningful demands which impose a far more frequent use of the sexual act for its relational function than could ever be brought into harmony with procreation itself. Man needs to express his mutuality with his partner, and in the sexual act this mutuality is both expressed and recreated; and in this sense the sexual act as a relational act is a genuinely purposeful act, and not mere play or unleashing of passion. Since this is the case, the couple cannot well dispense with the act and yet continue to live in a sexual relationship without doing extensive emotional damage to the basic stability of their marriage. Since the firmness of their relational cohesion with each other is the cement that holds the marriage together, and this, in turn, is the milieu in which the children which have been born are nurtured, the first ideal of marriage, the ideal of procreation itself mitigates against the use of a method of birth control which would undermine the stability of the sexual union of the couple. Thus the continued use of the sexual act for its relational purpose, even when its procreational purpose is impeded, may be said to be required by the procreational purpose itself, because the procreational purpose extends to the nurture of the child; and if the continued use of the sexual act is necessary in order to maintain the union of the couple and their ability to carry out their continued responsibility to the child, then the primary purpose of marriage itself points to the use of the sexual act for its purely relational function.

Thus in actual practice man has no real choice (except perhaps in the case of a couple both called to a life of virginity), but to find some method of birth control which allows him to continue to use the sexual act for its relational purpose and to do this under as ideal emotional circumstances as possible. Among these methods there are four main types: permanent sterilization, periodic continence, the mechanical or chemical contraceptive and the oral-steroid pill.

Permanent sterilization is undesirable chiefly because of its finality. It takes from man his ability to choose in favor of procreation and leaves him only with his previous choice against it. It thus dehumanizes him by depriving him of his freedom to make authentically human choices.

The rhythm method (which I shall examine in greater detail below) has several defects which cause a falling away from the ideals we have outlined. First, the method forces a mechanization of the affections of the couple who must artificially "schedule" their mutual affection at the time of the infertile period, and this takes from the couple their freedom to choose to love as an expression of true mutuality, and makes them subservient to an impersonal biological cycle which has no genuine relationship to their human expression of mutual love. Secondly, this method is very insecure and so forces a constant calculation and worry which is psychologically debilitating and tends to undermine the couple's stability and introduces fear and conflict into their relationship. Thus the rhythm method is undesirable for the same reasons as total abstinence, that its demands upon the psychological cohesion of the couple often exceed what can be reconciled with the stability of their relationship, and thus not in the best interests of the family as a whole. Thirdly, this method does not give fully effective control over procreation, but the natural fluctuations of sterility are such that the most careful use of the method (and we must remember that the method is being practiced by human beings, and not laboratory rats, and that the psychological tensions created by the method also are a permanent contributing factor to its ineffectiveness) will produce many accidental babies, often exceeding the total number of children the couple feels they can accept, and so it does not give the couple the freedom to fully affirm their desire for children—rather, in practice, the couple has to spend so much energy in trying to make the

method work, i.e. to get it to effectively impede procreation, that the freedom authentically to desire a child and
plan for his conception is lost.

The third method is that of the traditional contraceptive: condom, diaphragm, spermicidal jelly and the like.
All have the undesirable quality that they tend to intrude
themselves into the psychological dynamics of the sexual
act itself, because the couple must calculate the time of the
sexual act in order to be armed in advance, and they are
made psychologically aware of the means being used to
impede procreation in a way esthetically distasteful to
many people. However, one must make distinctions within
this general group of mechanical and chemical means.
Certain means, such as condom and *coitus interruptus*,
definitely do not allow for the full completion of the sexual
act as a relational act, and so they may be said to devalue
the relational aspect of the act in a way which is morally
intolerable. Other methods, such as the diaphragm, oper-
ate at the base of the cervix, or even within the womb.
They do not prevent the full and natural sexual play between the couple and the depositing of the seed in the vagina. Thus they can be condemned only if one condemns
any method which prevents the procreative fulfillment of
the act, and this, as we have said, is equally true of all
methods of birth control, including the rhythm method.
Some of these mechanical means are still inesthetic, and
this may cause some falling away from the ideal of marital
mutuality, but it is questionable whether esthetic criteria
alone can brand these methods as absolutely immoral. The
esthetic criterion is a highly subjective one, and many persons do not feel such methods are inesthetic or that they

prevent the full expression of mutual self-giving (in the relational rather than the procreational sense of the word). These people simply accept such means in the same way that one accepts a pair of reading spectacles, as an aid to nature which one uses but psychologically ignores.

Finally, there are the new oral-steroid pills, which, assuming that they are medically safe, would seem to hold out the best possibility for a reasonable balance of goals and ideals in marriage. First, this method is fully effective, and gives to the couple the power to hold their procreative powers in abeyance when this is necessary, and, in turn, to release these powers to create a child, when they can and do desire to so choose (—and this choice may often require a great sacrificial effort. We do not intend to suggest that this voluntary choice of procreation by which man dares to live up to the highest ideal of the sexual act will existentially be an easy one to make). Furthermore, when the woman discontinues the use of the pills, she has a jump-back of heightened fertility and so receives a "bonus" of added assurance that the desire for a child may actually be brought to fruition. Thirdly, the method is totally divorced from the physical and psychological setting of the sexual act, and as such it is preferable from the esthetic point of view. Finally, it allows the couple full freedom to use or control the sexual act according to the true laws of their love and respect for each other, without being forced into subservience to its external considerations, such as the "safe period," or the need to calculate the relationship in order to have the contraceptive in place.

I would like now to examine in greater detail the flaws

in the use of what is known as the "safe period." The theoretical understanding of fertility upon which the rhythm method has been based assumes too simple and schematic a functioning of human fecundity. It has been assumed, for example, that the sperm could live only about forty-eight hours, so that a couple had only to abstain for about two days before this time. Recent studies have shown that forty-eight hours is only the *average* life of the sperm, and that actually this is only the mid-point in a spectrum. Some of the spermatozoa may live only a few hours. Others have been found to be still viable in the mucus of the cervix after intercourse for as long as seven or eight days, and it is unknown how much longer they might live in particular instances.

The ovarian cycle of the woman is equally unpredictable. The twenty-eight day cycle is only a statistical *average*, but real women are not statistical averages. Many women have cycles which vary considerably, but it is absolutely normal for the woman's cycle to vary somewhat, that is from twenty-six to thirty-one days. When we try to put all these facts together: the variations in the woman's cycle, the difficulty in predicting the exact terminus in the life cycle of the sperm, the possibility of second ovulations, which occur quite often in some women, it becomes obvious that for the more fecund couple there may be no time when they can be sure whether an act of intercourse will result in conception. Fecundity is not a phenomenon which exists in the same way in all people. It is rather a group of variables which go from the very infecund couple, the couple where the husband has a very low sperm count, although not low enough to be classed as sterile, where the wife ovulates very irregularly to the highly fecund couple, where the man's spermatozoa may have a very high count and long durability, and the wife be subject to short cycles or perhaps to second ovulations. The relatively infecund couple may be able to use the rhythm method quite well; in fact, they might be surprised to discover that they would have done almost as well to have used no method at all. The highly fecund couple, on the other hand, may abstain for long periods during every cycle and still find that the method has inexplicably failed. The method, in effect, rewards the sterile, and penalizes the fertile.

R. E. Lebkicker, a biologist from Philadelphia, has done research on the ovarian cycle which indicates that the time of ovulation has no calculable relationship with the onset of menstruation and, therefore, that the Ogino-Knaus rhythm method, which attempts to predict the probable time of ovulation from the beginning of menstruation, has been operating under a fallacy. According to Lebkicker, ovulation is related to hormone changes which take place previous to menstruation at the end of the cycle at a time difficult to determine by overt signs. Depending on when these changes occur and depending on variables in the hormone structure of different women which create various patterns in the time of menstruation, the time of ovulation may take place as early as the fifth day after the onset of menstruation. This means that a woman could be ovulating and menstruating at the same time, a thing which is considered impossible according to the rhythm methods now being taught, which take the menstrual period as absolutely infertile. According to this research, however, even this period may not be infertile, but a woman who carefully followed the present calculation of the "infertile" period could actually become pregnant while still menstruating. Whether Lebkicker is correct in his criticism or not, in any case it indicates how little agreement there is even among experts as to when the infertile period actually is and how it is to be determined.

Another common fallacy found in discussions of the rhythm method, particularly by the clergy, lies in the attempt to promote periodic abstinence as a kind of ascetic discipline. Yet the clerical moralists themselves are somewhat of two minds about this. On the one hand, they try to laud the virtue obtained by abstinence as "heroic sacrifice" and, on the other hand, to denigrate any real hardship involved, so that they may not be thought to be imposing something beyond the reach of the average person. Now it is obvious that no married couple either needs or wants to make love every night, and it is perfectly normal to go weeks at a time without making use of the sexual act. The typical clerical query: "Can't you abstain for just a few days?" really misses the point of the criticism of the rhythm method. The present author, for example, is presently living alone while her husband works on a scholarship in India for twelve months. It is certainly a hardship to be separated from him, but it is *him* and not the sexual act which is the essence of the deprivation. The mistake which the clerical moralists tend to make in this matter is to assume that married people have some purely bodily drive which needs to be satisfied. This drive is seen on the animal level essentially as an egotistic need of each of the members of the partnership individually. In other words, the drive is understood by the clerical moralist primarily under the rubric of lust. Therefore he tends to assume that it would be "good for them" to repress this drive for a while, that periodic continence will "help" them to "humanize" their lust; otherwise they would be given over to unrestrained self-indulgence.

This point of view totally misses the essence of the marital relationship. This is so primarily because the clerical moralist unconsciously has patterned his description of the sexual drive on his own position, which requires the repression of a need, which, for him, is totally egotistic. If the priest has experienced the sexual drive at all, it is as a need of his own body, and without any specific link to another person. In other words, the sexual drive outside the context of marriage is and can be nothing else but a purely egotistic drive, because it does not exist in the context and as an expression of a specific I-Thou relationship with a particular person.

Unconsciously, the clerical moralist tries to apply some of the rationale of his own celibate existence to his understanding of the marital relationship. His line of reasoning goes something like this: "I have sublimated my sexual drive entirely. Why can't they do it for a little while each month?" What this kind of thinking fails to grasp is that the married person, if he is really a morally developed person, already has sublimated his sexual drive, but in a different manner from the celibate, and in a manner which makes any half-way application of the celibate's kind of asceticism quite irrelevant for the best fulfillment of the married person's state of life. The married person has sublimated the sexual drive into a *relationship* with another person. The sexual drive, for him, ceases to have any meaning or urgency simply as an egotistic drive, or self-centered bodily appetite. It is rather the intimate expression of one's relationship with this particular other person, this unique and irreplaceable other person. Thus it is quite clear that once my husband is gone, the sexual act is simply no longer relevant. It no longer has a purpose or need in my life. I don't miss it or need it at all because it is not a thing which I need to satisfy an appetite of my own, but it is entirely subsumed into a means of expressing my relationship with him. Once we are reunited, however, it again will become important as the act of communion by which that relationship is expressed.

Rhythm is debilitating to this relationship not because it is difficult in itself for a couple to abstain for a few days. Most couples tend to do this even without thinking about it. In fact, couples who use contraceptives and who know that they can use the sexual act without fear of pregnancy whenever they wish may well be far less preoccupied with sex than those who use the rhythm method. From my discussion with Catholics using the rhythm method and with Protestants who use contraceptives, I have noticed a kind of obsession among the Catholics which seems to be absent in many of the Protestants of comparable social and moral development. The very tension created by the rhythm method may make the Catholic couple more rather than less taken up with sex. By being constantly forced to worry about when "it is safe" to use the sexual act, they may well be being forced into a hyper-consciousness of the need for sexual expression which would not exist with some other method. Thus the rhythm method may really have an effect for many couples which is the opposite of the supposed ascetic virtues commonly predicated of it.

Essentially the rhythm method is debilitating because it imposes an abnormal regime on the expression of marital love. It treats marital love as an appetite which can be scheduled, like eating and sleeping. But marital love, if it is really developed, has been sublimated from the appetite level. It has been raised into the expression of a relationship, and therefore needs to follow the laws of that relationship, and to flow with the dynamics of that relationship. When a couple are busy, tired, caught up with other concerns, they may go for considerable periods without even thinking of using the sexual act. But at the moments when they need to turn to each other for solace, reassurance, renewal of their bonds with each other, it is precisely at this moment and not ten days later that they need to be able to use the sexual act.

It is this essential kind of psychological naturalness which the rhythm method destroys, when a couple must try to hold their sexual relationships to some rigid calendar schedule. Thus the effort to interpret rhythm as a kind of half-way celibacy is misconstrued and rests on an inability to understand the sexual act as the expression of the relationship, rather than merely the satisfaction of an egoistic appetite. Now it is obvious that if a couple were to really practice continence as a spiritual discipline, the last way they would do it would be according to the woman's monthly cycles of fertility. They would perhaps abstain for the forty days of Lent, or something of this kind, and meanwhile devote themselves to some special regime of prayer and contemplation. In this way abstinence might have a genuine spiritual function in their lives. But to ab-

stain according to the woman's monthly cycle can scarcely
be subsumed into an authentic spiritual discipline. It serves
primarily to disrupt the natural psychological dynamics of
the sexual life, and to reveal itself at every turn as a blatant
method for avoiding pregnancy. Anyone who has tried to
live by the temperature-taking, glucose-testing, chart-making
routine imposed by the rhythm method with its artificial
manipulation of the whole relationship can scarcely be led
to see this as any real spiritual discipline. The motivation is
obviously all wrong to begin with. It is like being asked to
fast during Lent not for any ascetic value, but because a
ten-ton block had been placed over the ice box which
would fall on your head if you opened the door. Obviously
such a situation, far from promoting the ascetic values,
would simply make a person obsessed with hunger and
filled with a sense of personal degradation. He would feel
that he was being treated like a rat in a laboratory, and
rightly so. Let this ten-ton block stand for the fear and uncertainty which accompany the rhythm method, and one
may see why the rhythm method is a debilitating rather
than an elevating adjunct to the normal marital relationship; and one must recognize also that this ten-ton block
will grow apace with each failure of the method to produce
the kind of control over fertility that the couple wants
and needs.

One might use this kind of analogy to explain the de-
humanization created by such a method of regulating fertility. Suppose one were not allowed to smile when one
really felt happy. The smile was not allowed to function as
a spontaneous expression of *joie de vivre*. Rather the smile
was treated as if it were some kind of appetite which had

to be kept in check, although being a forceful appetite, one must condescend and satisfy it periodically. The satisfaction of this animal smiling-drive was linked by some Grand Inquisitor with a lunar stopwatch which flashed red and green at intervals. When it flashed green the person could smile, when red he must stop. In addition to this, the stop watch had a few kinks in its mechanism so that it functioned very irregularly and inefficiently. The person therefore was not quite sure when it was flashing red and when green and he lived in constant dread of smiling at the wrong time, in which case he would be hit on the head with the aforementioned ten-ton block. Let the clerical moralist contemplate this analogy with care. Let him consider honestly what effect such a regime would have on his own psychic life, and perhaps he will have an inkling of why many Catholic married people object to the rhythm method.

As we have indicated at the outset of this essay, the ability to love and to procreate is a union of will and act governed only by the discipline of love itself: this is the full ideal of marital sexuality. But, in the existential situation, this cannot be attained at all times. Failing this full ideal in every act, it would seem that some such method as we have outlined earlier might give the couple the second best possibility of experiencing their full union and harmony of purpose from time to time, until they can give themselves to procreation in full generosity of spirit; and, on the other hand, it gives them the maximum freedom to develop the auxiliary perfections of their married life as much as possible. In the words of Augustine: *"Ama et fac quod vis."*

THE LESSONS OF BIOLOGY

JULIAN PLEASANTS

Looked at from the outside, living things seem to meet the requirements of life in simple, straightforward fashion. An action such as breathing or eating begins a definite process which then goes on automatically to provide the body what it needs in the way of oxygen or food. These simple observations can lead and have led to various generalizations about biological activity, e.g. that an action has one specific purpose, that an action once started naturally goes on to completion (except for accidental reasons) and that a living thing initiates an action according to the measure of need for its product.

This is what we might conclude from looking at the *net results* of living activity. When we go inside an animal, however, as the biologist does, this picture of a neat and tidy economy breaks down. An action usually has several specific purposes, not just one. The need for any one of these purposes will initiate the action, and the other effects, if unneeded, will be inhibited in some way, instead of going on to an automatic conclusion. Life would be impossible without this type of control, as I shall show later. But first let us see how these two pictures of life influence our thinking on birth control.

Catholic spokesmen have finally admitted that the *net result* of birth control activity, such as wider spacing of children in the family, safeguarding of health, slowing down of population increase, could be desirable under certain conditions. Arguing from an earlier, superficial biology, however, they maintain that the only *natural* way of limiting the result is by limiting the action to times when physiological conditions make the result impossible. This position demands that one should make the assumption that the marital act has only one specific purpose and that any other effects are subsidiary to it. The position also implies that inhibiting one purpose of an act while achieving another is unnatural. But, the closer look at life which modern biology provides indicates that, on the contrary, a biological action is ordinarily multifunctional, and that inhibition of a function which is not needed is the typical means of achieving the integrated control required by living things. Without such control, the body would be overrun by an accretion of unneeded materials which had to be taken in while the needed ones were being accumulated.

Breathing, for example, is not just a means of gaining oxygen, but also a means of disposing of carbon dioxide; and carbon dioxide is not just a waste product, but a means of maintaining blood acidity within safe limits. Breathing may have to be speeded up to dispose of excessive carbon dioxide even if no more oxygen is needed; the excess oxygen taken in will be breathed out again, rather than be accumulated in the hemoglobin. In man, breathing is also a means of activating the vocal cords. In this case, the pattern of breathing will be regulated by a need which is basically spiritual, rather than by complete subordination to the usual physiological controls.

The act of eating is even more a multifunctional action, since it must provide calories, building materials for growth and repair, and special elements, such as vitamins, for regulating metabolism. No meal can possibly provide these in the exact proportions needed by the body at a particular time. So the body balances its needs in various ways. Some nutrients, like sugars, are unavoidably absorbed, and then stored if not required at the time. The absorption of some others, such as iron, is inhibited as long as the body stores are ample; other types of minerals may be absorbed in excess of need but are excreted by the kidney. Illogical as it seems to take something into the blood and then put it back out again, the process is quite systematic and provides a very dependable way of controlling the level of different nutrients in the blood.

In man the act of eating can assume an additional role. To varying degrees in different cultures, the act of dining with others functions as an expression of acceptance and unity, more significant in some societies than any verbal expression. Under certain conditions this function would certainly justify a man's eating, even if his body did not need food. Would it also justify something more radical? This might be the place to give a biologist's view of the argument that contraception is wrong just as it would be intrinsically wrong to eat a meal and then vomit it out so that another meal could be eaten. Since this seems to be one of the most often used analogies to show the evil of contraception, it may be worth some consideration—although it must be acknowledged that it is drawn much less frequently than formerly.

Unless we are to assume that a professional wine taster is sinning all day long, we must assume that there is something decisive about the act of swallowing. Once food has been swallowed, it has been abandoned to the automatisms of digestion, and these presumably cannot be tampered with. But, of course, everyone recognizes that they can be tampered with if something harmful has been eaten, particularly if it is some harmful substance, barbiturates, for example, which the stomach cannot detect as harmful and will not automatically reject. But here it is a case of reversing an action which should not have been performed in the first place. What if it is a case of a meal legitimately eaten which becomes a liability to the body by reason of subsequent circumstances? In case of extreme stress, the same nerves and hormones which excite the heart, lungs, and muscles to greater activity simultaneously stop the activity of the digestive system. A stomach filled with stagnating food can cause considerable distress, for example, to a woman in labor. If the stomach does not quickly empty itself, no one would, on moral grounds, forbid giving the stomach a little help. So the real question is not whether we have a right to reverse the act of swallowing, but whether we have a right to do it for non-physiological reasons.

To bring the non-physiological function of eating into some semblance of analogy with the marriage act, we would have to invest eating with a ritual meaning which it does not have in our culture. We would have to imagine an anthropologist traveling among some primitive people for whom the willingness to share their meals is a sign of acceptance of their persons, of their personal value. Our imaginary traveler, who genuinely admires these people, has just gone a short distance from one camp site where he shared in an enormous festive meal, only to find that he has ridden right into the midst of another tribal group whose festival is just beginning. He cannot let them feel that he rejects them, yet he couldn't eat another such meal without getting sick in the middle of it, and this too might be considered a symbol of rejection. The thought also occurs to him that if he refuses to eat with them, his very life may be in danger. If only he could get rid of the first meal, which has already served its most important function, and thus be free to eat another one. Being convinced that it is intrinsically evil, however, he rejects the temptation at once. He is never heard from again.

This, of course, is an exaggerated picture as far as the act of eating is concerned. But it is not an exaggerated picture of the function of *meaning* in the marriage act, where meaning is far more important and far from arbitrary. We will come back later to meaning as purpose, but let us first review some other typical biological activities which the logician would call self-frustrating.

If it is unnatural to initiate an action and then frustrate some of its effects, we should all have our kidneys removed. None of us would be alive to read this if the first part of the kidney filter were not frustrated in its seeming desire to rid the blood of nearly all its water-soluble components. Looking at the net result of kidney activity, we marvel at the efficient way it takes urea and excessive salts out of the blood and disposes of them. But it does not do this by simply extracting these substances from the blood. Instead, the glomerulus, the initial filter, lets almost every small-sized molecule pass into the filtrate, including not only urea and unneeded salts, but also much-needed amino acids, sugars, and essential salts. If the lower tubules did not frustrate this prodigality by reabsorbing the needed materials, we would be dead in a short time.

The nervous system is equally dependent on such seeming frustration. A nerve impulse, as from an irritated pain nerve ending, must cross a junction to get its message to the central nervous system. To do this, it causes secretion of a hormone which then excites the nerves on the other side of the junction. But an enzyme present in the junction destroys this hormone almost immediately. This frustrates most of the work of the first nerve impulse, but in effect it clears the way for a new impulse to act, so that we can tell if the pain is still there. Besides this general type of inhibition, whole tracts of the nervous system are given over to inhibitory activity. Delicate coordinated movements would be impossible if some of our automatic reflexes occurred in the middle of them. These must therefore be inhibited. The importance of inhibitory tracts at a higher level can be appreciated by observing the actions of a drunken man or one who has had his pre-frontal lobes removed. He carries out ill-considered movements because his inhibitory tracts are not working well and not cutting in on his reflexive responses to certain stimuli.

In short, life would be impossible if the body were at the mercy of any action which once started had to be allowed to achieve all its possible effects. On the contrary, the body

commonly overdoes things, and then inhibits or frustrates
any excessive results. If this seems untidy, it certainly cannot be called unnatural. Our bodies evolved: they were not
engineered by logicians. Instead of developing a new organ
and a new action to meet every new need, the animal body
added new functions to existing systems and activities. In
the course of evolution, the act of circulating the blood first
transported oxygen through the body; later it transported
food, then body wastes, then materials for defense and repair, then hormones to regulate metabolism, then body
heat. The circulation of blood cannot shut down just because one of these needs is satisfied. Therefore the body
must limit any unneeded effects so that they will not be
overdone.

In biological activities, it is meaningless to speak of the
integrity of an action, as if it had to accomplish all its
effects at once. It would be worse than meaningless; it
would be fatal. What life depends on is the *integration* of
an action, the regulation of its effects by the needs of the
whole organism. What is crucial is the integrity of the
organism, not the integrity of individual actions. As long
as such actions are multifunctional, the organism's needs
will nearly always require at least the partial suppression
of some functions in order to balance its physiological
needs.

To fit the marriage act, and the possibility of contraception into the perspective of natural biological processes, we
must first ask if the marriage act is a multifunctional one,
or if it is, as many theologians imply, a single-functioned
act with other effects which are essentially "bait" to get
the main function performed. The answer to this question

does not require any biological finesse. It is an experimentally verified fact for millions of married couples that the marriage act has a psychological function which is more than mere pleasure. From experienced reality, they know the marriage act as a sacrament on the natural level: an act which accomplishes spiritually the unity which it symbolizes physically.

One could go into a comparison of the way in which mating in the lower animals is concentrated in the times when the female is fertile, while in man the action can occur at any time of the ovulatory cycle. Thus even in a highly fertile, very spontaneous marriage, about 98 per cent of the marriage acts will achieve only the psychic function, not the procreative one, indicating that in man the act of mating does not have the simple subordination to procreation that it does in lower animals. But no such comparisons can compare in cogency with the sheer fact of psychic union as it is experienced by married couples. Those who cannot know the fact experimentally and are unwilling to accept the testimony of those who do know, should still be able to reason to the fact by observing the psychic unity which characterizes happily married couples.

Therefore, as a datum of reality, the existence of this spiritual function of the marriage act needs no further substantiation than the experiencing of it. If the fact cannot be fitted within a given philosophical framework, then the philosophical framework is incomplete. The scientific profession has known for a long time that the Aristotelian framework is indeed incomplete, and that its principles must be expanded if they are to cover all reality, especially living reality. The progress of science has resulted from the

scientists' decision to abandon this framework, to expand
their principles, to redefine their terms, and to reorganize
their theories whenever they became aware of new facts
which could not be fitted into the old schema. This is
especially true for the biologist. It is not only his knowledge
of life which expands, but life itself which expands, actualizing potentialities never before actualized. This is how
evolution has come about. If you define a thing or an action
so as to say what it *cannot* do, you automatically cut yourself off from an understanding of living reality. What the
scientist has discovered is that the definitions of things
must be left open at the ends. What was valid yesterday is
still valid today but it may not be complete. What we say
positively about something, on the basis of present observations, can continue to be true, but what we say
negatively about it may need to be revised when the thing
reveals new powers in new situations, or when be become
aware of powers which once escaped our observation.

When we say that the marriage act has the function of
procreation, this is a perennially valid statement. If we say
that the marriage act has no other function coordinate with
procreation, such a definition can become obsolete as we
become aware of the coordinate importance of psychic
unity in marriage, and as man develops means for inhibiting one function while achieving the other. The scientist is
used to such revision of definitions. It might be called his
profession. The philosopher, however, seems to consider it
a sign of failure. Yet if the philosopher, too, is going to
keep in touch with reality, he also will be forced to the
conclusion that our understanding of reality is growing, and
that reality itself is growing, in the sense that hidden po-

tentialities can become actualized. His positive definitions will hold. His negative definitions may be subject to revision.

The tendency to hang on to negative definitions has been a frequent source of embarrassment to the Church, and an impediment to the spread of her authentic message. Her theologians once justified slavery on the ground that some men were naturally incapable of self-guidance. At other times theologians have relegated women to a "naturally" inferior intellectual status, or have opposed democratic regimes on the assumption that men were naturally unequal to it. They seem to have made a practice of selling human nature short, not because of any religious evaluation, but because they were following a particular pre-Christian philosophy. Once you try to enclose a nature within a negative definition, presuming to say what a thing cannot do, you must automatically view all progress as unnatural. This has been a sufficiently frequent and disastrous position among ecclesiastics to make us wonder if the Church should continue jeopardizing the Christian message in order to maintain an Aristotelian fondness for definitions that definitively put things in their place. The Church's present position on contraception is simply the latest of a series of such positions. My fondest hope is that in recognizing the incompleteness of their analysis of the marriage act and of contraception, ecclesiastics will also recognize for the first time the philosophical presuppositions which got them into this and similar situations. Thus we may be spared future and perhaps even more tragic repetitions of the same pattern.

Some things have to be taken as simple facts, no matter

how they disarrange our thinking. These facts are that the marriage act has more than one function, and that it is common in biological systems to inhibit one function of a bifunctional activity when only the other one is needed. One cannot therefore, consider contraception biologically unnatural. Besides, every adult nowadays is aware that an existing pregnant state inhibits, by means of hormones, the formation of new ova, and therefore the possibility of imposing a new pregnancy on top of the existing one. A similar but less absolute hormonal inhibition occurs during the nursing of a baby. So the real question is not whether inhibition of procreation is unnatural, but whether it is natural for man to inhibit procreation for some reason other than pre-existing pregnancy or lactation. There are certainly other good and legitimate reasons for postponing another pregnancy at certain times. The Church's spokesmen have recognized them as legitimate. The body alone cannot be aware of these non-physiological reasons, and so cannot direct in its hormonal apparatus to bring about inhibition of ovulation. Neither does the reproductive system have any process similar to that of the kidney, for withdrawing something after it has been put out, so as to keep it (the sperm in this instance) from reaching an undesired destination. Yet the mind of man is capable of devising means by which the reproductive system can follow a spiritually initiated cue in the same way that if follows physiologically initiated cues. We have seen that the fact that such means are new does not argue against their naturalness. Biology must be prepared for the actualizing of new powers, and so must any philosophy which expects to come to terms with biological reality.

What then makes the whole thing unnatural as soon as the mind of man enters in? Here I think we face a difficulty that has nothing to do with biology, philosophy, or theology, but is purely a matter of semantics. It is still being alleged that contraception is unnatural because it is artificial. Now none of us is immune from the tendency to use the word "natural" in two very different senses, one of which sets natural in opposition to artificial, while the other sense inevitably includes the artificial as soon as we start speaking of man. The biologist will speak of a natural amino acid or a natural sugar, meaning thereby the particular compounds prepared and used within the body. But he does not therefore consider it unnatural for man to prepare (as he has) tens of thousands of artificial compounds and to use them for his own purposes.

Even the most agnostic biologist who will not admit anything spiritual in man will still staunchly maintain that man is an art-producing animal, whose amazing adaptability to various environments cannot be understood without the clothing, shelter, tools, machinery, speech, organizations, etc. which act as extensions of his body and help to overcome its physiological limitations. In the case of man it becomes ridiculous to say that the physiological limitations are natural and the artificial extensions are unnatural. Other writers have used the example of clothing to illustrate the naturalness of art. I would only like to add a commentary of my own. When primitive man was trying to press northward from the tropics and was worrying about how his naked body would stand the winter cold, it is fortunate he had no witch doctors to limit him to three choices: 1. Don't go north (complete abstinence); 2. Go north only in the summer time (periodic abstinence); or 3. Go north as you are and trust in the spirits of your clan (accept all the biological consequences of your action). But man found a fourth choice, "instant fur," and became thereby the most adaptable mammal on the face of the earth.

Most people freely admit that they use the word "natural" in two different senses, only one of which excludes human art. Only a few people consider that every creation of man's mind has been a mistake, and these people (some nature poets, some nudists, some natural-food advocates) are not usually consistent in the position that all of God's creation is perfect, and all man has ever done is to spoil it. When we find theologians even remotely associated with such a position, equating artificial with unnatural, we can only assume that they do it on the ground that any stick will do to beat a dog. Surely they must be judging the dog on some other ground.

Within the perspective of general biological control systems, neither the frustrating character nor the artificial character of contraception lays it open in any way to the charge of unnaturalness. But this does not mean that the biologist is satisfied with any of the existing mechanisms of contraception. None of them is esthetically or physiologically ideal; each has its drawbacks or its risks which must be taken into account. But as we have seen, life is full of such untidy processes, because life evolved, trying to meet new demands by modifying pre-existing systems. This lack of perfection cannot be advanced as a reason for proscribing them, for the other choices offered also suffer from serious imperfections. The dangers of complete abstinence are obvious enough. The rhythm method, in addition to its present degree of undependability, has a remarkable tendency to despiritualize the marriage act, and to make it seem like an end in itself. When love making can be spontaneous, it can occur within a framework of what we might call family liturgy. It becomes an expression of the joy and unity we feel on Church feasts and on family feasts: anniversaries, birthdays, etc. It becomes an expression of worship for something especially admirable, or an expression of unity in the face of some difficulty that has to be surmounted by one or both spouses, or an expression of consolation in the face of a difficulty that was not surmounted. The rhythm method tends to take the marraige act out of this larger framework and make it something that has to be "gotten in."

Vast challenges remain for the biologist, therefore, to perfect the means of control not only for the sake of married persons themselves, but also for the sake of theologians who find these imperfections a stumbling block to understanding. Conceivably, the researches of scientists could solve the whole problem tomorrow, by the discovery of some new technique acceptable to everybody. No doubt many a council Father, like many a layman, prays devoutly for such a discovery. But this possibility cannot absolve any of us from facing our present responsibilities. Catholics are being asked to bear sometimes crushing burdens on the strength of an admittedly fallible interpretation of natural law. They are asked to credit this interpretation with a high probability of being right when in fact the interpretation has been made on the basis of very incomplete knowledge, by persons who have no direct experience of the marriage act and no biological perspective within which to place the contraceptive process.

The Church's present position may indeed be right, but if so, this is an accident entirely unrelated to the evidence on which the position was reached. Unless the council Fathers are willing to base a new definitive position on a new kind of evidence, namely an unambiguous, official, self-consciously infallible pronouncement, lay Catholics will continue to be asked to base very serious decisions on the human knowledge of private theologians. Since this human knowledge is obviously incomplete, the conclusions based on it cannot be said to have any special probability one way or the other, either of being right or of being wrong. It may be alleged that the position acquires some probability of being right simply from the fact of its enunciation by the pope, even when he labors the point (as he does in *Casti Connubii*) that he is not speaking *ex cathedra*. In this connection, a comment may be helpful which Cardinal Newman made about papal policies affecting the Irish Church:

I had been accustomed to believe that, over and above that attribute of infallibility which attached to the doctrinal decisions of the Holy See, a gift of sagacity had in every age characterized its occupants, so that we might be sure, as experience taught us, without its being a dogma of faith, that what the Pope determined was the very measure, or the very policy, expedient for the Church at the time when he determined. . . . I am obliged to say that a sentiment which history has impressed upon me, and impresses still, has been very considerably weakened as far as the present Pope, Pius IX, is concerned. . . . I was a poor innocent as regards the state of things in Ireland when I went there, and did not care to think about it, for I relied on the word of the Pope, but from the event I am led to think it not rash to say that I knew as much about Ireland as he did (W. Ward, *The Life of John Henry Cardinal Newman*, I, 388).

Substituting the word "marriage" for the word "Ireland," many lay married Catholics, particularly those who are biologists, would be willing to make such a statement their own.

The immediate responsibility of Catholic biologists is to try to offer theologians the kind of biological perspective they need for making a relevant judgment on contraception, hoping that they will give as much of a hearing to modern biology as they give to the biology of ancient Greece. But this can only supplement the primary communication of the primary fact: the dual function of the marriage act. This is the responsibility of married Catholics everywhere to communicate to their spiritual leaders, hoping that the latter will pay at least as much attention to their experimental data as to that of a fifth century Church Father who experienced the sexual union only in the context of fornication.

Precisely because of this fact, that the marriage act has two functions, and that the satisfaction of these does not necessarily coincide, the necessity arises for a way of balancing the two functions within the one action. What the biologist can show is that this is a regular problem in many biological systems, and that various processes of contraception are entirely analogous to solutions developed by living things for the problems created by multifunctional actions. These are the two relevant facts for making a decision as to the naturalness or unnaturalness of contraception. On this issue, a dialogue between theologians and married Catholics is not only desirable but indispensable, since the former are not in possession of the facts. Until their statements reveal an awareness of the relevant facts, we shall have to assume that their pronouncements apply to some world other than our own.

THE LESSONS OF ZOOLOGY

ELIZABETH A. DAUGHERTY

The natural purpose of sex in man as it may be determined by the use of right reason is the basis for the Catholic position on sexual morality, including the Church's stand on contraception. Certainly as Christians we have no quarrel with this, for God is indeed the designer of love and procreation, and we must honestly seek to use these gifts in a manner pleasing to Him. The reasoning of the natural law is based in part on biological data, however, and it is this area which is a cause of concern to so many thoughtful Catholics today.

Many are saying that the biologism of the act of love has been overstressed at the expense of its psychological values; in this they are correct, for human sexuality cannot be understood in purely procreational terms. For myself, I do not object to the fact that the Church has placed heavy emphasis on biologism, for sex is, after all, a biological phenomenon. What I do find so disturbing is that the biology was faulty in the first place and that the carefully reasoned position of the Church has been based on a false observation (at least false in the sense of being incomplete) of the purpose of an act.

According to my understanding, the Church has been teaching, most basically, that the natural purpose of sex in marriage is for conception, that this is the primary purpose of sex and that all other purposes are secondary at best. Pope Pius XI states it most clearly in *Casti Connubii:* "Since therefore the conjugal act is destined primarily by nature for the begetting of children, those who in exercising it deliberately frustrate its natural power and purpose sin against nature." Yet, in the three decades since this was written, much has been discovered in the field of mammalian reproduction which is in conflict with this statement.

My purpose therefore will be to set forth in this article the evidence which may be obtained from the biological sciences as to the sexuality of man and the regulation of his numbers, and to inquire if the insights provided by this evidence may not contribute to the solution of our particular dilemma.

Research has clearly established that the female estrous cycle regulates the reproduction of the lower mammals, while among the primates the menstrual cycle is common to women and to female anthropoid apes and to some monkeys. The menstrual cycle is thus seen to be a very recent evolutionary development.

The internal regulation of both estrous and menstrual cycles depends on gonadotrophic hormones from the pituitary, the follicle-stimulating hormone (FSH) which also stimulates spermatogenesis, and the luteinizing hormone (LH) which causes development of the corpus luteum, or non-ovulatory phase after ovulation has occurred. The LH hormone also stimulates the interstitial cells of the testis and ovary. Fluctuations in the relative amounts of FSH and LH and their interaction with other hormones produced by the pituitary and the ovary (estrogen and progesterone) are intimately concerned in the maintenance of the estrous cycle in animals with breeding seasons, and with the menstrual cycle of primates and human beings.

It is difficult to make an exact comparison between the menstrual cycle and the estrous cycle; yet the physiological similarities are so striking that the menstrual cycle has been called a serial estrous.[1] The most striking difference is the periodic bleeding of the menstrual cycle, which has nothing corresponding to it in the estrous, and the fact that each woman follows her own variable cycle, whereas in wild animals most estrous females come into heat at the same season or seasons. All the factors in the environment which determine the external regulation of the estrous cycle are not known, but there are indications that food supply and changes in the length of the day are motivating factors.[2]

The reproductive cycles of the sub-primate mammals are further classified as monestrous, in which there is only one annual breeding period, or polyestrous, in which there are two or more periods, or seasonally polyestrous, in which there are several serial estrous cycles at one season of the year. Animals which are monestrous in the wild tend to become polyestrous after many centuries of domestication.

[1] J. Z. Young, The Life of Mammals, Oxford 1957.
[2] Kenneth C. Greiser and Ludvig G. Browman, "Total Gonadotrophic Potency of Mule Deer Pituitaries," Endocrinology 58, 2, February 1956.

The dog and horse, the chicken, and the milk cow are all examples of alteration of reproductive cycles under domestic breeding.

A close relationship between ovarian condition, estrogen level, and sexual receptivity appears to be the rule with sub-primate mammals, according to Beach,[3] and sexual activity is dominated by the physiology of the periodic estrous cycle and rarely occurs except at a time when fertilization can take place. Thus conception as a result of mating holds undisputed primacy of purpose only among the sub-primate forms.

Human beings may have sexual relations at any time during the wife's cycle and this means that relations may take place during the period of lowest estrogenic activity as well as the highest, or during the period dominated by progesterone. The period of lowest estrogenic activity immediately after the menstrual period corresponds roughly to the anestrum of lower mammals; the period of rising estrogen levels to the proestrum, when the ovarian follicle is ripening, and the time of ovulation is the true estrus or heat in lower animals, and, as already noted, is the only period during which the females are receptive to mating. After ovulation, all mammalian females are under the influence of progesterone from the corpus luteum. This is a period of rapidly declining estrogenic activity which ends the sexual receptivity of the lower mammalian female, whether or not fertilization occurs; but marital relations continue during this progesterone-dominated period before

[3] Frank A. Beach, "Evolutionary Changes in the Physiological Control of Mating Behavior in Mammals," *Psychological Review* 54, 6, November 1947.

the abrupt onset of menstruation. It is the period of lowest estrogenic activity and the progesterone-dominated period after ovulation which are known as the "safe period" for marital relations.

Thus it seems to be clear that only the higher primates and man have the use of sex in excess of reproductive needs, and that this non-reproductive use is most pronounced among human beings. Most primates males are sexually responsive whenever a receptive female is available, but the menstrual-cycle female primates show receptivity to the males principally for a few days around the time of ovulation, and only rarely at other times. Only with human beings are both sexes relatively free from physiologically dominated sexual desires, so that we possess a more or less permanent sexuality from adolescence until old age.

In order to bring into bolder relief the differences in the life system of an estrous-cycle animal and human beings, let us consider the life cycle of a species of deer. The deer is monestrous, and the mating takes place in the fall of the year. The rest of the year is the period of sexual quiescence called the anestrum. The males do not have continual spermatogenesis, as men do, and the females ovulate only once a year, at the time of the mating season, when male spermatogenesis and female ovulation are synchronized. The first estrus occurs when the doe is about eighteen months old, conception occurs after mating in a very high percentage of mature females, and usually twins are born. Considering the life span of the deer, the young are matured in less than 10 per cent of the total life span of the mother, and about 85 per cent or even more of the life span is devoted to reproduction. The birth rate of a deer population might run to several hundred per thousand annually, compared with the present worldwide human birth rate of about thirty-five per thousand annually. It is important to note here also that the wolf is a rare example, if indeed not the only example, of an estrous cycle animal with true paternity and monogynous mating; with the deer and most other lower mammalian species there is a separation of the sexes as soon as the mating season is over.

With human beings, the child is dependent for about 25 per cent of its life span, and a woman's reproductive years are roughly 35 per cent of her life span. The sexual act is successful as a generative act less than 1 per cent of the time over the course of a normal marriage of forty years or so, even if no attempt is made to control conception.

Besides these very important and significant differences between man and the lower mammals, there are several other lines of evidence which demonstrate our non-reproductive use of sex. It should be worthwhile to examine this evidence briefly.

The continuance of the marital relationship during most of a normal pregnancy. Some primates are also known to have coitus during pregnancy, especially the anthropoids, but with estrous mammals conception marks the end of the mating season. During pregnancy progesterone is the dominant hormone, first supplied by the corpus luteum, in both lower mammals and women, and later by the placenta. Part of progesterone's role is to block out estrogen so that no further ovulation or uterine contraction will occur. Asdell further states that with estrous cycle mammals progesterone is protective in that heats and coitus during pregnancy are prevented.[4] Yet with human beings intercourse during pregnancy is considered normal and moral not only by the Catholic Church, but by almost all societies.[5]

The continuance of the marital relationship during lactation. In most species, the estrous cycle is depressed during lactation. It is known also that in women, ovulation occurs only rarely, so that complete nursing of the child is now advocated as a means of conception control; and for many centuries it was indeed nature's method of spacing births, possibly quite as efficient as the present rhythm system without nursing.

In those rare species, such as the Alaska fur seal, where the estrus occurs shortly after the birth of the young, delayed implantation of the embryo in the uterine wall may occur. This method enables such species to nurse the newborn young for a suitable length of time before the fertilized egg cell develops beyond the blastocyst stage. It might be mentioned here in connection with lactation that women are unique in possessing a permanent development of the breast rather then development only during lactation, which is the condition prevailing among lower mammals. Some biologists point out here the importance of the breast in sexual attraction and love making.

The continuance of the marital relationship after the menopause. The menopause itself is a unique feature of the menstrual cycle which ensures that no children will

[4] S. A. Asdell, *Patterns of Mammalian Reproduction*, New York 1946.

[5] Clellan S. Ford and Frank A. Beach, *Patterns of Sexual Behavior*, New York 1951.

be born after its occurrence, for the risk would be great, if fertility was unchecked, that the mother would not live to care for the child until it reached the age of independence. Old age is probably a rarity in wild animals, but there is no corresponding dramatic estropause. Animals with an estrous cycle often breed until very nearly the end of life, because their young are usually independent within a few weeks or months. Here we might suggest the possibility of an induced or stabilized menopause, utilizing progesterids, as one aid to conception control.

The absence of any accessory mechanisms for sperm retention. These mechanisms to insure fertilization are present in the lower forms when mating is not synchronized with ovulation, or with the optimal time of pregnancy. Examples are the spermatheca of insects, the uterine storage of spermatozoa in some bats, and the vaginal plug of spermatozoa in cattle, as well as the delayed implantation of the blastocyst mentioned above.

The chemical hostility of the vagina and cervix to sperm except at the time of ovulation. This coincides with the "safe period" of the rhythm method. Buxton and Southam[6] state that it is well known that infertile female patients may have a normal postcoital test containing large numbers of active sperm near the time of ovulation, but with complete absence of sperm post-coitally at other times in the cycle. This is correlated with definite changes in the characteristics of the cervical mucus which chemically changes from a pre-ovulatory acid level to an alkaline level at the time of ovulation and acquires a fairly high glycogen con-

[6] C. Lee Buxton and Anna L. Southam, *Human Infertility,* New York 1958.

tent (the glucose test methods for the determination of ovulation time are based on this phenomenon). Thus the glandular physiology of the cervix is such that migration of large numbers of sperm into the uterus is permitted only near the time of ovulation. In view of this, one may certainly ask why it is not proper during the sterile period to reinforce this natural phenomenon with the use of spermatocidal agents, or other agents impeding the migration of the sperm into the uterus.

A survey of studies which have been made concerning the rhythmic variations in the sexual desire of women is of value here. Ford and Beach[7] report studies made by Davis in 1929 and Terman in 1938 show that a peak of sexual desire occurs most often just before or just after the menstrual period, and that the peak of desire was reported least often as occurring around the time of ovulation. Over nine hundred women were questioned in the two surveys. A careful and impartial evaluation of the rhythm system, which so many lay people are now demanding, must certainly take into account whether or not women do indeed characteristically experience fluctuation in desire, at what periods, and of what magnitude.

If women do normally experience a strong peak of desire just before and just after the menstrual period, rather than at the time of ovulation, it is another indication of the evolutionary development of the non-reproductive use of sex, on the one hand, and on the other hand an indication that the practice of periodic continence is inherently easier for women than men. It must be remembered however that normal women are not unreceptive to their hus-

[7] Ford and Beach, *loc. cit.*

bands at times other than when the greatest desire may be experienced and that love making is more commonly initiated by the man.

Low fecundity associated with permanent sexuality and with the non-reproductive use of sex. I wish particularly to stress this point because I consider it of central significance in our understanding of the nature of sex and of human sexuality. Therefore it should be useful to discuss our understanding of the natural control of animal populations and the relationship of this knowledge to human fecundity and the population explosion. My discussion is based on the work of Lack and Wynne-Edwards.[8]

All animals and plants have great latent power of increase, so that even the slowest breeders could produce offspring in excess of what is needed to sustain population. Therefore in order to prevent geometric increase, some sort of brake must be applied. The application of this brake is said to be "density-dependent," so that when density is low, expansion is permitted, and when it is high and a limiting threshold is reached, the brake is applied.

The most important of these density-dependent factors appears to be food supply; other limiting factors are predation and disease. It is important to point out however that while food may be the ultimate factor it is not the proximate factor, and food shortages will not begin to take a toll of numbers until long after optimum density has been exceeded. Carr-Saunders outlined the principle of optimum numbers, as opposed to maximum numbers, in 1922. The

---

[8] David Lack, *The Natural Regulation of Animal Numbers,* Oxford 1954; V. C. Wynne-Edwards, *Animal Dispersion in Relation to Social Behavior,* New York 1962.

optimum number for human population has slowly increased with increasing technological development, but we
see now in many areas a very serious lag between technological progress and population. Also, even in the most
favorable conditions we must try to determine the optimal
growth rate as well as the optimum population, if the
population is to expand rather than be stabilized. Among
animals, both mortality rates and reproductive rates vary
with these density-dependent factors, but in order for an
animal population to be stabilized, it follows that a high
death rate is an inevitable consequence of high fecundity.

Animal populations are also kept stable by reproductive
adaptations which result in a reduction in progeny, and
here we see the general rule in operation that the average
number of offspring of a species is in inverse ratio to
the amount of parental care, and subsequently to the survival rate, of the young. The social insects provide a classic
example of this sort of adaptation, in which sex is limited
to one act performed by one pair in the life-cycle of the
colony, and the entire colony is responsible for the care of
the developing young. As I will bring out more fully later,
our reproductive specialization permits the choice of a mate,
love, and the family.

A pair of spawning fish may leave thousands or even
hundreds of thousands of fertilized eggs uncared for on the
spawning grounds. This number is reduced to the clutch
of eggs laid by birds, where true maternity appears, and the
litters of the smaller mammals. Because of the marvelous
system of protection, nourishment and care of the young
which has developed with the placental mammals, a reduction in the numbers of progeny has not only been per-

mitted, but is a necessity. Lack notes that since domestic breeds of animals have larger litters than the wild forms, it is reasonable to conclude that mutations for larger litters must be eliminated in the wild by natural selection. Wynne-Edwards goes further in saying that it must be advantageous to survival for animal species to control their own population-densities and to keep them as near as possible to the optimum level for each habitat they occupy, and that this tendency is thus favored by natural selection. This self-balancing system he terms population homeostasis.

Complex interactions of the primate characteristics of arboreal habitat and prolonged infancy and slow maturation has resulted in a further reduction in numbers in this group. Prolonged infancy keeps the nursing mothers from ovulating, and delayed maturation reduces the percentage of the life span devoted to reproduction. Anatomical and physiological adaptations permit the bearing of only one offspring at a time, and at widely separated intervals.

It may seem paradoxical in the face of a population explosion to say that man is not a fecund species, but comparatively such is the case and this should not be surprising in view of the above discussion. It may not be entirely accurate to say that man is, by absolute numbers of offspring, the least fecund of all animals; it is probably accurate to make such a statement in relation to his size, which is not much more than moderate, and his life span, which is one of the longest of all animals. Some of these differences have already been noted in the discussion of the deer.

The largest average family size probably ever recorded is

among the Hutterites of the United States and Canada, whose families average nine children (*Population Bulletin* 1954). This family size has occurred, however, under conditions in many ways optimal; good nutrition, no crowding, and in an age and country relatively free of epidemic disease and practicing a civilized level of sanitation. The general average per family for human beings has been less, possibly even five or six children born alive.

During the many centuries when human population needed expansion rather than stabilization, these same density-dependent factors which regulate animal populations inhibited the rapid growth of human populations. Predation, except secondarily by rats and insects, has never been a serious threat, but constant warfare has had a similar effect. Other density-dependent factors more peculiarly human are pollution control, pure water supply and the maintenance of social harmony.

It is our conscious control of disease and food supply which has destroyed the homeostatic regulation of human numbers, and is causing the population explosion. The annual birth rate in the United States in 1890 was 31.5 per thousand and the annual death rate approximately 17 per thousand; in 1962 our birth rate had declined to 23.4 per thousand, but the death rate had declined to 9.3 per thousand. Thus, despite a steadily declining birth rate, we now have more than two births for every death, whereas in 1890 there were less than two births for every death. It is also interesting to note here that the average wife in 1890 bore an average of 5.4 children.[9]

[9] Paul C. Glick, *American Families*, New York 1957.

The balance between births and deaths which we have upset by rational control must now be restored by the rational control of conception, rather than by the excessive control of the use of sex. Yet such excessive control has been seriously proposed by some Catholic writers not only within marriage itself by total abstinence, but by the delay of marriage.

Let me point out first of all that marriage is already delayed in civilized countries at least five years past that of primitive societies, and sometimes by as much as ten years. It would seem, then, that in civilized countries at least this means of control has already been fully exploited.

Marriage delayed past the early or mid-twenties could indeed reduce fertility. Guttmacher[10] investigated the relationship between age of the wife at the time of marriage and later involuntary childlessness and found that there is a decline of fertility with age; only 4 per cent remained childless if the wives were married before twenty, and this level of infertility gradually increased through the next two decades to a level of 69 per cent infertility for those who married at age forty to forty-five. A conservative estimate of sterility for all couples is thought to be about 10 per cent. Unfortunately, marriage delayed past the mid-twenties would coincide with an increasing rate of maternal and infant morbidity. The years of optimum fertility are also optimal for childbearing.[11]

---

[10] Alan F. Guttmacher, *The Complete Book of Birth Control*, New York 1961.

[11] Edith L. Potter, "The Perinatal Origin of Handicapping Conditions of Childhood," *Institute on Prevention and Management of Handicapping Conditions in Infancy and Childhood*, The University of Michigan School of Public Health, November 1959.

So far in this discussion we have established the point that the gradual phylogenetic decrease in numbers of progeny culminating in man has been accompanied by an abandonment of an ancient and efficient method of reproduction, that of the estrous regulated breeding season. This system has been replaced by a system which is much less efficient as far as achieving conception goes, but is even more efficient in over-all reproduction because of increased parental care. This system also permits the use of sex in excess of reproductive need.

The primates stand about halfway between man and the sub-primate mammals in this development. The breeding season has been largely obliterated so that the young may be born at any time of the year, but seasonal concentrations of birth occur in many species. The most outstanding mateship pattern of the primates, according to Ford and Beach in their survey work, appears to be polygynous with one male and several females and the young. Field studies of the gibbon, however, suggest a family of one adult male and one adult female and their offspring. The social group is a small band or troop of individuals, typically.

While true paternity (in the sense of the male as provider as well as protector and ruler) does not appear to be definite among the primates, a patriarchal social organization has been reported by Frisch[12] and others. The primate mother must carry her baby in her arms or on her back and the infant cannot be left alone while the mother forages,

[12] John E. Frisch, "Research on Primate Behavior in Japan," *American Anthropologist* 61, 4, August 1959.

as is the case with lower mammalian infants. Infancy lasts one year or more with monkeys, two years or more with apes, and sexual maturity is reached in two to four years in monkeys, eight years in apes.[13]

Among the primates therefore we see associated increased sexual activity, decreased number of offspring, a longer period of pregnancy and of dependency of the young, an increase in maternal duties, and an increase in brain size and socialization. It seems reasonable to conclude that all these characteristics are intimately interrelated.

With man, apparently the purpose of a permanent, continuous sexual relationship in excess of reproductive needs is to implement family life which is a necessity for the preservation of our species whose offspring have such a prolonged period of helplessness and dependency. An estrous-dominated mating cycle would be socially disruptive, perhaps disastrously so, with human beings. It is replaced by a method that is socially cohesive.

Young[14] states that human social organization is possible because men and women experience attractions that are more persistent if somewhat less insistent than the sweeping changes of desire of the anestrum and estrus, which may produce violent behavior. Other authors put the answer in a more positive way, saying that monogamous family life is dependent upon the continued and permanent use of sex.

The immense importance of the family and the basic reason for its universality is now generally recognized by

[13] S. L. Washburn and Virginia Avis, "Evolution of Human Behavior," *Behavior and Evolution*, New Haven 1958.
[14] J. Z. Young, *The Life of Mammals*, Oxford 1957.

anthropologists and other students of human biology, and it is generally conceded that our species could never have survived, let alone developed civilization, without this social organization. Loren Eiseley has said, quite poetically for a scientist, that man has survived not because he is tough minded, but because he is tender minded.[15] Harlow and his associates[16] are doing exciting work on the affectional relationships of monkeys, and Harlow states his opinion that even among primates the continuance of society is dependent more upon love than lust, and more upon happiness than hunger. Any mother of a two-year-old can testify to the passionate, overwhelming, and sometimes exhausting love which her dependent child shows for her. We are beginning to get a clearer understanding of the development of our own affectional system; the child who is cherished and nourished in the home and in the arms of his mother is learning a pattern and role so that he may in turn cherish his own mate and care for his children. The infant or small child deprived of tender loving care is incapable of forming or maintaining normal adult attachments, and his incapacity will be in direct relation to the degree of childhood deprivation.

I do not wish, therefore, to be accused of championing a one-sided hedonism as the basis of marriage. Man does not live by bread alone, neither does he live by sex alone; conversely we do not live without bread and we do not live in marriage without sex.

[15] Loren Eiseley, "An Evolutionist Looks at Modern Man," *Adventures of the Mind*, New York 1960.
[16] Harry F. Harlow, Margaret K. Harlow, and Ernst W. Hansen, "The Maternal Affectional System of Rhesus Monkeys," *Maternal Behavior in Mammals*, New York 1963.

Murdock has written that in the family are assembled four functions fundamental to human social life—the sexual, the economic, the reproductive, and the educational.[17] Without provision for the first and third, he says, society would become extinct; for the second, life itself would cease; for the fourth, culture would come to an end. Murdock also found from his studies that no society has ever failed to regulate the use of sex, and that while societies vary from regulated permissiveness to strict prohibition of extra-marital relations, no society has ever denied the use of sex to the married couple.

I have attempted to give a careful demonstration of the evidence, which can be voluminously documented, that human beings have a reproductive system unique in the entire animal kingdom where sub-primate reproduction is strictly physiologically controlled and regulated. This system permits the bearing of relatively small numbers of offspring who require prolonged care and training, combined with the continued and permanent use of sex in the marital relationship. My principal thesis is, therefore, that conception as a result of the sexual act is meant to be occasional, but the function of the formation and maintenance of monogamous marriage as a result of the act is meant to be permanent and continuous.

To this rather utilitarian concept the biologist may add one more thought. The great advantage of sexual over asexual reproduction is that the former permits the sharing and pooling of cytoplasmic resources, normally to the benefit of the new individual, and it is on this constant regrouping of hereditary resources that evolution is based. The great

[17] George Peter Murdock, *Social Structure*, New York 1949.

advantage of the human marital union, freed from physiological domination, is that it permits a sharing of personalities, a psychic union, and a growth of love. This is to the great advantage first of all to the couple so united, and secondly to the new individual, born not necessarily of one specific act, but of that union.

I believe that, seen in this light, the permanent use of sex in marriage represents a major evolutionary development and may indeed be compared in magnitude to the development from asexual to sexual reproduction, which must have occurred in the very dawn of life.

Reproduction of a human being does not end with conception or childbirth; it ends when a skilled and educated young adult is ready to leave his father's house and assume a responsible role in society. It is in this latter function of the sex act to which we married people can give evidence from our own experience. In the past, we have been largely ignored in formulations of the theology of marriage; at the present, I believe that we have gained the ear of the Church.

I do not mean to disparage or minimize the very real development by many Catholic theologians of a positive appreciation of the values of sexual love. Recognizing this, some ecclesiastics have called for the marshaling of research to perfect the rhythm system, and Cardinal Suenens has said that it is not right to demand that men obey a law without doing all within our power to make obedience possible. Yet at the same time there is also a school of thought that is very strong within the Church which holds to the idea that if a limitation of births is indeed required, it is the sexual life which must be limited. But is this idea at all in accord with the demonstrable fact that nature has endowed us with the lowest of all fecundity and with the fullest and most permanent use of sex? Family life could never have survived seasonal matings; yet extended periodic abstinence can come perilously close to just that situation, particularly that abstinence enjoined by child-birth and the vagaries of the postpartum period, or during the erratic menopausal years.

Theological insistence has been predominantly on the preservation of the integrity of the anatomical and physio-logical processes, to the exclusion, if necessary (and all too often it is necessary) of the integrity of the marital rela-tionship. It is the integrity of the relationship which must be given much more careful consideration. We did not in-vent the normal marital relationship, any more than we in-vented the underlying physiological and anatomical proc-esses. We must also face the fact that in order to control conceptions, we must interfere with some phase of the sys-tem, and that this interference will be an unnatural regula-tion of a natural function. Periodic abstinence is actually an artificially patterned marital relationship; with the use of the progesterids we produce an artificially patterned physiological cycle, and with the use of the older types of contraceptive we have an artificially produced anatomical barrier. As I pointed out, spermicidal jellies may actually imitate a natural function of the sterile period.

The insistence on the control of normal marital behavior as the only permissible means of conception control should have its limits, just as we rationally set limits on other methods. The limits to the control of behavior should ex-clude total abstinence as a method of conception control, and a limit should also be set on the duration of the period of abstinence. A suggestion of a practical limit might be five days. Many lay people have pointed out that the rhythm method should be submitted to the same careful scientific investigation as to its effectiveness and freedom from harmful effects which we demand of any other form of contraception.

At the present time we suffer in the Church from a kind of loophole mentality, with the liberal theologian or pastor looking for every possible help for desperate couples, and the conservative theologian or pastor just as busily engaged in plugging up every new loophole. I admit myself to have presented two new loophole methods for consideration.

Over and over in my reflections, I have come back to the question, why do we call secondary the ends of the sexual act which have been accorded in fullness only to us, and why do we call primary the end that we share with the lower animals. If the thesis which I have presented here is accepted, we may then ask if it is not actually more proper to control or suppress the function of conception after this function has been fulfilled in the bringing forth of children, than it is to control or suppress the function of the sexual act which is meant to be permanent. A re-examination of the whole question of contraception thus becomes possible.

As a practical consideration, it seems almost too much to hope for that any one method of conception control, whatever it may be, will be effective and acceptable to all people everywhere regardless of age or occupation, economic status or education, religion or culture. The real dilemma of Catholic leadership is made that much more acute by the approval of only one method.

We are still talking about the spacing of births when, with civilized death rates, it is actually necessary to strictly limit births. We must remember that an average of only three children per couple will keep the population of civilized countries multiplying all too rapidly. The present average in the United States is three children (*Population Bulletin*, February 1964); yet our population will double in size in only thirty-seven years if the present annual growth rate continues, and will give us a population of eight hundred million, eighty years from now. On the other hand, the medical care and years of education which we must now provide were unheard of even a century ago. Is not this decline in numbers of our children thus in accord with the general principle that the greater the parental care, the fewer the number of offspring?

I hope that I have adequately demonstrated the basis for my belief that, after children have been born to a union, it is wrong to frustrate the non-reproductive use of sex through prolonged abstinence. The integrity and natural purpose are destroyed in this way just as surely as when a couple, without good reason and by employing contraception, refuse to reproduce at all.

Responsible Parenthood and the Population Dilemma

William V. D'Antonio

It is five years now since the ominous warnings about a population explosion had their first impact upon the American public. Early reaction in Catholic circles was cautious or negative. The phrase "population explosion" was roundly attacked as a propaganda term, a terror expression, and the population projections of the demographers were dismissed as hypotheses, or mere "guesstimates."

At the same time Church leaders were quick to perceive that the focus on the population explosion would lead to new plans to broaden the dissemination of birth control knowledge and devices, and this move, too, was roundly condemned. Insofar as a problem of excess population did exist, it was felt that such measures as large-scale migration, better distribution of wealth, and large-scale improvements in agricultural outputs would go a long way toward solution. Family limitation via the "rhythm" method was accepted as legitimate under certain conditions. For the rest, *Casti Connubii* was still clearly the law, still clearly *the* authoritative statement.

As we head into the mid-1960s, the whole tenor of the

argument has changed. Catholic leaders around the world are aware of the population explosion, they use the phrase themselves, and they recognize that, as John A. O'Brien of Notre Dame warned, something must be done "to deal effectively with the problem of a population increasing with a speed unprecedented in history." Gradually, the focus of discussion has changed, so that the population growth problem can now properly be placed within the more fundamental problem of love and parental responsibiilty. *Casti Connubii* may be part of the deposit of faith, but it is now clear that it need not be viewed as the final and definitive statement on Christian marriage.

The rapid social and technological changes of the past two centuries and especially of the past two decades are not only responsible for the fact that the world population will double itself in thirty-five to forty years, but they also have brought on the need for a re-evaluation of the most fundamental of all human institutions, marriage and the family. Thus, the primary focus of this article is on conjugal love and responsible parenthood, with only secondary consideration given to the population explosion itself. Population control must be achieved, but it is necessary first to establish a satisfactory basis for marriage and family life.

For, as most demographers recognize, even if a "perfect" population control mechanism were available today, it would not be employed in many parts of the world because of the traditional family patterns that persist and which resist change. For example, the distinguished demographer, Irene Taeuber, analyzing the problem of population growth in underdeveloped areas, observes that "the faith and culture of Islam are perhaps most conducive to high fertility. The ethical ideals, the family values, and the roles assigned to women are all structured to maximize fertility. And fertility is high indeed in the great crescent from North Africa through Malaya and on eastward to Indonesia and north to Mindanao." [1] And Notestein, Kirk and Segal argue that there is substantial evidence that *coitus interruptus*, known throughout the world for thousands of years, "began to be widely practiced in Europe when birth rates began to fall." They conclude that "the failure of birth rates to fall in other parts of the world clearly turns less on lack of effective means than on the absence of strong motivation." [2]

A basic premise upon which the following discussion is based is that man is a rational creature who is in some sense free, that is, that his behavior is not determined by forces beyond his control. Rather, as a rational animal he is able, potentially at least, to control his behavior, and this control can extend over virtually all aspects of human life. The amount of freedom an individual has seems to vary with the sociocultural conditions of his life and, most importantly, to vary with the degree to which he is oppressed by the degrading forces of poverty, or the suffocating embrace of traditionalism, that non-rational orientation to the past. Through the use of his reason man has gradually come to realize that human life and human history are an unfolding, an evolutionary development. Reason has helped man to look ahead, to systematically plan and

[1] Irene B. Taeuber, "Population Growth in Underdeveloped Areas," *The Population Dilemma*, Philip M. Hauser (ed.), New Jersey 1963, 43.

[2] Frank W. Notestein, Dudley Kirk and Sheldon Segal, "The Problems of Population Control," Hauser, *op. cit.* 128.

control his environment, and to believe in the ability to ameliorate the human condition.

Furthermore, as Christians, the most important guide for the use of our reason is to "love our neighbor as we love ourselves for the love of God." Thus, reason and love are combined in such a way that we work out our own salvation through striving to help others to achieve theirs.

It is a difficult task to try to give an adequate definition to such a term as "love" because of the wide variety of situations, social and divine, in which it is employed. Nevertheless, the task before us requires that the effort be made. The definition will be restricted to the human situation, and the adequacy of the definition can be judged in some measure by the degree to which it conveys the essentially dynamic character of love. Human love, as the sociologist Nelson Foote has suggested, is that relationship between two individuals which seeks to achieve the optimal development of both of them. We may say that married love is the most complete kind of such relationship knowable to man, with love of parent and child and love of one's fellow man expressing other degrees of that relationship.

Building generally upon a strong physico-sexual foundation, love gradually becomes that relationship between two individuals which is concerned with the fullest development of both in all of their human potential. Seen in this light, a true love relationship can never be exploitative nor self-sacrificing. It is noteworthy that Christ admonished us "to love our neighbor as we love ourselves," neither more not less than ourselves. The unique aspect of marriage is that this social relationship offers to human

beings the opportunity for the most complete fulfillment of the commandment of love, binding man and
woman together physically, emotionally, intellectually and
spiritually. And in every aspect the concern of the partners
is for mutual satisfaction and growth. As Bernard Häring
states, it is an "unselfish giving of oneself and a grateful
acceptance of the giving of the other." [3] From the point of
view of daily experience, love manifests itself in many important ways, two of which Professor Foote calls patterns of
equality and reciprocity.

Equality here does not mean a mere equal distribution
of goods or services. A formal equality might be manifested
in each person's receiving the same size piece of pie at
dinner, or with children at play, each one having the same
amount of time to ride on the swing, or with married couples, granting equal time to each one with the use of the
TV set. The kind of equality that expresses and at the same
time creates and recreates the love relationship is of an
interior or psychological nature. Love comes not because a
person has an equal size piece of pie or an equal amount of
TV time. Rather it comes in sharing experience with the
loved one. You enjoy the pie yourself and you have pleasure in knowing that the one you love is also enjoying the
pie. In conjugal love the joy of mutual fulfillment comes
not only with the personal gratification that sexual intercourse provides, but with the realization that the beloved
is fully sharing in the same pleasure. Thus, you do not sacrifice yourself for the good of the other, but learn to share

[3] This and the other quotations of Father Häring are taken from
"Christian Marriage and Family Planning: John A. O'Brien Inter-
views Bernard Häring C.Ss.R.," *The Problem of Population*, Donald
N. Barrett (ed.), Notre Dame 1964.

the joy and pleasure of the act. For many husbands this means learning how to help their wives to achieve the full pleasure of conjugal union, and thus of experiencing the added pleasure that ensues from a much closer union. For many wives this means developing a recognition that sexual union is a good in itself, not needing extrinsic reasons to make it a good, and thus not having to feel guilty about enjoyment of the act.

Reciprocity is also a fundamental form of social relationship. Man has always been doing things for his fellows, in return for favors done or hoped for, or for goods or services rendered. We reciprocate Christmas cards, all too often not as expressions of love and affection, but as formal social requirements, or out of fear of some negative sanction. I well remember the complaint of the housewife who said that she "did so many things" for her husband who never did anything in return. People in love do not need to be reminded to reciprocate; they are constantly performing such acts for one another, as an expression of their love. Again, the idea of mutuality must be emphasized. If the husband, for example, is always doing things for his wife, and making it impossible for her to reciprocate, then only a dependency relationship can develop, and not true love. It is all too easy, even inadvertently, to snub, belittle, or ignore the proferred gift or act of the spouse, or simply to fail to recognize the important meaning of a small action. Reciprocity in love can only be for the sake of the beloved.

As the love relationship deepens to include concern for the total personality growth of both spouses, the other comes to matter as much to you as you do yourself. Then, as the noted psychiatrist, Harry Stack Sullivan, has observed, "it is quite possible to talk to this person as you have never talked to anyone before. The freedom which comes permits nuances of meaning, permits investigation without rebuff which greatly augments the consensual validation of all sorts of things."

Thus, sexual intercourse, the most perfect expression of the love relationship, can become for most married couples who are striving to achieve this love a central action of mutual pleasure, tenderness and other satisfactions both social and psychological. Sexual intercourse in marriage, mutually desired, is in itself a good and needs no excuse to make it a good. No other human action expresses so many levels of true and abiding love. Indeed, Ignace Lepp asserts that "certain theologians speak of coitus between husband and wife as a sacramental act which 'opens up the floodgates of sanctifying grace'."

Now the question arises, what is the relationship of sexual intercourse to parenthood? If conjugal love is a good in itself, how is one to evaluate canon 1013 which emphasizes the primacy of procreation-education? To accept the primacy of procreation-education in the way this canon has been traditionally understood would seem to require giving an undue emphasis to the biological aspect of coitus. Daniel Planque and others now interpret this canon to have only a juridical meaning. But it remains true that on the popular level, the laity are still told that "the sexual faculty is primarily for reproduction." Certainly *a* biological function of the sexual faculty is reproduction. But in man the sexual faculty has many other vital functions as well, and these must be taken into account if we are to establish a sound basis for married life.

To put undue emphasis on reproduction is to distort marriage. As Father Häring says: "A natural-law consideration which places the accent only on a right biological performance of the conjugal act remains on the level of mere animals and considers as primary what man has in common with the animals." It is necessary to see the situation in a different perspective. If love is the central focus, then married love is, as Father Häring expresses it, "the *causa formalis,* the very essence of the marriage as a sacrament and the image and likeness of the covenant of love between Christ and the Church." Hence, we do not enter marriage because *we have to have* children, nor do we enter marriage as a kind of bargain by which we gain sexual pleasures in return for which we guarantee to God that we will keep the race going. Rather it should be seen that a couple in love wants in their love to have children. Procreation and education of children should be seen as the way by which the couple fulfills their love, brings it to its *full* unity. Procreation should not be a process which in any way diminishes conjugal love, any more than conjugal love should diminish the value and importance of procreation. The two processes are inextricably intertwined. It would seem to be impossible to give primacy to one over the other because of the injustice and, indeed, damage done to the one given the lesser value. It is love and not obligation that should bind man to woman. Thus, God provides for the preservation of the human race through love, his guiding principle.

The dilemma for us in our time seems to lie in the question how much procreation should be fostered or encouraged for the optimal development of love? For now it becomes clear that while we enrich the original love relationship in procreation, we also enter into a new love relationship, that between parent and child. A different set of emotional and intellectual responses is called up, and a different order of physical and sociopsychological needs and actions are called into play. With the addition of more children, the web of social relationships is extended even further.

In recent years social scientists have given increasing attention to the parent-child relationship and its implications for love among human beings. This research has become important because of the unparalleled historical change which has taken place in the last two centuries. Two of the most important aspects of this change have been the decline in mortality rates at all age levels, and the changing nature of economics. Improvements in sanitation, medicine, and food production have all combined to reduce drastically mortality rates, especially during infancy and early youth. Indeed, for most of human history, the key question for man was one of survival, and a high birth rate was necessary to offset the high death rate and insure survival of the race. Now it is no longer a high death rate which threatens man's survival, but a continuing high birth rate, the same birth rate that was so essential just a few centuries ago. There is nothing in God's law that demands a high birth rate; it was simply a natural adjustment to living conditions. Unfortunately, we have come over time to grant a "sacred" quality to high birth rates and large families.

These large families were deemed necessary for survival in an agricultural society. Married couples needed many

children to help them run the farm. And because of the
high infant mortality, multiple pregnancies were necessary.
The family was a producing as well as a consuming unit.
Adequate production depended on having children who began their work career at an early age. A child was an economic asset, whatever else he might have been in the eyes
of God and his parents. He is no longer an economic asset
in this sense. We don't need the labor energy of our children to survive. In fact, children who do not at least finish
high school are rapidly becoming social and psychological
problems because there is no place for them in the labor
market. As parents and citizens we must be prepared to
spend an increasing proportion of our wealth on the formal
education of children in colleges and universities. In an important new sense, we have become a child and youth-
centered society. The structure of society has changed and
our understanding of marriage and the family must change
with it. We would be less than true to our nature were we
not to use our reason to help marriage and family to adapt
to change and to develop their own meaningful structures.

One of the exciting things about contemporary society
is that for the first time in history we have the opportunity
to control our behavior and to offer a fuller life to large
numbers of people. The opportunity to control and direct
for large numbers of people and not just for a small elite
is a challenging one indeed. It requires a new look at the
question of freedom and personal autonomy, and what
these entail for marriage and the family.

Married couples are responsible for their actions. They
have personal control over their behavior. This control is a
God-given gift and not a denial of a God-given gift. This

must include control over procreation as well as other facets
of married life. Probably few theologians still believe that
married couples should accept children as "God gives
them," without planning or spacing, or even, for that matter, without a sense of personal responsibility for their
birth. This belief is the "sacred" hangover from the past.
Evidence for the continued vitality of it may be found in
a recent issue (January 1964) of the *St. Gerard Bulletin,*
which was devoted to the question of planned v. un-
planned families. The issue was made up entirely of letters
from parents, both pro and con. The following excerpts
are from those who do not believe in family planning:
". . . Although we had planned on a sixth someday, God
sent him a little sooner than we had hoped . . ." "If the
good Lord wants us to have another child, he will give us
one regardless . . ." "Can a couple really say how many
children they are going to have?" "We are so grateful for
these eight beautiful 'wee ones' and any future ones God
in His goodness sees fit to send us. Our friends ask us: 'Do
you really want a great big family?' They cannot seem to
understand it is not what we want that counts; it is what
God wants. We simply have no 'druthers' either way." Or
the following: "One hears a lot of talk these days about
planned families; somehow I think we are going over our
heads when we start planning life. I do not think this
should be planned by us poor mortals any more than
the weather or the course of the stars." "When we say we
are 'planning' our family, is not this the same as saying we
no longer trust God, but only ourselves? Does God know
what He is doing? Can we improve on His definite plans?"

The answer, of course—and it is the answer of most

responsible churchmen today—is that family planning does rightly rest in the minds and consciences of married couples in accordance with their rational nature. As Bishop Bekkers has expressed the idea, the married couple and they alone are responsible to make the decision when and how many children they will have. It is a sign of their lack of freedom and moral choice if they will not take this responsibility. It is a sign of faulty theology if they believe that God does all the planning. And most serious of all, perhaps, non-planning is a sign that this may be the only resolution they can find for the problem of conjugal love in their lives. Their proliferation of children are signs of sexual attraction that cannot and should not be put off. If they are to adhere to a teaching which accepts only rhythm as a means of control of family size, they may not be able to exert any control unless they wish to jeopardize their love.

One of the women who was quoted above admitted as much in her letter. She explained that she and her husband had decided to practice rhythm after their sixth child. "But by the time our baby was ten months old we could no longer go along with this method. Our love making was not spontaneous; the 'calendar' always stood between us. And, in a sense, we sometimes felt that we were trying to play God (in that we wanted to be the ones to determine when our children should be conceived or born). . . . Now we no longer keep our love making regimented and find that we are not under such *stress* and *tension* as when practicing rhythm" (my italics). It must be questioned whether this thinking can be said to represent the Christian concept of man.

I have quoted extensively from this letter because I think it reveals some of the most important aspects of the problem of married life for Catholics today. Like so many other Catholic couples, this couple is trying to live in accord with the traditional Church teaching on marriage and the family. The couple finds rhythm to be an "unnatural" method of family control. This finding is hardly unique with this couple. So they resolve "to accept whatever God sends," in the hope of being able thus to foster their conjugal love. This is hardly an act of personal responsibility, and the long range consequences may be disastrous.

What is involved here? Consider the couple quoted above. These people already have six children. They are not in an economic position to give these children all the attention they need. The husband works at two side jobs part of the year. Bills mount up! There is no way out. The sociopsychological pressures are intense. But this couple and many like them may try to keep on going as long as they can believe that this is God's plan for them. It is necessary to reiterate nevertheless that husband and wife have the responsibility to decide when and how many children they will have, based on their resources of health (mental as well as physical), home conditions, educational aspirations, general economic conditions, and societal needs.

What then is the obligation, if any, to procreate? How can we know what we should return to God for all that he has given us? Clearly, what we can and should return is more than mere numbers. We must learn to balance quantity with quality, that is, we should have no more children than we can hope to help to their and our optimal development. We should return to God a human being capable of knowing and loving him—and this necessarily means a human being capable of loving other human beings, of being concerned about the optimal development of other human beings. For some couples this may mean having only one or two children; for others, possibly ten or eleven.

And yet another element intrudes itself here. The question of responsible parenthood is not completely a personal judgment made with regard only to personal feelings or capabilities. We must begin to consider the consequences of our decisions for our communities, societies and ultimately for the world population. If we are to act responsibly for God's sake, we must place ourselves in the context of his total universe.

An average of two children per family does not quite reproduce any given population. An average of three produces an increase in population size. As we try to define what responsible parenthood should mean to us as Christians, we should keep this fact in mind. *The world is already overpopulated with human beings who have no chance to grow to fulfillment of their potential, nor anywhere near it.* We cannot call them irresponsible, but rather non-responsible. It hardly seems in accord with the Christian view of the world that we should foster or condone uncontrolled and/or undesired growth among the underdeveloped areas of Asia, Africa or Latin America, or our own big-city slums, or even among our middle-class families. The question of responsible parenthood must include the more immediate question of world population growth. And we must be concerned because our neighbor is every man, and we must find a way to help all men to a life consonant with their nature.

Thus, both from the perspective of our responsibility as citizens of the larger community and as parents trying to fulfill ourselves as well as to help our children, it would seem that the smaller size family which prevails today in the developed areas of the world is, potentially at least, a pleasing response to God's gifts. For I cannot conceive it as a *good* just to have the earth populated with starving creatures, whose lives are lived in chaos, misery, and without the slightest notion of love. Nor can it be a good to encourage such large families that the spouses become alienated from each other because of the pressures that build up in trying to rear large numbers of children in a metropolitan environment, and the pressures entailed by trying to avoid another pregnancy. These pressures are not the figment of the imagination of an anti-baby mentality. They are the empirical experience of everyday living in contemporary society. And we cannot simplistically denounce the society, for despite its temptations to materialism, it offers man more hope for self-fulfillment than has any society in all previous history.

In trying to develop a firm basis for married life, we must consider carefully the world of reality within which we try to educate our children, and into which children from widely varying social backgrounds are thrust. It is apparent to most social scientists that it is much more difficult to educate children today than it has ever been before in human history. It is much easier to bring them into the world, and to be sure that the children will live beyond infancy. But education is a part of the process of rearing children and that is the part that has become so very complex. And I mean education here in the broadest sense of the word, to include formal schooling as well as personality formation in the home. This fact is not to be regretted, but to be applauded, for it signifies the enrichment of opportunity, at least in the developed areas of the world. Nevertheless, it is often charged that selfishness and crass materialism rather than concern for the complex problem of education are the real motivating forces which limit the size of families today. The empirical evidence does not seem to support this negative criticism, and Catholic critics especially would do well to avoid becoming fixated on this theme. We should be reminded here of the acute observation made by Yves Congar that all too often in the past we have been fixated on the idea that "obedience is the only virtue just as the sin of the flesh is the only vice." Such fixation prevents us from seeing the whole reality, and drains our energy so that we are unable to take advantage of the positive opportunities available to foster the teachings of Christ.

An interesting trend in contemporary American society is that post-World War II college-educated couples have tended to increase their family size compared to pre-World War II counterparts. These are the more advantaged couples of our society, generally able to satisfy their material wants, and knowledgeable about birth control so that if they wished, they could limit themselves to one or no children. Instead, they tend now to have two, three, and occasionally more children. These people are becoming the leaders in demanding better educational facilities for their children. Few of us are satisfied with our educational system, but it must be recognized that we are just becoming fully aware of the implications of the great revolution of our times, and we are in fact enriching the quality of the educational experience.

Can we seriously claim that the children of the better-educated members of our society are more selfish, less oriented to the great commandment of love, than the children of lower educational levels? Have these children and their parents in fact made a lesser or a greater contribution to the common welfare? Does the affirmation that the large family is automatically the God-centered family hold up under scrutiny? Individual examples of outstanding large families should not blind us to general social reality either here in the United States or in the world at large. Again, it needs to be reiterated that each couple alone should be in the best position to know what its capacities are for a full life.

This assertion leads to the final question and that is: how to achieve responsible parenthood? If the principle of responsible parenthood is accepted, then it is clear that Catholic couples are caught in a bind. This is so because the only method now generally available to them apart from living together as brother and sister, is rhythm. Let me say this about rhythm: it cannot be easily dismissed as a means of family limitation. It does work. But the cost may be great.

A University of Michigan fertility-control study using a U.S. national sample showed that about half of the Catholic couples in the study who used any control used only rhythm to control family size. But the scientists also learned that there was a clear-cut pattern by which Catholics, once they had achieved the family size desired, or found themselves with a larger family than desired, resorted to contraceptives. Again, the more education the Catholic couple had, the more rhythm was likely to be resorted to exclusively. However, even one-third of the college educated who admitted to trying to regulate fertility resorted to the use of contraceptives.

The primary problem with rhythm is that of the duration of the period of continence required. For a small percentage of couples a period of only five or six days of abstinence is required. This short period of abstinence may not be burdensome. In fact, it may be beneficial. For this group we can say that generally abstinence makes the heart grow fonder. But for the great majority, periods of from ten to fifteen days or more of abstinence may be required, and this is where conjugal love is jeopardized and family life disrupted. There is probably no other single problem today which so disturbs practicing Catholics and the clergy who are trying to counsel them. The evidence is mounting for all to read. And it comes in from all over the world. The letter from which I quoted says it admirably: the spontaneity of conjugal love is destroyed. Psychiatric evidence suggests that the necessity to practice extended continence tends to produce an obsession with sex, which manifests itself in tension and hostility between partners and toward their children.

A study of one thousand French Catholic lay leaders, who might be termed the elite of Catholic laity in France, reported in *Jubilee* magazine (November 1963) stated that the data were so shocking on the question of procreation that it was deemed unwise to publish the findings. However, some general statements were made which can be summarized as follows: these Catholic people do try to live a Christian marriage; multiple pregnancies near-in-time produce psychic imbalances and nervous depressions; continence heroically practiced also leads to psychic imbalances and nervous depressions; many of these Catholics have resorted to the use of contraceptives.

It may be that within ten years a drug will be produced that will not only regulate the fertility cycle, but also make it possible to know exactly when ovulation is going to take place within the female. Under these conditions a period of continence of only five or six days would be necessary. And the certainty of the method might be appealing to many non-Catholics as well as Catholics. It could resolve the problem most of the time for the majority of the people in areas of the world where literacy is widespread, the drug easily obtainable, and family values such that conjugal love can be fostered.

If not rhythm, what? One possibility that has received increasing study is Dr. John Rock's pill, Enovid, and others like it. Under the principle of double effect, theologians have been considering the pill as a possible legitimate aid following pregnancy, that is, as an aid to a natural process. In a recent news release it was reported that Dr. Nino Pasetto of the University of Rome's gynecological and obstetrical clinic has emphasized that the pill does not induce temporary sterility, but merely results in temporary ovarian repose. This finding was reported to have led Antonio Nalesso, professor of morals at the Roman medical school, to state that, "therefore, if Pope Pius XII judged the use of the pill illicit solely for its sterilizing property, opposition today should dissolve." [4] The recent article by Canon Janssens, who urged that the pill be considered as licit for couples who do not find rhythm feasible, seemed eminently sensible and showed a sensitive awareness of the reality of married life.

What about other forms of contraception? It is clear that large numbers of Catholics are resorting to one form or another of contraception. And it is also clear that the Church leaders must uphold the principle that what is essentially against nature can never be justified. But many Catholics are wondering if contraception is essentially against nature. The grounds on which this argument is based no longer seem compelling to many Catholics. If they do not use contraceptives, it is not because they believe that the theological argument is cogent, but rather because they respect the teaching authority of the Church.

If the primary function of married sexuality is procreation, then the statement of Pope Pius XI that "any use whatsoever of matrimony exercised in such a way that the act is deliberately frustrated in its natural power to generate life is an offense against the law of God and nature" might be unassailable. But the arguments put forth here and elsewhere in this book would seem to raise a grave question that the primary function of married sexuality is procreation. The phrase "to generate life" could perhaps mean the enrichment of the life of the spouses themselves and, through this act, the generation of life through love with their already existing children and their fellow man. In other words, it is the experience of married couples them-

[4] Quoted from *Our Sunday Visitor*, July 5, 1964, "Pill Distinction Rules Out Sterility," 1.

selves that conjugal union does indeed "generate new life" in them, even when this does not mean the birth of another child. And certainly couples practicing rhythm do so with the positive hope of avoiding pregnancy, while seeking the other generative function of the act. It also seems clear from the evidence that where uncontrolled procreation is the practice, it is difficult if not impossible for the couple to achieve a sense of "two in one flesh." At least subjectively, a contraceptive device like the diaphragm or the intrauterine ring may provide many couples with the freedom from fear-of-another-pregnancy that will make possible a more satisfying conjugal union. Again, it is difficult to see *a priori* why at least some contraceptive devices vitiate the act, or destroy the integrity of the act. If the contention is true, it should be evident upon reasonable reflection to the couples using such devices. Is it so evident?

While there may be no change in the papal stand against contraception, there is a discernible change in attitude toward those who for one reason or another are not able to use rhythm to manage responsible parenthood. Certainly pressure from the laity is one of the major factors involved in this change of attitude toward "the sinner." But it is also true that the theme of love has received new and exciting emphasis in the writings of some of the most eminent spokesmen of the Church today, particularly Cardinal Suenens and Bernard Häring, as can be seen in their respective books, *Love and Control* and *The Law of Christ*. All of these various factors indicate that a radical revision of traditional positions is taking place today. Much of this revised thinking is evident in the various essays in this book written from a biological, philosophical, and theological perspective. Such exploratory studies need to be fostered by all laymen.

It would seem that at this juncture in human history, the Catholic Church must attempt to establish guidelines or "norms" of a very flexible nature to confront three distinct groups of people: first, people in the advanced areas of the world who have achieved a relatively high standard of living; second, people in underdeveloped areas and in big city slums whose aspirations for a better life are just emerging; and third, people in underdeveloped areas who still cling to traditional, archaic ways. The needs of these three groupings are so divergent that no single set of guidelines serves adequately. But whatever the divergences, it is clear that common to all three as a basis for modern family life is the question of freedom.

Since man's dignity is grounded in his reason which makes it possible to actualize his freedom-potential, the begetting of children should be a free act, an act of positive choice, not a matter of chance, and most certainly not a mere concession for the privilege of sexual union. Only the individual couple has all the facts to know how many such choices it can make. For some couples no fertility control may be necessary, for others rhythm may be a most satisfactory solution. Many couples will find the progesterone pill to be the means most satisfactory to their situation. Yet for others neither of these means will be feasible. Are they then to be denied freedom of choice? Will not a greater good be served if they can be free to seek a means of control commensurate with their needs and abilities? Is not the question of goodness or evil in the act to be found in the motivation for the act?

Never before in human history have we been so close to an understanding of Christ's dictum to "love our neighbor as we love ourselves." It is incumbent upon us to find a viable means by which this love can be fostered, between husband and wife, between parents and children, and gradually by extension between man and his fellowman, for the love of God.

CONTRACEPTION AND THE PHILOSOPHY OF PROCESS

E. R. BALTAZAR

Introduction

Today, with the universal longing for ecumenical unity, one of the major stumbling blocks to its realization is the position of Protestants and Catholics on the morality of contraception. For the Protestants, birth control or contraception is allowed for the justifiable purpose of limiting the size of the family; for the Catholics, any "artificial" method of contraception is not allowed—only such methods are tolerated which allegedly do not frustrate the procreative character of the sexual act. Both the above positions are well-intentioned, both are sincere in their belief in the validity of their respective stands and, because freedom of conscience is the ultimate subjective norm of morality, both are subjectively right. Our problem, however, is the objective truth of the question, and in this regard, both positions are open to re-examination.

The Catholic position on birth control is based mainly on philosophic arguments. Thus a Catholic writer notes that:[1]

[1] Paul Quay S.J., "Contraception and Conjugal Love," *Theological Studies* 22, April 1961, 19.

There would seem to be small grounds in Scripture for a strictly theological position, nor does tradition in its other forms make up for this lack. In point of fact, the papal documents which have specified the Catholic position seem to argue from revelation very little if at all; rather, the emphasis is upon the natural law and upon the role of unaided reason in the establishing of the norms of human conduct. The arguments adduced by moralists have followed along this same path.

From the passage quoted above, we find that the argument (even of papal documents) is based on the scholastic doctrine of the natural law and the role of unaided reason in the establishing of the norms of conduct. In other words, the argument rests on a purely philosophical basis. Now, in a re-examination of the Catholic scholastic position, all writers, to my knowledge, who have disagreed with it, have not probed deeply enough into the very root of the problem. They have not questioned Aristotelian-Thomistic philosophy as such. To be sure, certain aspects of scholasticism have been questioned, e.g. the natural-law doctrine, but there have been no radical departures from the scholastic framework. As long as this framework is not questioned, either because of ignorance of its nature or because of its adoption as a starting point, it is futile to attack the scholastic conclusions on the morality of contraception which are deduced within this framework. For given the scholastic premises, the conclusions follow logically. Our procedure, therefore, is to question the very adequacy and pertinence of the scholastic framework for the understanding of the nature of the sexual act. The main philosophic task of this paper is the establishment of an epistemological framework in which the nature of the sexual act and the morality of contraception can be derived.

For Aristotelian-Thomism, reality is approached as having already become, as having come from the Creator's hands as *substantially* finished. Hence to know reality, one knows it as *being*, not as *becoming*. For this philosophy, what is becoming is *per se* unknowable scientifically (i.e. in the classic sense of science) because science is of universals, of the unchanging. When the Thomist approaches man, he looks at him as a universal, as a nature and from this unchanging nature he derives ethically the natural law as basis for morality. This ahistorical epistemological approach is applied to all Thomist questioning. When the Thomist asks for meaning, he asks: "What is the essence?" for an essence is, to him, that which makes a thing what it is.[2] He carries this approach over into theology, and looks at revelation as an unchanging body of propositions which he then enshrines in thesis form. Relative to our problem of contraception, when the Thomist asks what is the sexual act, his method is to abstract it from time and contingency in order to arrive at its unchanging essence.

In contrast to the static Aristotelian-Thomist, most contemporary thinkers would maintain that the greatest find of our modern world is the fact of history and evolution. On all levels of our constructions and formulations, our outlook is radically evolutionary and historical: we look on nature in terms of a natural history and on man in terms of cultural history. Instead of approaching man in terms of his human nature, we now approach him evolutionarily. We have developed the sciences of embryology, of child, adolescent, and adult psychology. Because of our evolving

[2] See Edmund Hill O.P., "Aristotle or Jung; or Psychology Whither?" *The Clergy Review* 48, December 1963, 779.

concept of man, we have even begun to change our concept
of the natural law itself. In theology we now look on revelation, not as a static body of propositions but as salvific
events, as a history of salvation. We no longer regard the
Church as a static juridical structure as scholasticism would
present it, but as a Mystical Body which is in process of
growth toward the *pleroma Christi.*

The Epistemology of Process

But how do we know process or becoming? This is our
main problem. First, we make the observation that anything which becomes or evolves can never be dissociated
from its context or environment either for its physical
existence or for its intelligibility. In other words, the meaning and intelligibility of a given evolving reality is derivable
from its evolutionary context. To put it another way, to ask
what a thing is is to ask what is its evolutionary context.
Let us take several examples to illustrate our point. If one
has a temporal continuum represented by a line *ab*, with
stages x, y, thus: a . . . x . . . y . . . b, then one cannot
dissociate, let us say, a seed, from the context *ax* and place
it at the context *xy* or *yb*. A seed is a seed precisely because
it is in the context *ax*. The time or stage *ax* is what constitutes the seed to be what it is; the seed is this temporality we call *ax*. This particular temporality evolves and
at the stage *xy* becomes a seedling and at the final stage
yb, it becomes full grown and is fruit-bearing. Again, take
human growth. The child is a child precisely because it
is at the early stage of human growth, or more properly, we
should say that the child is the early stage itself. Just as it

is the stage that constitutes being, so it is the stage that likewise determines the norm for judging the character of a thing. In man, for example, what is natural or unnatural, rational or irrational is determined by the context or stage one is in. At the childhood stage, it is unnatural to act like an adult; at the adult stage, it is unnatural and irrational to act like a child.

If we move from the micro-level to the macro-level of reality, we find that one's place in the evolutionary line is essential to the constitution of what one is and of one's intelligibility. On the one hand, the common-sense view is accustomed to putting inanimate, vegetative, sensitive and rational beings all in the same time context, abstracting them out of this temporal context in order to arrive at their meaning. But on the other hand, from the evolutionary view in which there are successive stages, namely matter, vegetative life, sensitive life and then rational life, we see that man is man precisely because he is the last stage of the evolutionary process toward consciousness. Man could not have been there at the beginning, contemporaneous with matter; the meaning and essence of man is derived from his position in the evolutionary line.

The evolutionary epistemology just outlined is more adequate than the Aristotelian-Thomistic for the understanding of the meaning of the sexual act. The failure to use this evolutionary and historical pattern of thinking has made our traditional ethics and moral theology absolutistic and unbending. But before we apply this epistemology to the problem of contraception, some observations are in order.

We agree that the morality of an act has three sources or fonts: the nature of the act itself, the intention, and the circumstances. But we recognize the need to add a fourth: the evolutionary stage in which the human act is located. It should be observed that the evolutionary stage is not a circumstance the way that place or time is a circumstance in the scholastic sense. In scholastic ethics and moral theology, *time* and *place* are purely accidental. *Time* and *place* should not be equated with the abiding evolutionary context of a thing which is not at all circumstantial, i.e. accidental. Perhaps an example may make the difference clear. Let us take two human beings both within the same evolutionary stage, that of adolescence. Though they are within the same stage, their actions may be circumstantially different. What is essentially common to both their actions is that they are adolescent acts and must be judged as such; what is accidental are the circumstances of time, place, etc. A second necessary observation is that this view has nothing in common with situation ethics which claims that the circumstances alone determine the morality of an act, the circumstances being unique to the person who exercises his freedom. That there is some truth to this ethic is undeniable. But what we are advocating is a context which is objective because it is common to all that belong to the same context.

Application of the Epistemology of Process

Our contention is that marriage is an evolutionary reality and therefore that the epistemology of process is the more adequate epistemology by which to understand it. Empirically, we see marriage to be evolutionary. Thus within it there are two observable stages: first, the stage of procreation or building of the family, and second, the stage of preservation or the rearing of the family.

The stages of procreation and preservation in marriage seem quite obvious. Even the Thomists unconsciously accept these two stages when they say that the primary purpose of marriage is the begetting and the rearing of children. However, true to their ahistorical mentality, the Thomists isolate those two purposes from their temporal setting. Properly, in terms of an evolutionary view, we should say that there is first the begetting and *then* the rearing of children. Thomists do not see the significance of this temporal connection, and fail to realize that procreation has a limit after which rearing takes over. There are still very many scholastically trained preachers who give as the ideal of the family the more children the better.

Accepting this evolutionary character of marriage, we are now in a position to determine the meaning and essence of the sexual act. The presupposition here is that sexual union has meaning and value only within the context of marriage and that any such union outside of marriage is morally wrong and therefore irrelevant to our purpose. Within the context of marriage, the scholastic view is that the sexual act is essentially for procreation. However, no scholastic would maintain today that procreation in each and every sexual act must be attained, for if this were so, then acts placed during periods of natural sterility would be immoral, being contrary to the very nature and finality of the act. Rather, scholastic moralists claim that intercourse, irrespective of context, that is, whether it is performed during periods of fertility, or during periods of infertility, as long as no "artificial" birth-control technique is used, is procreative in character (*de jure* procreative), although it may not be procreative *de facto*.

Empirically, there are two classes of sexual acts: first, those placed before menopause, and second, those after menopause. These two divisions are not arbitrary because they are based on the two natural stages of woman's sexual life: the reproductive stage (the menstrual life) and the non-reproductive stage (popularly called the "change of life" or menopause when menstruation ceases). In the first class the sexual acts are further subdivided into those which are procreative and those which are not, e.g. acts during periods of infertility. In the menopause all the sexual acts are non-procreative. Now given these classifications, how can the Thomists generalize from a few instances in which the sexual act is procreative and say that *as such* it is procreative? There is no empirical foundation for so saying. The traditional view would call periods of infertility and the final period of menopause accidentally nonprocreative. In this view, the ideal sexual life is seen as one where there is no period of infertility and no final period of menopause. But this is to reduce woman to the level of the female animal. Let us take woman as nature constructed her and not restructure her sexual life according to some preconceived notion as to the meaning and essence of the sexual act. In an evolutionary context, the menopause stage is a natural one in woman and not something accidental, not a defect of nature. Thus we have to conclude that the sexual acts after menopause are naturally or *de jure* non-procreative.

If the sexual act as such is not permanently procreative, then what is its ultimate finality? It is necessary to answer this question in the context of an epistemology of process. By an analysis of anything which evolves, we find that the meaning of a thing is based on the final stage of a process, not on the early stage, for it is the final stage that fully unfolds and reveals a thing for what it is. Furthermore, the early stages are known in relation to the final stage and are specified or named in terms of this final stage. For example, in the case of a fruit-bearing tree, it is the fruit (the final stage) that specifies or names the intermediary stages: the seed, the seedling and the plant itself. Thus we specify the seed by the kind of fruit it is, for instance, an *apple* seed. Likewise, we call the seedling an *apple* seedling and the plant an *apple* plant. The fruit, however, is specified by none other than itself. Hence we do not call the fruit an "*apple* apple," but simply apple. Because of his unfamiliarity with the epistemology and logic of process, the scholastic will find that what we say here is heterodox. He can analyze that which has come to be, but not what is in process of being. In his framework, he logically relates the effect to the cause. Since the effect comes after the cause, he looks for meaning in the beginning, not in the end. Instead of looking for meaning in the ultimate stage of the process, he looks for it in the initial stage. But if we reduce the final stage to the initial stage, then we would have to say, for example, that the oak is nothing else but an oversized acorn or that the human adult is nothing else but an oversized child, which is patently nonsense. In the case of growth, it is not the beginning or growth as such which is the finality of the process: the beginning and the middle are only the means to the end when growth ceases, and the preservation of the mature size is the natural end.

In the case of marriage with reference to its two stages, the natural and final stage is the fully grown family. This final stage is preservative in character and purpose, rather than procreative. From this stage we see that the sexual act in its ultimate finality and purpose is preservative. In determining the essence of the sexual act, it is wrong to abstract it from its context and conclude that it is essentially reproductive. It is within the evolutionary context that the nature of the sexual act must be seen. And even when we try to see the it within this context, it is bad epistemology to absolutize the early stage and say it is natural, while the later stages are relative and accidental. In the context of process, the sexual act at the early stage of marriage is for procreation, but we cannot conclude from what is true for this stage to what is true for marriage as a whole; such a conclusion would be an invalid extrapolation and generalization. In fact, in the context of process, since the full meaning of the sexual act is to be found in the final stage, we would have to say that it is relatively for procreation, and primarily and ultimately for the preservation and raising of the family.

For this reason, St. Paul tells us to see the relation between husband and wife as the image of the union between Christ and his spouse, the Church (see Eph 5:21-33). Hence, just as Christ and the Church are made one flesh through the sacrifice of Calvary which Christ called his baptism and whose commemoration we call the sacrifice of the Mass, so husband and wife are made one flesh through the sexual act.[8] Furthermore, just as the baptismal character

---

[8] Although the parallel between the nuptial act and baptism is clear all through Scriptures and even among the fathers of the

of the Mass brings forth children to Mother Church, so sexual union brings forth children to husband and wife. On earth, the mystical act of union which is the Mass is for the building of the Mystical Body until it reaches the fullness of Christ (the *pleroma Christi*), after which the Church is assumed into heaven. In heaven, the Mass goes on eternally, as we are told in the Apocalypse, being the eternal nuptials of Christ and his Church. However, in its ultimate finality, the Mass is no longer for the *building* of the Mystical Body but for its continued *preservation*. Again, if we see the Mass in relation to believers and unbelievers, we find that while its graces are for the bringing of new members to the Church, yet they are more basically for the preservation and growth of those who are already possessed of the Christian life. These theological confirmations have great relevance and value for the understanding of the meaning of sexual union for we are dealing here not only with the biological but also with the spiritual dimensions of the act. Pius XII himself tells us that to properly understand the meaning of sexuality, it must be considered in its totality, not only biologically and psychologically, but spiritually.[4]

Church (creation as a baptism and marriage; the various types of baptism in the Old Testament, the baptism on the cross, the rite of baptism as a marriage between Christ and the soul, etc.) this view is lost to us today due partly to scholasticism with its emphasis on univocal expression and its ignorance of the epistemology of symbols and partly to the Manichean view (and later puritanical) prevalent among many Christians of identifying the sex act with the sphere of darkness, of sin and of evil.

[4] See his address to the Second World Congress on Fertility and Sterility, May 19, 1956 in *AAS* 48, 1956, 470.

To the superficial onlooker and to the unreflecting view of common sense, procreation is the only aspect seen relative to the family. But a deeper analysis and reflection will show that sexual union makes for peace and harmony in the family, and that these effects are not confined to the couple alone, but flow into the well-being of the children —a well-being which is not merely an accidental finality of the sex act, but an essential one. Sexual union is not meant by God merely for the engendering of the family, after which it becomes accidental; nor is it meant merely as a consolation for assuming the heavy burdens of marriage. The present social situation reveals the undiscovered dimension of sexual union. For at no time in history has the raising of a family been more complex and burdensome than it is today, so that great love is needed as a motivation for sacrifice in the fulfillment of one's duties as a parent; and the ordinary means of fostering this love is sexual union. Just as from the Mass flow the sacraments—the source of spiritual nourishment of the Mystical Body—so from the sexual act flows the life-giving love that binds the family together. Sexual union is sacramental and like all sacraments and sacramentals, it is for growth and sustenance.

The scholastic view appeals to papal documents in support of its contention that sexual union is only for procreation in its essence; true, this view admits that it is also for the mutual service of the married partners, but this is purely secondary and accidental. Thus, it is pointed out, Pius XI in *Casti connubii* speaks of the conjugal act as designed for the generation of children, and Pius XII speaks of sexual union as the order established by God for the beginning of human life.[5] However, it is the contention here that these statements must be understood *sensu aiente*. In other words, the sexual act is divinely instituted for the beginning of life, yes, but *also* and much more fundamentally, for the continuance of life already constituted.[6] One may agree, therefore, that sexual union is life-giving in nature and that this character should not be frustrated, but this life-giving character must not be confined only to the procreation of children but extended to the preservation of the family already existing. The scholastic view which sees the life-giving character of the sex act as purely procreative is as narrow as to say that food is for *growth* alone, and to ignore its life-giving purpose relative to the *preservation* of the full-grown tree.

The Morality of Contraception

At the outset, it is necessary to note that the obligation to limit the size of the family is an ordinary obligation imposed on all married couples by the more basic end of marriage which demands that children be brought up in a Christian way relative to the social conditions of the times. As Thomas Burch, Director of the Center for Population Research at Georgetown University, observes, in our present social situation, the regulation of fertility is an integral

---

[5] AAS 43, 1951, 835-36.

[6] If Papal documents do not give this deeper meaning and dimension of the sexual act, it is because they are not intended to be exhaustive treatises on the topic, their main purpose being to stress that aspect of the act which at that time was being ignored, violated or frustrated.

part of modern life, irrespective of levels of living.[7] If, therefore, limitation is an ordinary obligation because it is incumbent on all, then there must be an ordinary means of limitation available for all. An extraordinary means may be used by the heroic, but one cannot impose this on everyone. Let us now see whether the means of limitation proposed by scholastic moralists meet the specification of an ordinary means.

Concerning periodic continence or rhythm there are two reasons why it is not an ordinary means. First, since it works only for some couples, it is not a means applicable to all or even to the majority. And secondly, even for couples who can make rhythm work, we believe that it is an extraordinary means, for while it limits the family, it does so at the expense of other great values. The foregoing of sexual union affects adversely not merely the parents but the children as well, since the well-being of the parents necessarily flows into the well-being of the family. Hence, the parents are obliged by their calling to maintain and enhance peace and love between themselves, not only for the sake of the so-called secondary end of marriage (mutual service), but above all for the sake of the second part of the primary end of marriage—the proper upbringing of the offspring. The ordinary means ordained by God for the fulfillment of this obligation is sexual intercourse—the common denominator for all couples, cultured and uncultured. Besides, the practice of rhythm involves a contradiction, for on the one hand parents are obliged to regular sexual intercourse for the sake of the unity of the family

[7] See his "Population and Parenthood," *The Commonweal* 80, June 5, 1964, 330.

and the proper upbringing of the children; and on the other are obliged to forego the regular practice of intercourse to meet the obligation of limiting the family. The scholastic moralists, however, because they do not appreciate the adverse effects both on the parents and on the family of foregoing regular sexual intercourse, do not recognize any contradiction in their position. For they hold fast to the premise that the essence of the sexual act is procreation alone, and that the only means that do not jeopardize the structure and finality of the act are total abstinence or rhythm. In saving the integrity of the sexual act, they endanger marriage itself and not only marriage but the peace and even salvation of human beings who go on practicing contraception, avoid the sacraments, or defect from the Church altogether.

The solution being proferred here is that there is an objective situation in marriage in which contraception is justified. From the epistemology of process we learn that there are two stages in marriage—the procreative and the preservative. Furthermore, we showed that it is the latter stage that gives meaning, structure and finality to the sexual act. At the first stage it is procreative in character, physical structure and finality; at the second stage it is non-procreative in character and consequently must be so in its physical structure, for its finality is the enhancement of the life of the family already produced, not the production of a new life. Thus, once a given couple has reached the preservative stage (the time is relative to the couple) sexual union takes on an essentially preservative character. Therefore, to restructure the sexual act by the use of contraceptives in order that it attain the finality intended for it by nature cannot be unnatural.

The scholastics do not see the heterogeneous character and two-dimensional structure of the marriage process. Rather they see marriage univocally and homogeneously as one procreative situation, menopause being a defect in this context. Consequently, sexual union for them remains essentially and *de jure* procreative throughout. There is no time or situation in which it sheds this character. Ultimately, therefore, the objection to the scholastic view of sexuality is philosophical. The scholastic sees first what the sexual act is outside of time in order to know its meaning in time. For to him, meaning can only be found by abstracting a thing from its temporal setting. The reason he abstracts from time is that for him time is contingent; it is a series of discrete moments without pattern and without direction. It does not evolve, it does not have stages, it is not dimensioned or structured but it is one homogeneous, univocal flow. This is time for him philosophically. He believes, too, that one does not have to study all the various classes of sexual acts, for one can abstract the essence from a single act. Once he has arrived at what he thinks is the essence of the act, in this case, procreation, he then replaces it in time. He believes that this notion of the sexual act defines the entire marriage process. He thus sees the whole of married life as essentially procreative and explains away menopause and periods of infertility as defects of nature.

On the contrary, however, it is not the sexual act that lends meaning to the marriage process, rather it is the mar-

riage process which lends meaning to the sexual act. This
is possible because time for us is not a mere succession of
moments which is unknowable. Time for us is evolutionary;
it has stages; it is patterned, structured, oriented, and
hence it is knowable. It should be pointed out that all of the
scholastic objections to this viewpoint are valid if we take
the sexual act *absolutely*, i.e. apart from any temporal
context; but they are invalid if we take it relative to a
whole (the family) of which it is a part. A simple example
may illustrate what the significance of this distinction is.

To nip a bud is a frustration of its ordination to life,
hence it is an unnatural act. But situate the same bud in
the context of the whole tree so that it is an overgrowth,
i.e. a growth that jeopardizes and threatens the life of the
tree, and the same action takes on a different value. It is
now justified, for it is the life of the tree we are concerned
with, not the life of the bud which has ceased to be absolute. Similarly, if we take the sexual act in and for itself,
then to frustrate it is an offense against its very ordination
toward a possible new life. But situate this same act in the
context of family living, and it ceases to be absolute and
cannot be thought of apart from the welfare of the family.
Opposed to this view, the scholastics, true to their epistemological pattern, still see the sex act absolutely, even in
the context of a full-sized family; consequently, they cannot
very well justify any type of contraception. The result has
been the sacrifice of the whole (family life) for a prospec-
tive new life; the sacrifice of the real for the possible. It is
like sacrificing the whole tree for the overgrowth.

Let us now compare the solution being maintained
here with the papal documents forbidding contraception.

Casti Connubii states that "any use whatsoever of matrimony exercised in such a way that the act is deliberately frustrated in its natural power to generate life is an offense against the law of God and nature, and those who indulge in such are branded with the guilt of a great sin." This statement could be taken to mean that *each* and *every* sexual act cannot be deliberately deprived of its natural power to generate life or that the sexual acts taken collectively cannot be deprived of that power. In other words, the papal statement could be taken divisively or collectively; absolutely or relatively. It is more probable that the sexual act here is regarded divisively and absolutely, for the encyclical is an expression of scholastic morality. Relative then to the scholastic pattern of thought, the statement of the Holy Father is logical and valid and if we accept that pattern of thought, we may be obliged in conscience to follow his directive. However, there is no papal directive that obliges one to think in a scholastic way. The problem of birth control today shows not that the papal statement of it is wrong but that the scholastic categories are inadequate for understanding fully the morality of contraception. Furthermore, the validity and worth of the present conclusions must be gauged within their own epistemological context. They can only be proven wrong by proving the epistemological context from which they have been drawn to be wrong. What is right or wrong is relative to the context; and we might note too that these contexts are not so much "right" or "wrong" as "more" or "less" adequate.

On the other hand, if the papal statement may be taken collectively, then it confirms the present solution rather than contradicting it. There is some reason to believe that the term "sexual act" in the quoted papal statement is used collectively for it does not say: "Any use whatsoever of matrimony exercised in such a way that *each and every act* . . ." but: "Any use . . . in such a way that *the act* . . ." If this interpretation be valid, then the papal statement is not so much concerned with safeguarding the sexual act in and for itself as in safeguarding the institution of marriage as the one and only valid means of generating life. Thus, for example, the divine command to increase and multiply is given to man collectively and not divisively, for otherwise the practice of celibacy would be a frustration of the divine command. In like manner, in order that the life of a person may be ordered to salvation and grace, it is not necessary that each and every act be a baptism. One baptism, one act of faith, ordains that life to eternal life. So, too, it is sufficient that the first stage of the marriage-process be ordained toward procreation for the marriage as a whole to be so ordained. Just as one can look at the whole series of human acts collectively and call it his life-act, so we can look at the whole series of sexual acts in matrimony collectively and call it the act of matrimony. If we are to rephrase the papal statement to harmonize with this viewpoint, it would read thus: "Any use whatsoever of matrimony exercised in such a way that the act (of matrimony) in *its totality* is deliberately frustrated in its natural power to generate life . . ."

There is a final argument against contraception in general which indirectly challenges the view being defended here. This argument, which is based on the demands of interpersonal and intersubjective relations, affirms that to put a barrier between the ovum and the sperm is to mean that the love-giving is not complete.[8] The fallacy in the argument derives from a false notion of marital love common to both the scholastic and secular views, namely that love can be thought of apart from procreation, either as a secondary end of marriage (the scholastic view) or as an absolute and independent end of marriage (the secular view). In the light of Scriptures, the scholastic and secular notion of marital love is not only inadequate but un-Christian and therefore in need of revision. In the Scriptures, conjugal love cannot be thought of apart from the child since the child is the fullness of it. Thus the fullness of the conjugal love between Yahweh and Israel is the Child, Christ. To conceive of the union of Yahweh and Israel apart from Christ is meaningless, empty, barren, for Christ is the fruition and incarnation of that love. Again, the fullness of the conjugal love between Christ and his spouse, the Church, is the outpouring of the Holy Spirit resulting in spiritual children to the Church, and finally, the love between Father and Son is the Holy Spirit, the symbol and personification of that love. To think of the love in the Godhead as dualistic and not trinitarian is impossible. In like manner, conjugal love is essentially trinitarian, not dualistic. Consequently, couples who have children or at least desire to have children possess the fullness of marital love, while couples who deliberately exclude children from their marriage do not have even the semblance of love, for love to be true must be sacrificial. Through the child the couple give of themselves—their

[8] Paul Quay S.J., *op. cit.* 36: "Even one act is a consenting to the building of a barrier to their most intimate connection. In one single act the integrity of their mutual word of affection is sacrificed to their pleasure."

lives, their very substance, so to speak. Without the ordination of the sexual act toward the child, love ceases to be
other-centered; it becomes self-centered (on the couple
themselves). This is egoism, not love. With regard to the
sexual act which puts a barrier between the sperm and the
ovum, there is no denial of love if the parents are directing
the act toward their children, who are the incarnation and
fullness of their conjugal love. By rendering a fertile sexual
act infertile, the parents are in fact removing a threat to
their love. In the context of a philosophy of process, contraception may be practiced without necessarily being a
barrier to interpersonal conjugal love, rather, it could be for
the enhancement of that love.

On Discovering Natural Law

Justus George Lawler

Introduction

It is impossible to believe that the unprecedented statement of Pope Paul on birth control (June 23, 1964) was
intended to terminate all discussion on this question,
though such an interpretation was placed upon it by some
secular journalists and some diocesan weeklies. The apparent aim of the Pope's remarks was to foreclose any
definitive and in the end embarrassing judgments from being rendered either by individual bishops or by national
hierarchies. The statement, then, was a clear recognition
of the collegiality of the whole Church, for if the bishops
are to restrain themselves from issuing decisions on this
question it can only be in order that the theologians and
the concerned laity may express themselves more freely and
thus bear witness to the beliefs and aspirations of the
whole body of the faithful.

American Catholicism, by reason of its popular devo-
tions which are mainly Latin in origin, and its religious
communities which are for the most part either Latin or
Irish in origin, has always had a strong ultramontanist cast.
American theologians, therefore, tend to treat the various

allocutions of recent popes, and particularly of Pius XII, much after the manner of the biblical fundamentalist interpreting the sacred text, and they are affronted by such a statement as Newman's that "The Church moves as a whole; it is not a mere philosophy, it is a communion; it not only discovers, but it teaches; it is bound to consult for charity as well as for faith." [1]

Toward the end of his life, Cardinal Newman told the young Wilfrid Ward that what was most needed for the Church was "fair and candid discussion between the representatives of the specialized sciences and the theologians." [2] Strangely enough in all the recent furor over the question of contraception, it has been the theologians who seem to have insulated themselves against any "fair and candid discussion." An outsider would almost believe that the Church is not made up of bishops and laity at all, but only of professors of canon law and moral theology. What Newman said of the ultramontanist bishops at the time of the First Vatican Council is true today of many moralists and canonists: "They have not come into contact with the intellectual mind of the times." [3] And the nineteenth-century bishops, like many contemporary scholastic theologians, could not come into contact with this "intellectual mind" because the laity were not formed to bear open witness to what they believed as well as to the culture in which these beliefs were held.

What Newman was saying in England had been affirmed

[1] Wilfrid Ward, *The Life of John Henry Cardinal Newman*, London 1912, II, 296.

[2] *Ibid*. II, 468.

[3] Cuthbert Butler O.S.B., *The Vatican Council*, London 1930, II, 29.

a few years earlier by his great contemporary, Matthias Joseph Scheeben, and it is as relevant to moral as to dogmatic teaching, and to 1964 as to 1864:[4]

It follows that the public profession of doctrine by the body of the faithful, being a witnessing of the Holy Ghost relatively independent, ought logically and briefly to precede the precise declaration of the teaching body, and in such circumstances influence, as a means of orientation, its future judgment.

But the layman has an obligation not only to testify in union with his pastors to the religious tradition; he has a further obligation to bear witness to all the legitimate longings and aspirations of the faithful. Apart from the question of contraception where the lay voice has been muted, the obvious example of an area in which there has been effective lay witnessing is that of the arts. Two decades ago it was not uncommon to find clerical critics condemning certain realistic works of fiction or of the cinema on premises that were so completely detached from the actual conditions of a Christian living in the twentieth century that these condemnations often had little effect other than to lead to a disregard for authority itself. Concerning the arts, for example, a moralist can rarely justify defining occasions of sin simply on the basis of abstract principles and his own personal response to this or that artifact. Rather, what would be required is a profound knowledge, certainly of theology, but also of esthetics, of the social structure of various groups, of the psychology of attention, and of a host of other factors which generally come within the scope of specialized lay research.

Should an occasional theologian be found conversant

[4] *Dogmatik*, Freiburg 1948, Sect. 14, 99.

and capable in all these fields, there will probably yet be lacking to him that empathic awareness of conditions in the large body of the faithful which the layman possesses, as it were, connaturally. And if this can be maintained of so relatively public an area as that of the arts how much more nearly true must it be of the whole domain of sexuality where not only modesty but prudery and a score of other inhibiting influences prevent any easy understanding—above all by theologians who are celibates. Moral teachings as the human though not fallible expressions of the immutable ethical code, are not precisioned in a vacuum, nor even in a confessional, a pulpit, or a lecture hall. They are generated at that point where meditative reason, enlightened by theological wisdom, comes to grips with concrete realities; they are not the product of the isolated mind, nor of the group "mind," but they are defined by the entire Christian community acting as a complete *person.* It might be said that their "body" is given in all its physical and pragmatic richness primarily by the layman; their "mind" is that ordinance of reason which moralists— whether lay or clerical—discern; and their "soul" is the sanction of the bishop which purifies and enforces them. Moreover, since it is the Christian community that defines this teaching, then grace acts both to enlighten and inform it.

Christian moral doctrine, then, is an expression of that collegiality which dogmatic theologians have rediscovered only recently, and which should be characterized by a kind of perichoretic harmony, as among equals. Recent efforts on the part of moral theologians to silence the lay voice are simply Sabellian in intent.

The Search for Sources

There is an anti-intellectual doctrine known as traditionalism which maintains that man cannot by the power of reason alone come to a knowledge of God's existence or of any absolute truth. The traditionalists or fideists in order to explain the knowledge of a supreme being therefore posited some kind of primitive revelation which had been handed down from generation to generation, had been refined by the philosophers and purified by the teaching of the Scriptures and the Church. As we all know, this notion, widely held even into the middle of the last century through the influence of de Lamennais, was condemned definitively by the First Vatican Council in its affirmation that the existence of God is a truth naturally knowable. Traditionalism was in part an expression of that general and not entirely unwholesome denigration of reason which stemmed from the *devotio moderna* and which was consummated in the exaggerated "supernaturalism" of the romantics, whether Catholic or not; but traditionalism was also, paradoxically, an expression of a very reasonable desire to understand the widespread denial of the existence of God in post-Renaissance Europe. For, so the traditionalists argued, if the existence of God is a truth attainable by unaided reason, how can one explain the fact that people, as obviously endowed with reason as any theists, can simply reject all arguments for his existence. To ascribe such disbelief always and invariably to intellectual or moral perversity was in effect to question the honesty, sincerity, and intelligence of great numbers of people who appeared to be no less gifted with those virtues than any believers.

A similar problem faces those who argue on the ground of natural law against all forms of contraception. It is quite obvious that many people as earnest and as capable of scrutinizing nature and its laws as are the opponents of contraception have not been persuaded by the natural-law argument employed by Catholics. This raises a number of questions concerning the value of a natural teaching that is unattainable by human nature which I shall consider in a moment. But, first, one must inquire as to the origin of the notion that contraception is intrinsically immoral. Only three solutions would seem to be possible for this problem. Either the teaching on the immorality of contraception is part of revelation, in which case one must determine its source; or it was a conclusion reasoned to by the creators of the now traditional view, in which case one must determine why reasons cogent in the past are no longer cogent to men of good will in the present; or finally, it was based on certain sociological, cultural, and biological presuppositions which are no longer valid or binding.

There is perhaps a fourth and corollary possibility: that the conclusion while attainable by reason alone, given the power of concupiscence was in fact rarely attained, and that therefore the light of faith was required to illuminate the teaching. There are, as we know, certain natural truths, even in the physical order, that can be known with certitude only through faith: thus the implications of the doctrine of the Immaculate Conception seem to have made it fairly clear that a human person comes into being only when the fused sperm and egg, the gamete, are capable of further cell division. This is quite a different teaching from the old scholastic view that a person exists only after the vegetative and sensitive soul have been subsumed in a rational soul, a process which was believed to occur some months after what we know as mitosis; it is also quite a different teaching from that of Anglo-Saxon jurisprudence which allows human rights only to a viable fetus. But though these radical discrepancies between canon law and civil law, and between a position not universally accepted —at least in theory—before 1854 and the subsequent position which is implicitly *de fide*, do raise problems regarding the relation of natural law and revelation, these problems are not essentially different from those raised by our first hypothetical answer to the initial question: that is, that the condemnation of contraception as intrinsically immoral is a part of revelation.

Setting aside momentarily all arguments in favor of the official position founded on natural law alone, the basic issue now concerns the role of revelation. There is virtually a unanimous consensus of fathers and doctors throughout the Christian tradition of the past that the condemnation of contraception can be based on the story of Onan in the Old Testament. This consensus of the tradition was reinforced by Pius XI's citation of that same scriptural passage in *Casti Connubii*. Similarly, it is a unanimous consensus of fathers and doctors, and of acts of the ordinary magisterium, which has led contemporary theologians to view the present teaching as irrevocable. However, as has been pointed out frequently in current discussions of the question, there are large numbers of biblical scholars today who do not believe the punishment of Onan to have any bearing on the matter of contraception as such. Unfortunately, what has been overlooked with regard to this last fact is not merely that if the consensus of theological opinion is no longer unanimous in finding the story of Onan as a revealed source of the condemnation, then that unanimous consensus which resulted in condemning contraception on those grounds is dissolved, but also that if unanimous consensus is the indispensable note of an irrevocable teaching, then obviously we are going to have to revise our ideas of unanimous consensus. For what was a unanimous consensus in the case of the interpretation of the story of Onan over the last fifteen hundred years, and what was therefore believed irrevocably taught, is no longer unanimous, and the interpretation has been generally revoked. The same may certainly be true in the case of contraception as such, above all when the revealed basis for the condemnation has been shown to be very possibly nonexistent. May it not theoretically be, then, that there can be no such thing as an irrevocably binding unanimous consensus of the theological school and of the ordinary teaching of the magisterium until true unanimity has been attained, that is, until the end of time?

If the immorality of contraception is not explicitly revealed, yet, it has been suggested, it may be implicitly revealed in St. Paul's condemnation of homosexuality and other perversions. Thus Fathers Kelly and Ford observe:[5]

But might not St. Paul's repudiation of one or several unnatural sex practices be taken to include implicitly a condemnation of other unnatural sex practices that are not mentioned explic-

[5] John C. Ford S.J. and Gerald Kelly S.J., *Contemporary Moral Theology*, Westminster 1963, II, 272.

itly? If such an interpretation is correct, then the immorality of at least some forms of contraception (*coitus interruptus* and condomistic intercourse) would be implicitly revealed.

But with regard to condomistic intercourse it is very difficult to see how such an interpretation could ever be correct, since it is based on a patent begging of the question. What we are seeking is to determine if the immorality of contraception has been revealed; we cannot rely on arguments based on natural law alone, since these arguments are not cogent; nor can we rely on a consensus of the school because this consensus is based on a seriously flawed scriptural interpretation. Obviously if the question were only of homosexuality, or probably were only of *coitus interruptus*, one could invoke St. Paul in proof of this confirmation of natural law by revelation, since homosexuality, and probably *coitus interruptus* whether culpable or not, are also condemned on the grounds of natural law. What we are seeking ultimately to determine is why theologians believe contraception immoral. The basis for the condemnation must be either reason or revelation or some coalescence of the two. But since reason has proved unable to yield any such basis it is impossible to stigmatize contraception as unnatural and to group it with various other unnatural practices condemned by St. Paul. For if that were a valid line of exegesis, why confine it to this passage in St. Paul? Fratricide, incest, and a score of unnatural vices are all condemned in various places in the Bible, and with this loose canon of interpretation one could take the biblical repudiation of one or several such unnatural practices as including implicitly a condemnation of every other allegedly unnatural practice that is not mentioned explicitly.

Certainly one may do this: but it offers no real solution unless one knows antecedently that the "other" practices which are not explicitly mentioned are really unnatural: and this is precisely what we don't know, and what we are trying to determine.

The question remains, therefore, from what source did churchmen derive their condemnation of contraception, if it is neither explicitly nor implicitly revealed, and if it cannot be certified clearly and cogently by reason. Fathers Kelly and Ford suggest as a third possibility that the "entire natural law is implicitly contained in the two great commandments and the Decalogue." This argument parallels that in the preceding paragraph, but since these two distinguished and generally forebearing authors seem to find it an important proposition, it may be discussed further. They note that:[6]

> . . . every pope who has distinguished between natural law and revealed law was conscious of the fact that some of the natural law (e.g. the Decalogue) is explicitly revealed. It seems to us, therefore, that the real purpose of such assertions is to vindicate the Church's power to teach and to apply the natural law, whether it be revealed or not. Thus, such papal statements leave open the question whether the natural law is also contained in revelation, at least implicitly.

However, while unquestionably some of the natural law is explicitly revealed, none of it is explicitly revealed *qua* natural law: the determination of what in revelation relates to natural law can be made only by reason. After it has been determined by reason that something falls under the scope of natural law, the Church may illuminate the iden-

[6] *Ibid.* 274.

tity or similarity between this particular natural law principle and revelation, and such illumination may even enrich our understanding of the original principle, even as
christology has enriched the philosophical understanding
of the nature of the person. But what is not possible is
for the Church globally to legislate that teachings which
cannot be verified by reason can be shown by revelation *to
be verifiable by reason.* Nor, as we have seen above, is it
possible for the Church to proclaim that an allegedly natural law principle is contained in revelation without also
disclosing where in revelation it is explicitly or implicitly
contained. Either such disclosure will carry one back to the
Scriptures or it will not: if it doesn't, then one will have to
assume that there is such a thing as a constitutive tradition,
that is, a body of revealed truth which is entirely independent of the biblical revelation. One is free or not to embrace such a concept of tradition, though it flys in the face
of a large body of contemporary theological opinion to do
so.

The circularity of the arguments used to relate revelation
to natural law is again brought out in Kelly and Ford's
final statement:[7]

But even if all these possibilities [considered above] were rejected, there would still remain the consideration of whether
the entire natural law (and this would include the *immorality
of contraception*) is not a secondary object of infallibility because it is intimately connected with revelation. The idea here
is that, since supernatural salvation is certainly a part of the depositum fidei, *all the requirements for the attainment of salvation* are intimately connected with the depositum fidei, even
though not in themselves revealed. It seems to us that at least

[7] *Ibid.* 274-275.

in this minimum sense, the *natural law* must be considered an object of infallibility, and that this, as well as the other possibilities explained in this section, should be more thoroughly discussed by the specialists in fundamental theology. It is our conviction that, whatever be the explanation, there can be no reasonable doubt that the Church can infallibly interpret the *entire natural law* (italics added).

All of this presumes that natural law has made it unmistakably clear that contraception is immoral. There seems to be no awareness when speaking of "all the requirements to salvation" that there are large numbers of non-Catholic Christians who believe contraception to be an aid to marital union, and therefore to the sanctification of themselves and their children. Unless this position can be shown to be a contradiction of the natural law, it is difficult to see how revelation enters into the discussion here at all.

What is to be noted in the above passage is the peculiar statement: "whatever be the explanation, there can be no reasonable doubt that the Church can infallibly interpret the entire natural law." One would have thought that the mode of explanation would be essential, and that any such explanation would have to take as its premise that such and such a truth is in fact a determination of natural law. This indifference to explanations is characteristic of much Catholic writing on contraception, so that the impression is sometimes given that Catholic theologians are intent above all on reaching a predetermined conclusion, no matter what rules of logic may have to be dispensed with en route.[8]

[8] The tautology that underlies much argument against contraception is evident in some recent and highly intemperate remarks, which implicitly deride the witness of the layman, by John J. Lynch S.J.,

If the condemnation of contraception cannot be based on natural law, cannot be based on revelation, cannot be based on ecclesiastical faith—unless one accepts the notion of a constitutive tradition—one again is compelled to search for its sources. I do not think it a novel assumption to say that it may well be founded on certain cultural and sociological factors which have conditioned Catholic theologians and therefore Catholic theology in its course through the centuries. In many cases these factors have influenced the generality of western men as well, but since these comments are centered on a specifically Catholic problem, I will confine myself to some brief instances of what I have elsewhere called the celibate *Denkform*.

It would be impossible to do any kind of justice to this subject in this short essay,[9] as it ranges over such peculiar notions as Justin Martyr's denunciation of the *Iliad* as being concerned with only one thing, "woman," [10] to the clerical editors, of *Sign* magazine condemning Governor Rocke-

---

who argues against the liceity of anovulants on the grounds that their use means the temporary suppression "of the generative function as such, that is, precisely as generative" (*Theological Studies*, June 1964, 241). Unfortunately this kind of circular logic is not very compelling to most Christians because the very point at issue is whether this "function" is properly denominated only as "generative." After all, it is by the names of things that we first come to know their natures and properties, and no one except those inexperienced in precisely this field refers to intercourse, physical union, coition, copulation, etc. as the "generative act."

[9] I have discussed certain historical influences relating to this theme in "The Christian Understanding of Love," *The Christian Imagination*, Westminster 1955.

[10] *Discourse to the Greeks* I (provenance dubious), in Christian Heritage, *St. Justin Martyr*, New York 1948, 432.

feller after his divorce as unworthy of the presidency, and this notwithstanding the fact that the only other announced candidate had publicly stated that he wanted "a test of strength with the Soviet Union," and that he was "against all disarmament." In general this mindset, which is not confined to clerics, shows a greater preoccupation with personal and individual morality than with social; demeans the place of woman because it sees in her only an instrument for breeding or conversely elevates her to a quasi-deity (where she is safely beyond reach of all cloying human passion); consequently it warps the understanding of sexuality by apotheosizing it (hence the spate of recent naive clerical works glorifying sexual union) or demeaning it (hence the pre-twentieth century Augustinian tradition of regarding sex as smirched).

In the clerical and legalistic conception of sexuality the law of charity is sometimes lost sight of entirely, whether it be, for instance, charity in that relationship between spouses which may make the limitation of children through means other than abstinence psychologically, and even physically indispensable, or charity toward priests who have fallen from their state and married. Concerning the latter, whose plight is often ignored, there are the best of grounds for being distressed at the scores of good and godfearing men who for one reason or emotion or another have had to abandon their state, and who have been the victims of an almost systematic social revulsion and reprobation on the part of Catholics. The religious, to say nothing of the social and economic condition of these priests is worse than that of Catholics who are divorced and also destined by our moral legislators to live out their lives in a

permanent "state of sin," unless they can abandon their
legal spouses and families. Certainly if Christ could embrace the Magdalen some accommodations can be made in
the name of charity for all these people; but that canon
law treats them so severely, can provide them with no solace until their deaths, points up how much more emphasis is placed on sexual union by the clerical adjudicators of
human existence, than sexual union in fact deserves to
have. It is not necessarily the laity seeking an adaptation
of the laws concerning contraception who are preoccupied
with sexuality; it may as well be those clergy who cannot
see it in its place as only one among many elements determining a man's nature, and who, like Augustine, imagine
that if it weren't for the need to copulate Adam would
have found a better helpmate in another man.[11]

The Social Matrix

The present sharp divergence of opinion between great
numbers of laity and a majority of the clergy points up how
fully Catholicism has been institutionalized around the
written work. Given a biblical cult, this focus was almost
imperative. But it is enormously exaggerated by the fact
that for centuries the only literate people were celibates
and the products of a celibate training which itself contained a strong admixture of false asceticism and implicit
heresy. As with all such closed cultures the predominantly
theological literature which this literacy begot reflects only
an intermarriage of congruent and related ideas, and it
would be sociologically impossible to expect to extract from

[11] *De Genesis ad litteram* IX, 5, 9.

it any strong indications of variant views. It is only in the last four centuries—and even more recently for Roman Catholics—that the voices from the underground so long suppressed are now dissolving the hegemony of celibates and clerics (the word *clericus* itself points up this relationship of literacy and celibacy) and creating a religious literature which includes the worldly and the laic. It is understandably a shock to the theologians to realize that truths which they had so long nurtured, exchanged, and rarified in their debates are regarded by the now-literate masses as fragmentary or simply irrelevant.

But because in the pre-Renaissance world the lay currents which did find expression in the popular culture were never recognized by the theologians, the result was the same kind of inbreeding of ideas and mores among the masses as among their political and religious overlords. Whenever any stratum of society is cut off from interchange with the other levels the result can only be the kind of cultural monstrosities which in the present instance are evident in the Goliardic literature, in the literature of *l'amour courtois,* and in the Augustinian doctrine on marriage—strictly a doctrine, as a score of events, such as the influx of prostitutes to Constance at the time of the general council or the widespread clerical concubinage would suggest. It is therefore only in our time that there can be a fruitful dialogue between the celibates, clerics, theologians, and the married, worldly laity.

Sitz im Leben, an important catchphrase in modern biblical exegesis, means that a given scriptural text must be set in the context for which it was written by its human author. The results of this kind of approach to the Bible have been truly revolutionary. Strangely enough, however, while biblical theologians have been willing to apply this critical method to the sacred text, moral theologians have been less liberal in extending it to various opinions of the school or decrees and formulations of the magisterium. Moreover, for the present student of sexuality, it is a question not merely of knowing the disputes that provoked a particular decision of authority, but rather of understanding the whole social ambit in which these disputes occurred. For example, it seems apparent that the doctrine of the primary end of marriage would be considerably more applicable to a society which was devastated by periodic plagues, and which had no knowledge of elementary hygiene or prophylaxis, than to a society such as ours in which the birthrate is outstripping—Colin Clark notwithstanding—the manifest capacities of the economy to create new resources.

Man is not only the passive subject of evolution; he controls it. And it is quite conceivable as he more and more grows in self-awareness, and consequently in the power of directing his own evolution, that the problem of contraception may resolve itself—even to the satisfaction of the theologians. If we are now in a stage of thinking on this problem radically different from that of the nineteenth century when contraception was universally condemned by all major Christian bodies, that is, if we are now in a stage when contraception is seen by many Christians as essential to deepening the interpersonal aspects of marriage, we are entitled by every law of history to forecast a future stage in which sexual love may not be rooted primarily in genital union, but will be incarnated and expressed in other forms.

The traditional canonical position may thus be organically reasserted as intercourse will be seen as primarily directed to procreation. For this reason one can accept the conclusion of Paul Chauchard—the great interpreter of the work of Teilhard from the perspective of neurophysiology—that "the brain is the principal sexual organ." [12]

It is also in the light of this evolutionary principle that one must understand Aristotle's opinion that sexual intercourse is an inferior good because it involves an abdication of reason. Copulation, which in its human beginnings was a brute act,[13] during the Christian era has been artificially controlled by religious and social constraints; but in the present age it is finding its basic order not in any external and institutional requirements but in the demands of the human person as person. This whole evolutionary process has paralleled and been nourished by the emergence of a sense of selfness and of interiority in western man. In that process—what Aristotle called "reason" and what we would call "spirit" has taken possession of itself—the old assumption of sexuality as a rupturing force in a world of continuity, an assumption defended in our time by Max Picard,[14] has been set aside. Discontinuity is a characteristic of matter, of that world of the absolutely "physical" which is essentially fragmentary and which is defined as

[12] Cited by A. Plé O.P., in *Vie affective et chastété*, Paris 1963, 176; see also the forthcoming English translation (New York 1965) of Chauchard's *L'Etre humain selon Teilhard de Chardin*.

[13] It is noteworthy that Leo XIII speaking of the corruption of marital love among the pagans emphasized that "the wife had sunk so low" that she was viewed only "as a means for the gratification of passion, or *for the production of* offspring" (*Arcanum Divinae Sapientiae* 7; italics added.)

[14] *Hitler in Ourselves*, Hinsdale 1947, 190-191.

part-outside-of-part. And so long as sexuality was understood on that plane only, the Aristotelian notion of "abdication of reason" was valid. But with the emergence of spirit, with the conscious awareness of human interiority, the purely genital act has more and more come under the regency of the whole human person. It is in fact the meaning of the present sexual revolution—which has its counterpart in every aspect of human activity—that sexuality must transcend its merely biological limitations.

By way of one specific application of these large statements, it may be suggested that what the sexual revolution implies is a kind of space-time continuum with regard to conception and contraception, even as it more obviously implies a continuum of the primary and secondary ends of marriage. In the classic philosophy time and space exist because of matter or its analogues. Yet because of a primitive folk cosmology space has been viewed by Catholics as more "material" than time: a spatial object is obviously palpable and visible—as when we think of the disciples literally seeing Christ "ascend into heaven"; whereas temporal reality is intangible, seemingly ethereal, and therefore more "spiritual." Thus a directly contraceptive practice which places an obstacle in time, such as the "safe period," is moral, while a practice which places an obstacle in space is absolutely forbidden. What is imperative is to recognize the common material root of the temporal and the spatial and their subordinate role in the service of spirit.

Moreover, this entire evolutionary development has even affected canonists and moral theologians, no matter how ingeniously they may attempt to cling to certain historical formulations as absolutes. Thus for many centuries the "natural" use of sexuality meant for the official teachers a use which in no way and in no circumstances interfered with the physiological processes. Once coitus, whether voluntary or involuntary, had been engaged in, any attempt to frustrate the biological order was viewed as immoral. Whereas in the present under the influence of humane sentiments and quite apart from any subsequent rationalizations, many theologians now teach that a woman who has been raped may make use of a vaginal douche with the direct intention of expelling the alien and unwanted seed. Thus the "natural" use of sexual powers no longer means, as it did for theologians before the twentieth century, their functioning entirely apart from the will and intention of the subjects, entirely, that is, as mechanical acts so that any interference with the "machinery" would be regarded as intrinsically immoral. And there is at least one moralist, Charles McFadden O.S.A., who would extend this concern for the innocent victim of rape to permitting the use of an intrauterine spermicidal douche. The justification for this is: [15]

. . . ovulation occurs only once a month, that a month involves about 720 hours, and that the ovum possesses a life-span of, perhaps, eighteen hours (some authorities would place it as low as twelve hours, others as high as twenty-four hours), we are confronted with the fact that the odds are about 40 to 1 against a live ovum being present at the time of rape.

Since this author has gone to great lengths to explain that any fertilized egg is in every sense of the word a human person with all the rights of a person, and that therefore destruction of the fetus is simply murder, it is difficult to

[15] *Medical Ethics*, Philadelphia 1961, 144.

follow the reasoning that would say that even on the basis of a remote possibility, that is, on the basis of a forty-to-one chance, it would be permissible to use a spermicide which would directly kill a fetus if present. Yet however hesitant one may be about embracing this line of argument, it is only necessary here to point out the radically greater willingness there is now than in the past to interfere with the "natural" ends of the sexual act.

A similar such evolution is evident in Pius XII's condemnation of the practice of homologous insemination whereby the seed drawn directly from the testicles or derived in some other licit manner, is inserted in the genital tract of the wife. The condemnation is not so important here as is the basis for it:[16]

We formally prohibit artificial insemination in marriage. The conjugal act by its natural structure is a personal relation, an immediate and concurrent collaboration by the husband and wife who as such and in accord with the nature of the act express by it that reciprocal gift which according to the sacred Scriptures engenders "union in one flesh only."

On the ground, then, of the secondary end of marriage, the attainment of the primary end was interdicted by Pius XII. If that is so, it is not entirely impossible that on those same grounds of "union in one flesh only" a similar interdiction of the attainment of the primary end would be allowable in other cases of great necessity. The Pope himself went on to explain that the marriage bond did not confer a right to "artificial impregnation," but only a right to the "natural marital act"; the slight shift in accent is important because

[16] Address to the Italian Catholic Union of Midwives, *AAS* 43, 1951.

the natural marital act is not being defined as the depositing of the semen in the vagina with the direct intention of procreating, it is now being defined in terms which can only be characterized as highly personalistic.

However, everything depends, again, on the definition of "natural," for the Pope added that the "marriage contract has not the 'child' for its object, but the 'natural acts' which are able to beget new life and are destined for that end." Yet an act using a contraceptive is intrinsically no more able to beget new life than is an act posited during an assuredly "safe period." Moreover, it is impossible to say that a pre-determined safe period is either intrinsically or by the intention of the agents "destined for" procreation. It is, then, to the role of natural law that one must always return; and it is with some reflections on this theme and on its relation to ecumenism that I would like to close this portion of the present discussion.

The Implications of the Natural-Law Doctrine

It is a tenet of the natural-law doctrine as developed by Catholic moralists that the primary principle, "avoid evil and do good," is known by all men whose reason is normally developed. Secondary principles which are direct deductions from the first principle are also regarded as knowable by all men of reason. Concerning the tertiary principles, which are "conclusions of rather involved processes of reasoning," [17] it is affirmed that a man of developed reason may at times be invincibly ignorant of *some* of

[17] Thomas J. Higgins S.J., *Man as Man: The Science and Art of Ethics*, Milwaukee 1948, 121.

them; this ignorance will, it is alleged, be due to the influence of immoral customs, generally accepted evil practices, etc. There is some circularity to the argument here as well as some dubious sociology, since it is not clear how the initiators of the "immoral customs" and "evil practices" could have disseminated them so broadly and have given them such widespread currency in the face of the developed reason of all other members of society. It is also difficult to see why honest and objective investigators, seeking to set aside so far as possible their prejudices, could not work their way back through the customary evil practices to a determination of the pristine virtues. That in point of fact they have not suggests that the natural-law doctrine is really a kind of gnosis attainable only by the initiates of the mystery.

Otherwise how explain that contraception is not universally acknowledged as immoral, particularly since the principle on which it is condemned entails no "complicated processes of reasoning"? Rather it involves only the most elementary enthymeme: the essential purpose of the conjugal union is procreation, and therefore any frustration of that purpose is immoral. The crux of the problem is not a matter of accurate or defective reasoning, but of the basic premise. Regrettably, the attainment of such basic premises is not the work of ratiocination, but of revelation, intuition, instinct, or cultural conditioning. To avoid a wholesale condemnation of the great majority of non-Catholics, natural-law theorists would have to say that the evil of contraception falls under the tertiary conclusions of the natural law. But it is apparent that so far as the distinguishing note of tertiary conclusions goes—the complexity

of the reasoning involved—it may as well be viewed as falling under those of the secondary order. One Catholic moralist has even stated that:[18]

> . . . a principle of the natural law is: Foster offspring; unite
> with the opposite sex in a union of love; avoid anything that
> would be contrary to the natural use of this power of procrea-
> tion, that would be contrary to the natural attraction existing
> between male and female. . . .

Of this and similar principles enumerated, this author observes that they "are as self-evident as the most fundamental principle *do good and avoid evil.*" In this instance contraception would be directly included in those acts which
are "contrary to this natural power of procreation." Thus
if we root the intrinsic immorality of contraception in *any*
principles derived from the natural law, whether primary,
secondary, or tertiary, we must conclude that no man of
normally developed reason can be invincibly ignorant of
the unnatural character of this evil—a conclusion which
necessarily foredooms any ecumenical efforts on the part of
Roman Catholics.

One may also consider the following similar ecumenical
barrier that the present natural-law argument raises. Catholic moralists teach that for a couple to enter into marriage
with the intention of bestowing on each other only the
right to contraceptive intercourse is to render the marriage
invalid. (We have seen only recently in a decision of the
Roman Rota how exemplarily this principle can be invoked
to ease the strained consciences of multimarried celebri-

[18] Michael V. Murray S.J., *Problems in Ethics*, New York 1960,
234.

ties.) Let us suppose two people refuse to accept the distinction between "natural" sexual relations and contraceptive intercourse—since we know it is perfectly licit to have intercourse without the *intention* of procreating—would their marriage be invalid? If this is so on the ground of natural law, then the inference would be applicable to overwhelming numbers of non-Catholics, all of whom must therefore be viewed by *their* separated brethren as living, at least formally, in a state of concubinage.

Since the natural law is the expression of the divine mind, there can be no cancelling of any part of it, for such cancellation would be a contradiction and a denial of the existence of a supreme lawgiver. But Catholic moral philosophers do teach that divorce and polygamy—also seemingly inalterably condemned by natural law—may be allowable in certain circumstances. The Pauline privilege allows what is by strict definition divorce; and polygamy was sanctioned by Moses. In both instances the Catholic natural-law theorist maintains that this does not mean the natural law admits of exceptions, but rather that what unaided reason has attained, in concluding to the immorality of divorce, is erroneous; for, according to these moralists, natural law does not say, do not grant divorces; what it says is, do not grant divorces unless the supreme lawgiver approves. Obviously, such a notion makes the classic notion of natural law absurd, since it either means that only explicit biblical revelation and the Church which interprets it can verify the nature of natural law, or it means that God's mind can change. Both illations are untenable, and the only humanly logical line to follow is that many of the premises employed by natural-law theorists as well as many of the conclusions deduced are false. This is to say quite explicitly that we have not yet discovered entirely what the supreme lawgiver approves: which is hardly surprising, since the rational faculty which is the proper discerner of natural law is itself in a process of self-discovery.

Conclusion

In conclusion it is to be hoped that what the council will do, given the widespread confusion the present position has created, is make a simple decree leaving this whole area open to further exploration, and allowing the determination of specific means of birth limitation to be left to the judgment of individual married couples. Psychologically, this would be advisable because it would be a clear indication that Catholics have finally shucked off that tutelage which often in the past seemed to require a manual of casuistry to assess the licitness of a particular act. Sociologically, this would be advisable because it would create a countercurrent to the present clerically imposed orthodoxies, and thus result in a genuine *consensus fidelium*. Most important of all, sacramentally such a decree would be advisable because the whole basis of religion is that union of God with his people which is figured forth in the marriage bond. The union of the couple is a sacred sign of the promised return to integrity from the state of the divided image in which man after the fall has had to live.

For all these reasons one may criticize those laymen who have seen little benefit in a conciliar statement that would leave this issue to "private conscience"—worded in those terms, of course, one may agree. But in fact there is no such thing as "private conscience." As the French word *conscience* illustrates, conscience is not just the inner moral imperative, but is the ethical and intellectual response of the entire human person to all outside stimuli. Conscience in this sense is not rightly formed by definitive decrees to which the will must demand submission, but by a multiplicity of factors of which authority is only one. To suggest that the council should leave the specifics of birth limitation to the consciences of the couples involved is not to advocate a subjective morality or a situation ethic, for morality is not subjective in any sense; its norms are eternal and unchanging. But our apprehension of them can only be by personal appropriation, and for this no other man or institution can be substituted.

Casti Connubii AND THE DEVELOPMENT OF DOGMA

LESLIE DEWART

Introduction

The purpose of this essay is to study the relation between a hypothetical future teaching of the magisterium permitting the use of "artificial contraception" [1] in Christian marriage and the previous official teaching to the contrary effect. For the sake of brevity we shall consider here exclusively the principal and most authoritative document in which the Church's teaching has been set down—that is, Pius XI's encyclical *Casti Connubii*. Thus, the purpose of this paper is not to demonstrate the morality of artificial contraception—although some of the conclusions that it reaches may suggest the theological grounds on which such an argument might be attempted. This inquiry will, at best, clear the ground for such an attempt.

---

[1] In this paper, except where otherwise noted, the term "artificial contraception" does not distinguish between anovulants and the older mechanical or chemical devices. However, it does distinguish these from every other contraceptive means, specifically from the practice of *coitus interruptus* or any variation thereof in which sexual intercourse is physiologically abnormal or incomplete. The term "onanism" shall be used to refer to these.

I shall suppose that the question of whether the infallibility of the magisterium was involved in the Church's
teaching against artificial contraception is to be answered
negatively. This issue is, of course, far from settled. If the
answer were negative it would begin to smooth the way
for a reformation of the teaching, but even then the status
of Pius XI's treatment would have to be determined. The
possibility of scandal could be safeguarded against, in such
a contingency, through sincere and exact explanations of
the ways in which the magisterium *is* fallible. But even this
would scarcely solve every problem. It would still be desirable to ascertain in what way and to what extent the earlier
doctrine was erroneous and—perhaps most important of
all—how the error managed to introduce itself into the
teaching of the Church. If for no other reason we should
know this in order to avoid, insofar as possible, the repeti-
tion of a similar sequence of events in the future. Moreover,
it might well be inexact to conclude that a hypothetical
future teaching permitting artificial contraception would
simply mean that Pius XI was in error. It could be that the
Pope was partly in error, but partly not; or that he did not
in fact teach quite what he had been assumed to have
taught; or that *Casti Connubii*'s teaching was basically correct given the circumstances of its composition and the as-
sumptions on which it was founded, but that in a different
context a modified teaching may be needed; or, finally, a
combination of these and, perhaps, other factors.

The question, therefore, arises: if we suppose a future
authoritative teaching in favor of the morality of contraception, must we also account for the reformation of the
doctrine exclusively in terms of fallibility? Might we not

also do so in terms of dogmatic development? Is there any sense in which we could truthfully speak of a continuity between the two positions within the teaching of the Church? We should know in what way and to what extent the reformed doctrine would confirm and amplify the earlier one, and upon what truth of the one the other would expand. We should enquire whether otherwise startling modifications in the teaching of the Church could be explained in terms of the normal evolution of the Christian faith and of the processional variety of its cultural forms.

These are some of the questions to which this study may be relevant. I propose to investigate, through a critical analysis of the text of *Casti Connubii*, the theological and dogmatic factors which dictated the formulation of the encyclical's teaching against contraception. To this end we shall inquire, first, what is the exact nature of the document's teaching against contraception and, second, what is the wider dogmatic context in which this doctrine takes its place. Once this is done we may be in a position to appraise the encyclical in relation to the development of Christian dogma, and to determine which aspects it developed and which, if any, it may have left in an insufficiently developed state. But since the total historical situation that resulted in the formulation of *Casti Connubii*'s condemnation may be safely presumed to have had a wider compass than that of theology and dogma alone, it should be useful to begin by considering the cultural context in which the teaching occurred. A serious investigation of this last topic alone would be much more than the scope of this essay permits. A few schematic indications of possible heuristic value will have to suffice.

The Catholic Attitude to Sexuality and Its Origin

It would have been impossible for Pius XI or for the theological advisors whose views he underwrote in *Casti Connubii* to have been untouched by the attitude toward sexuality prevailing in the Catholic culture of the times—an attitude which had a long history (and which in the intervening period has become only slightly modified). Those treatises of moral theology which though written in the vernacular nevertheless found it necessary to treat *De Sexto et Nono* only in a less accessible tongue, were perhaps atypically prudish, but only in their exaggeration of a common trait. The Catholic conscience has long been especially horrified and its feelings have been unusually outraged by sexual immorality—even while it has intellectually judged that "sins of the spirit" are generally graver than "sins of the flesh." Something of this feeling is conveyed, for instance, by *Casti Connubii*'s apparent regard of contraception as a more repulsive sin than abortion.

There is little doubt that a moralist is entitled to inveigh against the shamefulness of sexual immorality. Nor is the propriety of the Pope's feelings being put in question here. What is being suggested is simply that *Casti Connubii*, rightly or wrongly, shows evidence of a certain attitude toward sexuality which might be fairly described as reflecting the same uneasiness and disdain which is to be found in much Catholic theological literature. At the same time, we must be careful not to magnify this. It might be best expressed negatively: sexuality is not an ennobling feature of human nature. It may have a proper and, accidentally, even an honorable place in human existence. But it cannot be considered in itself a proper foundation for human achievement or Christian spirituality. We stop short of concluding that God would have been wiser had he created an androginous mankind, or if he had disposed otherwise than sexually for the reproduction of man. But we do not ordinarily experience vividly, or with awe, God's wisdom in having created man male and female—along with all the personal sexuality of the individual which the generic bi-sexuality of man implies. We are not often *glad,* precisely as Christians and in virtue of our faith, that sexuality exists. At best, we refrain from contempt. This attitude can be detected in *Casti Connubii* as readily as in many another Catholic document. Pius XI reflected it; he was not its source.

It was fashionable at one time to ascribe the origin of this attitude to the theology of St. Paul. More recent New Testament scholarship has rendered this proposition a very doubtful one. With our improved undertanding of his anthropology we are no longer likely to interpret dualistically St. Paul's contrast between "flesh" and "spirit," and in the light of our rediscovery of the eschatology of the early Church we can wonder whether "Paul's reasons for advising celibacy were [not] apocalyptic rather than dualistic." [2] We no longer tend to read him in the same perspective as Marcion and other Manichean Gnostics did, though we recognize that there was a Hellenic strain in the writ-

[2] W. G. Cole, *Sex in Christianity and Psychoanalysis,* New York 1955, 37. St. Augustine's *De Sancta Virginitate* could be interpreted as teaching why the Pauline eschatological reasons for prizing virginity remain valid even within a different apocalyptic perspective.

ings of the Apostle which made certain theological and doctrinal developments more likely than others.

Even St. Augustine's attitudes toward sexuality appear to us much less determined by his Manichean antecedents when we consider his lifelong anti-Pelagian pastoral concern: "For, while either one is an error, either to make nuptials equal to holy virginity or to condemn them, these two errors, in their overeagerness to avoid each other, attack from opposite extremes, since they have refused to cling to the middle position of truth . . ." [3] Neither marriage nor virginity is commanded. The counsel of virginity may be more perfect—for *spiritual* reasons, as he abundantly explains—but the vocation of marriage is not to be despised: this is the substance of St. Augustine's doctrine. It is a doctrine which, for all its warnings to the contrary, easily lends itself to a justification of contempt for marriage and the married state—as soon as one forgets the reasons why virginity is worthy and to be valued for its own sake. But it may be difficult, unless we read St. Augustine out of historical and cultural context, to uphold the view that the last of the fathers condemned sexuality as such or the married state; whereas it may be argued that he did not introduce a Manichean disposition into the Christian tradition or transmitted any element which of itself required such a development. On the other hand, when a Manichean strain was later imported into the Christian culture of the West, St. Augustine's theology could not but facilitate the rationalization of attitudes of hatred, fear and contempt for human sexuality under the mantle of orthodoxy.

[3] St. Augustine, *De Sancta Virginitate* 19.

In point of historical fact, Manichean beliefs as such were reintroduced into western Christendom early in the second millenium of Christianity from the direction of the Balkans and quite independently of any Augustinian tradition. After a period of incubation in the fertile hotbeds of the deep social and political changes of the age, the germ burst into virulence a century later in the form of the Catharist movement (from *katharos*, clean, pure), which spread so rapidly that by the third quarter of the twelfth century it threatened to overwhelm the traditional Christian faith by the force of numbers alone.[4] The extent to which the previous development of Christian dogma (particularly on account of Christianity's early adoption of Hellenic cultural forms) may have provided the ideological basis for the strength of Catharism and for the passionate conviction with which it was held, remains a matter for further research. Given the depth of the anticlerical component of the movement, it is possible that the dogmatic predispositions were not nearly as significant a factor in its propagation as were social causes, such as the increasingly marked stratification of the Church into clergy and laity which had accompanied the feudalization of Europe and the advent of the Holy Roman Empire. Catharism was as much a socio-political movement as it was a religious one.

[4] The earliest recorded instance of Catharism in western Europe is that of a heresy trial at Orleans dated 1022, but evidence exists of contemporary occurrences in Germany and northern Italy. However, it was not until the late twelfth century that Catharism became a mass movement, especially in southern France, northern Italy and northern Spain. See Philip Hughes, *A History of the Church*, rev. ed., New York 1949, II, 343. The last burning of Cathar heretics seems to have taken place in 1330; see Steven Runciman, *The Medieval Manichee*, Cambridge 1947, 146.

The Catharist belief in the intrinsic sinfulness of all sexual behavior and the "impurity" of all sexual desire[5]
—hence the Cathars' exhortation to the unmarried not to
marry, and to the married to abstain from sexual relations
—was grounded upon the evil nature of the body and of
all corporeal being, which had been created by the "principle of darkness." If for this reason alone, the Catharist
doctrine of marriage and sexuality was repeatedly condemned by the magisterium of the Church in the most uncompromising terms. Nevertheless, through a slow, drawn-
out cultural process, Catharism succeeded in generating
within Christianity itself certain sexual attitudes which
have been strengthened by time and hallowed by history
as they have been handed down to our own day. Our contemporary knowledge of sociology assures us that this was
not unusual: it would have been abnormal if the religious
conflict between orthodoxy and Catharism had *not* exhibited the sociological process of "acculturation." In cultural
struggles the victor's triumph is often achieved through the
ingestion of the opponent; the digestion of the victim
means, in part, its assimilation. The result is usually a synthetic cultural compromise.

To understand how the acculturation of Catharist sexual
beliefs took place, we must remember that this movement
was associated with an antinomian practical outlook upon
sexuality—much as had earlier happened with Gnosticism.
The reason for this can be easily surmised. The conviction
that the body is thoroughly and irredeemably evil, that

[5] Curiously, the NCWC translation of *Casti Connubii* renders *cu-
piditas* as "impure desires." The English Dominican translation of
St. Thomas' *Summa Theologiae* translates *pudicitia* as "purity" in
II-II, 151, 4.

only the soul is good, naturally tends to degenerate into indifference to what the body does and to whether *it* behaves
sinfully. Catharism was noted not only for its sexual hor-
ror, but also for its sexual excesses. The Catharist distinction between the "Perfect" (*perfecti*) and the mere
"Believers" (*credentes, imperfecti*) reflected this ambivalence quite accurately. Thus, the complete materialization
of sexuality, potentially permitted the emergence of a "spiritual" or "true" love between woman and man. But what
could be the nature of a "spiritual," non-bodily love between the sexes? If such a love involves man and woman,
is it not by definition sexual? And if it is sexual, is it not
therefore corporeal?

In Catharism itself the consequent follows. The Christian adaptation of Catharism began when, for *Christian*
motives, early medieval culture actualized the potential "spiritual" love of man and woman which Catharism spontane-
ously suggested. The adaptation consisted in devising a
concept of love which permitted a logically viable and a
(seemingly) dogmatically orthodox distinction between
"spiritual" sexuality, as it were, and corporeal sexuality.
This "spiritual" love between man and woman was made
possible by de-genitalizing the sexual attraction of the
sexes. For instance, intense and even consciously fostered
sexual desire, endlessly verbalized and thought about, was
"spiritual" insofar as it was deliberately unconsummated
in sexual, genital union. This type of love could obviously
not obtain in marriage. It must be by definition extra-marital or pre-marital. Marriage, thus, was thought to be too
gross a man-woman relation, since it involved sexual relations and procreation. The true love between the sexes

could take place only outside marriage, where its beauty and its holiness could remain unimpaired. The "pure" sexual love of a man for a woman should not prosaically beget obstreperous proles: it should beget music and poetry (love poetry, that is). Because this concept of love grew with the refinement of manners and the cultivation of the arts in the ruling courts, it became known as *courtly love*.

Courtly love developed, therefore, as the Catharist belief in the absolute evil of sexuality was *rejected* by Christendom under the influence of orthodox Christian teaching. But Catharism's emphasis on the evil of sexuality suggested to the Christian culture the possibility of a "pure" love between the sexes. Strict Catharism desexualized love absolutely, because it equated love with physiology. Courtly love, more modestly, simply de-genitalized love. Love remained sexual, but its purity was guaranteed by the displacement of all the physiology of love to the wounded heart, to the fevered brow, to the pain of thwarted desire (is parting not a "sweet sorrow"?), to the sighs of unrequited affection, and to swooning at the sight of the beloved. "True" love was made possible by the simultaneous separation of sexual intercourse from sexual love, and of sexual love from marriage. This complex cultural phenomenon found a new means of expression—and a powerful vehicle for its propagation—when the "novel" literary *genre* of the "love story" or *roman* (OF. *romanz*, English *romance*)[6] was discovered—whence the later name given

[6] The substantive *romanz*, a story written (or told) in the vernacular, was derived from the adjectival noun of the same form referring to the vernacular tongue itself (LL. *Romanicus*). *To romance*, (OF. *romancier*), meant to write or sing in the vernacular.

to the same sociological and cultural institution, *romantic love*. Western lyric poetry and the vernacular literatures were born under this mystic sign of unconsummated sexual love.

Naturally, practical antinomianism was an implicit possibility of this concept; wherever romantic love has flourished loose sexual morality has ordinarily been harvested. The devotees of courtly love did not always succeed in purifying their baser instincts. Too ardent a spiritual wooing of one's lady love (*ma demeisele*, she who is loved *par* [*vrai*]*amour*) by even the "purest" lover, sometimes sets the bodily tinder afire, as Francesca da Rimini belatedly found out. Indeed, courtly love often rationalized "mixed love" (i.e. partly "spiritual," partly bodily) as permissible under the laws of "courtesy." For this reason the terms "courtesan" and "paramour" acquired the promiscuous connotations which now remain the only meaning of the terms. *Promiscuity* itself, in the sexual acceptation of the word, comes from the same concept of "mixed love."

Modern philological research has contributed singularly to our awareness of these processes. It is no longer a novelty to suggest that "all European poetry has come out of the poetry written in the twelfth century by the troubadours of Languedoc," [7] and although the exact relation of the tradition of *amour courtois* to Catharism remains the subject of some debate, it is difficult to deny any longer "that courtly lyric poetry was *at least inspired* by the mysticism of the Cathars." [8]

[7] Denis de Rougemont, *Love in the Western World*, New York 1957, 67.

[8] *Ibid.* 96. Italics in the original. Several authors have regarded the troubadours as crypto-Catharists. At the other end of the spec-

But it should be underlined that the *motive* which found the inspiration for its cultural devices in these exotic dogmas was thoroughly Christian. For it had been distinctive of Christianity that it had introduced into human civilization a powerful force which tended of itself to the universalization of charity as the norm of *all* human interpersonal relations. This extended specifically and explicitly to the relations between the sexes. The full authority of Scripture stood behind it: "There is neither Jew nor Greek: there is neither bond nor free: there is neither male nor female. For you are all one in Christ Jesus." [9] The inherent tendency of Christianity to further the cultural conception of a love of friendship within the scope of sexual relations had been partially checked, however, in the course of the first thousand years of Christianity, not so much by any hesitation in reconciling Christian supernatural love with the physiology of sex,[10] (after all, Gnosticism and Marcionism had been effectively dealt with by the Church), as by the difficulties of overcoming the historical inertia of culture and of learning to grant to womanhood the fullness of the human personality. Catharism suggested to Christians the possibility of *Christian* sexual love, that is, a supernaturally desirable *sexual charity* between woman and man. But given the historical circumstances of this Christian discovery, western Christendom was able to envisage sexual love only in the guise of "spiritual," extra-

---

trum, the late Alexander Denomy C.S.B. believed that "the origin of the courtly conception of love as ennobling is to be found . . . in Arabian philosophy and specifically in the mystical philosophy of Avicenna." *The Heresy of Courtly Love*, Boston 1947, 29-30.

[9] Gal 3:28.

[10] See Anders Nygren, *Agape and Eros*, London 1954.

marital, romantic love, and at the expense of the de-genitalization of sexual love relations.

The cult of romantic love, however, eventually led not only to the relaxation of extra-marital and pre-marital sexual morality; it also produced a confusion about the nature of sexual morality. In the Christian tradition the matter of the vice of lust (*luxuria*) is sexual desire and pleasure, but the vice formally consists in "departing from the reasonable order and mode of sexual behavior." [11] The "spiritualization" and the de-genitalization of romantic love, however, made it difficult to distinguish between the moral formality of sinful sexual love, that is, its disorder, and the matter, namely sexuality, since this cultural institution inculcated that the superiority of romantic love over married love resulted from the indulgence of sexual desire and the repression of sexual consummation. Once the culture became persuaded that a cerebral, sublimated sexuality was noble because it was actually "love" and not really "sex," the culture was bound to perceive the immorality of sexual sinfulness as formally consisting in "gross," overtly somatic, sexuality itself. Gradually a social morality arose in which a social premium was put upon the repression of genital activity at the same time that sexual desire was exalted by almost every means available to the culture. It is not a coincidence that one of the earliest personal accounts of a *grande passion* in western literature, the letters of Heloise to Abelard, dates from the end of the twelfth century at the same time that it exhibits this precise moral concept:

[11] St. Thomas Aquinas, *Summa Theologiae* (henceforth *ST*), II-II, 153, 3. I use throughout my own translation of the Marietti edition.

Heloise regretted, not having "loved," but having sinned. Nor should we marvel that our contemporary culture, in direct line of descent from the age of Chretien de Troyes and Eleanor of Aquitaine, constantly assaults everyone of us through every sense modality with the frustrating ambivalence ("naughty, but nice") of our age's sexual obsession; or that it mercilessly teases the young with the glamour of forbidden sex and with the tinsel of the ecstatic, sexual *mystique* of romanticism at the same time that it surrounds sexual behavior with an aura of guilt, shame, and revulsion.

Christian moral theology has not altogether escaped the influence of the cultural institution of romantic love. For instance, whenever a moralist excoriates sexual sin and impresses upon us its uniquely sordid and sickening quality with the admonition that it reduces human sexuality to the level of a beast's, or that it allows man's animality to overwhelm his spirituality, he betrays a degree of this culturally conditioned confusion. Similarly, we have tended to think that there is something especially sinful about sexual sin precisely because it is sexual and bodily. From this we have often taken the short step to the idea that sexual behavior can be without sin if sexuality is, as it were, redeemed by virtue, circumstance or sacrament—for instance, by marriage. Thus, little by little we have arrived at the attitude from which we view marriage as justifying and *legalizing* sexual activity—indeed, as an economic, social and religious institution which partly in order to achieve its own ends, partly as an incentive and a reward to those who agree to enter upon it, provides a license to man and woman to indulge their baser (though now, of

course, perfectly legitimate and morally permissible) bodily
desires. In this concept, therefore, the principal relation
between marriage and sexuality is permissibility (as contrasted with the forbiddenness of extra-marital sexual activity). Sexual relations which are otherwise within the
bounds of the moral law *may* obtain within marriage. But
marriage itself is ordered to better—that is, spiritual—
things.

Sexuality and Christian Marriage

In 1225, when the Count of Aquino sired his seventh
and youngest son, Catharism had been all but exterminated
in Europe by sword and fire a decade before, though the
last pockets of significant resistance were not overrun until
1249. Yet, when in the 1250s the young friar Thomas
wrote his commentary *On the Sentences of Peter Lom-
bard,* the budding attitudes toward the sexuality of marriage had already introduced themselves into Christian
theology and were revealed in certain curious ambivalences
of the new Master's doctrine. For example, St. Thomas condemned, on the one hand, the opinion that the marriage
act is sinful as "a most wicked heresy" (*pessima haeresis*)
which he associated with the "madness" of belief in the
creation of bodily beings by an evil god,[12] that is, with
Gnosticism and Catharism. But when he asked whether
it was sinful to "know" one's wife for the sake of pleasure
alone, he became somewhat inconsistent. Asserting that
pleasure was not the relevant moral consideration, since
"pleasure in a good action is good, and bad in a bad ac-

[12] *ST, Supp.* 41, 2.

tion," he judged that if sexual pleasure were to exclude the "honesty" of marriage (as it would if a man were ready to use either his wife or another woman indifferently), the seeking of pleasure would be sinful. Yet, if a man "sought pleasure within the limits of marriage, in such a way that he would not seek it in a woman other than his wife, it is a venial sin." [13] And elsewhere: "There are only two ways in which the spouses may come together without any sin, namely for the sake of begetting offspring and in order to pay the debt. Otherwise it is always a sin, at least a venial one." [14]

St. Thomas never explained why this should be so. There is no question that it had to do neither with the evil of sexuality itself nor with the disorder of heedless pleasure, since both are explicitly ruled out. For St. Thomas, evidently, there was no marvel in the fact that, nevertheless, the marriage act should be even venially sinful. It is fairly clear that this was an attitude he had osmotically absorbed from his world. By this time married love had become doubly suspect: to the secular culture of courtly love because it *was* married, to the Christian mind of the theologian because the only sexual love exhibited by the culture was *unmarried* sexual love. The cause of sexual love in marriage had few or no champions on its side. It had only secular enemies behind and theological suspicion ahead.

Admittedly, in the text of St. Thomas quoted above, the "payment of the debt" could be understood in a wide sense, so that it would be possible to reconcile this doctrine with

[13] *ST, Supp.* 49, 6.
[14] *ST, Supp.* 49, 5.

the opinion that sexual intercourse for the sake of mutual love is not only legitimate, but meritorious of grace. In fact, it is most probable that St. Thomas thought so. Nevertheless, the underlying attitude of St. Thomas toward sexuality, though certainly not one of revulsion or aversion, is evidently one of diffidence and misgiving. Since then these feelings have never been absent from moral theological thought. On the contrary, hesitations have grown into preoccupations, worries have caused apprehensiveness, fears have generated disdain. In this sense *Casti Connubii* takes its place in the increasingly common tradition of the later Christian culture. From St. Thomas' commentary to the document of 1930 stretches the long, thin line of a Christian theology of sexuality which has not always avoided the consequences of admitting cultural attitudes toward sex which have been miscengenated by Christian zeal out of exotic concubines.

The full history of the concept of courtly love, especially after the defection of the masses from the Christian faith beginning at the end of the eighteenth century, and the further degeneration of romantic love into libertinism, and its ultimate profound effect upon the sociology of contemporary marriage, can be incorporated here only by the merest allusion. We should note, however, that the twentieth century has suggested to Christianity for the first time the possibility of a genuine love of a sexual nature within marriage—I mean, a fully genital married love—a love whose "purity" would not derive either from asexuality, or (to use the psychoanalytic term) from pre-genital sexuality, or from extra-matrimoniality, but from the interpersonal nature of genital, marital relations. This suggestion has come from a source which has not been generally well received in Christian circles: Sigmund Freud.

Yet, Freud destroyed the basis of romantic love and, therefore, made possible the emergence of a Christian *eros* within the Christian culture of today. He did this when he laid waste the two myths upon which romanticism had been erected: the physiological nature of human sexuality, and the identification of "gross," or "bodily" sexuality with the genital. For one of the most enduring of Freud's contributions to human knowledge was his discovery that human sexuality is primarily a psychological and social phenomenon—that human beings do not merely copulate but, indeed, have sexual *relations*—relations which can be reduced neither to the physiological nor to the genital, but which can be understood only as interpersonal. Only since Freud have we been able to understand human sexuality as a phenomenon sufficiently complex and organismic to involve the deepest levels of the human personality and the highest aspirations of the human spirit.

In a sense, therefore, only in the twentieth century has it become possible for Christian theology to understand that the love relations of husband and wife are properly those of sexual love—or better, conversely, that the sexual relations of husband and wife are, in their very sexuality, interpersonal relations which of themselves aspire to the perfection of charity.

Chronologically, *Casti Connubii* was written when Freud had less than a decade to live, and when his work was for all practical purposes long since complete. But culturally, *Casti Connubii* is a pre-Freudian document. We must read it in that context, as a pre-Freudian document, if we are to understand what it truly means. The future development of the Christian doctrine of marriage will surely take place in a different cultural context, and it will hopefully offer its moral guidance to the married Christian only after having taken account of contemporary experience and of man's increased cultural awareness of himself. If so, perhaps the magisterium's teaching on artificial contraception might be more complete than *Casti Connubii*'s found it possible to be.

The Basis of Casti Connubii's *Condemnation of Contraception*

It is generally known that in *Casti Connubii* Pope Pius XI condemned contraception. This condemnation applied indiscriminately to all contraception, whether onanistic or by means of mechanical and chemical devices. No moral distinction between the two needed to be made—or was implied—since the reasons why the practice was immoral applied indistinctly to both. Allowance was made only for "periodic continence," which is not contraceptive in the proper sense of the word, since it did not deliberately deprive the conjugal act of its natural power and aptitude.

So much is incontestable. However, the ground on which the condemnation rested seem to have received insufficient critical attention. *Casti Connubii* may well have settled at the time the question whether artificial contraception was immoral, but it never settled the problem *why* it was immoral—on the contrary, it lent new interest and relevance to the topic. Unfortunately, the ensuing discussion has not always been fruitful. A review of the literature discloses a variety of interpretations, often mutually contradictory. Moreover, in practice some theologians have not always adhered to the distinction between theological inquiry and apologetics. Consciously or unconsciously assuming as their basic objective the defense of the authority of the magisterium of the Church, they have sometimes written as if the question *why* the Pope's condemnation was valid were somewhat impertinent. Only this hypothesis explains why some have been more concerned, apparently, with persuading the reader that Pius XI's reasons for teaching as he did were sound, than with showing *what* reasons the Pope himself actually offered, or with explaining, fully independently of the papal teaching, what the truth of the matter might be.

The first of these two tasks has been singularly neglected. Textual studies of *Casti Connubii* which attempt not to demonstrate how the document can be used to repel attacks upon Christian morality, but to analyze precisely what the text actually says, are rare.

Speculative studies are more numerous than exegeses, but their number is pared down if we omit those in which not only the legitimate premise is accepted that Pius XI did in fact condemn contraception, but in which a certain gratuitous interpretation of the reason why this practice is immoral is also introduced under the guise of self-evidence, or common sense, or demonstrable truth. However, given the difficulties under which theological investigation has operated in the last hundred years or so, one could not have reasonably expected fewer studies to suffer from this defect. In this matter, earnestly to have asked the question *why* has not always been a prudent pursuit for a theologian unless he began with reassurances that his conclusions would support Pius XI. Thus, the development of theology in this area has been an almost impossible task even for those who had the will to undertake it.

These and other reasons have conspired to spread widely, I do not say disputable, but baseless opinions concerning the reason *Casti Connubii* proferred for its condemnation. For example, everyone knows that contraception is wrong, according to Pius XI, because it is "against nature." Those are, indeed, the exact words of the encyclical. But what do they mean? What is that the nature of which contraception is against? The question is not often asked. Even when it is asked, it is not asked of the text of Pius XI. Consequently, much has been attributed to the Pope which in reality could be hardly justified from the words and meaning of the encyclical. In brief, the question *why* Pius XI condemned contraception cannot be considered as settled.

However, the reason *why* any given species of human behavior may be said to be immoral is of both practical and speculative significance. The question exactly *what* is condemned by a moral teaching (that is, under what formality) depends very largely upon the reason *why* it is immoral. For the reason *why* is the formality that defines the *moral* truth of a moral proposition.

A lie, for example, may well be definable as the lack of adequation of speech to thought. But lying is not immoral insofar as speech and thought, and the incongruence of the two are mere events; its immorality obtains insofar as thought and speech are *human*, moral events. A lie is not immoral because of that lack of adequation in itself, which as such is only a fact of nature. The immorality is comported by a deficiency which, being voluntarily introduced into the *communication* of thought, contravenes the right use of the powers of expression. Lying is sinful because it is deceptive; that is why even the truth can be used to lie.

To murder is not to cause that physiological condition which we call death: it is the taking of life. To understand what "Thou shalt not kill" actually forbids (does it forbid killing in self-defense? in war?) it is necessary to know why murder is wrong. Shedding blood is a physiological event; as such it is only the matter of fifth-commandment morality.

This does not mean that morality formally depends upon *subjective* conditions or events, such as the reason why the doer may intend it—although these subjective conditions, of course, (very particularly the envisaged intention), affect the morality of the act in various ways. Sometimes they may affect it radically (e.g. a fatal poison is administered by unavoidable mistake) but they always do so accidentally. The formality of the moral act depends upon the reason why the act is *objectively* right or wrong. The objectivity of morality is distinguished not only from the subjectivity of the subject's intention and other "inner" conditions, but also from the objectivity of the physical, "external" event. The objectivity in question is a *moral* objectivity, that is, it refers to the objective nature of *human conduct* as such. Thus, morality accrues to *the human act*, to human behavior, not to "natural," that is, physical events—not even to physiological, biological or mental events occurring in man insofar as those events have their own entitative character. A few examples should illustrate the point.

Fornication is not sinful because it consists in the use of

certain given bodily organs or because it is a pleasant bodily experience of a certain type. It is wrong and morally forbidden because of an objective *moral* defect of the fornicating sexual act precisely as human. Fornication is a type of sexual misbehavior or misconduct. It is wrong because it is misbehavior, not because it is sexual. In what does the objective defect of fornication consist which renders its performance human misconduct? As St. Thomas explains, it is a defect in the properly human relations that ought to obtain between man and woman. Fornication is a male-female union which objectively vitiates the due nature of the union; for according to its nature, the sexual congress of *human* male and female should proceed from and, reciprocally, generate those interpersonal relations which we call the society or covenant of marriage. The defect of fornication is that it excludes marriage.[15]

Similarly, masturbation is wrong and "against nature" (*contra naturam*) not because it produces the ejaculation of semen, or because it produces such an ejaculation without insemination. Physiologically, there would be nothing unnatural about it (unless, perhaps, the superstition that it is physically unhealthy were correct). Nevertheless, it is unnatural precisely as a moral object, for it contains a moral defect against the nature of the generative powers and the use of the sexual organs: it is "solitary" sexual behavior. The moral perfection of the use of these organs requires the congress of man and woman—needless to say it also requires several other conditions. Thus, as St. Thomas explains (in a doctrine which would appear not false but meaningless to someone who ascribed the immorality of

[15] *ST*, II-II, 154, 2.

masturbation to the "loss of seed") masturbation is "against nature" (and, thus, a much graver sin than simple fornication) because it is the use of the sexual organs "without any copulation" (*absque omni concubitu*), and this is "contrary to the natural order of the sexual act as befits the human race" (*repugnat ipsi ordini naturali venerei actus qui convenit humanae species*).[16] It is wrong, then, and unnatural, because of the sexual isolation in which its practitioner places himself. The sexual disorder of this sin is not physiological, nor specifically that the masturbator succumbs to the intensity of his sexual desire and thus loses his self-control. The unnaturalness results from the exclusion of the natural and proper object of male sexual desire, namely woman—and, of course, vice versa. Thus, it is necessary to understand the reason *why*, if we are to understand the moral nature of, say, contraception. To understand *Casti Connubii* we must understand why, according to the Pope's own teaching, contraception is *objectively*, that is, *intrinsically* (*per se, intrinsece*) wrong and contrary to nature.

The foregoing examples were not chosen at random. Probably the least uncommon interpretation of *Casti Connubii* has placed the unnaturalness of contraception in the "spilling of seed." A historical factor in the creation of this view suggests itself immediately: the long and uninterrupted Christian tradition concerning the immorality of "onanism."

Now, the matter of the sin of onanism involves—in part —the "spilling of seed." But this physiological occur-

[16] *ST*, II-II, 154, 11.

rence is not what constitutes the moral formality of the sin. Onanism is sinful, in the first place, because it is contraceptive in the sense condemned by Pius XI, that is, because it deprives the conjugal act of its natural generative power and aptitude. It is sinful, moreover, for a second reason which Pius XI did not discernibly consider in *Casti Connubii*, namely because of the unnatural marital sexual relation between the persons of husband and wife which it implies—so that if, *per impossibile*, onanism were not a contraceptive act it would nevertheless remain sinful, against nature, and morally forbidden. By the same token, even if in the future artificial contraception were declared by the magisterium of the Church, *contra* Pius XI, to be morally permissible, *Casti Connubii*'s condemnation of contraception would remain unaffected in what pertained to onanism.

The confusion which somehow has introduced itself into the Catholic mind is best illustrated by the frequency with which at a certain level of discussion the term "onanism" is used to signify "masturabation"—nor has this mistake been absent from every theological treatise. Somewhat less often, perhaps, the practice of onanism is described as a form of masturbation. Yet the only common element between the two is a strictly physiological one, namely the "loss of seed." From the point of view of moral theology they are specifically distinct sins, for the reason why they are sinful is different in each case. Thus, let us suppose that masturbation were performed in place of sexual intercourse, for the sake of obtaining venereal pleasure while avoiding the risk of an undesired conception: the immorality of this act would not consist in the act's accidentally contraceptive effect, but in its being "the solitary vice." Conversely, onanistic intercourse may well be sinful, both as contraceptive and as a perversion of natural sexual intercourse, but its sinfulness could not very well be said to consist in its being sexual solitude: thus, onanism would sin against oneself, against the other spouse (if the couple is married; otherwise, against the female's womanhood), and against the society of marriage—but not, like masturbation, against mankind.

The confusion in question antedates *Casti Connubii* by several centuries. It would be possible to trace its remote historical origins, perhaps, to primitive superstitions of the same nature that have produced, for instance, fertility rites and phallic worship out of mankind's natural and universal experience of awe upon awareness of the seemingly magical —and certainly wondrous—power of human semen to produce a new life which will grow to the attainment of human consciousness, that is, into another *self*.

We should recall the more immediate influence of Catharism upon the western world in this very respect. Semen was the bodily fluid by which human evil, corporeity, was perpetuated. Moreover, in the vehemence of sexual behavior man perceives his bodiliness much too brightly, in much too harsh a light, in too primitive colors, to be able to deny the bodily condition that substantially belongs to him. The religious fear and contempt of corporeity, thus, are naturally focused upon physiological seminality. The powerlessness to actually achieve emancipation from sexual desires by a mere act of will, the wounded pride of him who aspired to the condition of a "pure" spirit yet who was bound to his body most humiliatingly of all by his own sexuality—these frustrations could be much too easily turned back upon the ultimate, substantial, inner cause of it all. To spill the seed was not merely to indulge the body: it was to witness one's own human degradation. Probably not by simple coincidence, feelings of aggressiveness, hostility and contempt, both toward oneself and the opposite sex, lie etymologically just below the surface bluster of many of our vulgar sexual metaphors; and many allusions to the period have been retained by our common sexual lexicon[17]—though probably many fewer than in the conventions of our love poetry and romantic literature.

In more recent times certain early modern biological theories contributed, among other factors, to making the quasi-mystic aura surrounding human semen appear more rational. The biological theory that semen contains an "homunculus," a pre-formed embryonic human being which the mother nourishes and rears *in utero* to the maturity of birth, would be of obvious relevance to Christian morality.[18] On this assumption, any "waste of semen" might well be considered as almost a sort of ante-conceptional abortion. If so, it must be forbidden in itself, that is, quite apart from the relation of the physiological occurrence to one's sexual duties toward other persons or to oneself.

[17] Catharism spread in the West directly from the Manichean beliefs of a Bulgarian sect, the Bogomils, so called from the name of their "pope," Bogomili. It was commonly (but mistakenly) thought that the Bogomils and the Cathars advocated sodomy. Hence the LL. *Bulgarus*, a Bulgarian, became in the West a synonym for a sodomite. From this derived OF. *boulgre*, Fr. *bougre* and more recently Eng. *bugger* and the transitive verb of the same form which, partly euphemistically, partly by back formation, became the abbreviated *to bug*, the same word which, cut off from its origins, has very recently ascended from obscenity to slang.

[18] See below, note 64.

Casti Connubii did not create or authorize this confusion, but neither did it dispel it. Indeed, it served accidentally to compound it. For some persons, having interpreted *Casti Connubii*'s doctrine of *contra naturam* to mean that contraception is wrong because of the physiological "loss of semen," appear to have drawn some startling moral theological conclusions: for instance, that fornication or adultery are especially malicious if performed contraceptively, and that the use of artificial contraceptives within these acts constitutes a specifically different sin. Granted the premise, the conclusion follows. But neither is self-evident; and, indeed, the conclusion is so repugnant to common sense and to prudence that not very many theologians have drawn it without hesitation, even among those who would grant that sound logic demands it of the Christian conscience in the light of the teaching of *Casti Connubii* thus understood. For what prudent conscience would not in real life judge that an adulterer or a seducer would be especially guilty if he deliberately failed to ensure that his lust remained uncompounded with cruelty, injustice, and callous unconcern?

But in point of fact, the encyclical did not base its teaching against contraception on the physiology of sexual behavior, any more than it accepted physiological reasons to excuse it. It condemned without discrimination every contraceptive device or practice, presumably even those which would not result in the "loss of semen." Thus, if the prohibition is to be understood as applying to the use of a pessary or of contraceptive jelly (and there can be no reasonable doubt that it so applied) the reason is that it forbade not the loss of semen, but the deprivation of the conjugal act's "natural power to generate life." [19] Conversely, if the Pope's condemnation had been based upon the view that the intrinsic moral nature of the conjugal act is violated because the physiological act of insemination is prevented, it would not be clear why certain artificial techniques which do not prevent insemination, yet prevent conception, should be comprised under the prohibition.

Some theologians have tried to avoid this dilemma by so defining insemination that its completion requires, not only the placing of semen as it ordinarily occurs in sexual intercourse, but also in the unimpeded actual or possible contact of spermatozoa with ovum—in other words, by making an essential part of insemination its aptitude for fertilization. But this is clearly a spurious argument. This identification is made *a priori* and in the light of the conclusion to be defended. There is simply no empirical reason, common sense or scientific, to believe that the act of sexual intercourse is truncated unless fertilization is aptitudinally or actually about to begin[20]—an event which usually takes place not less than several hours, sometimes as much as a full day, after what most people would call a completed act of sexual intercourse.

[19] In this view, therefore, the condemnation applies to anovulants also and, indeed, to any conceivable contraceptive yet devised or devisable, since in order to be effectively contraceptive any device must effectively nullify in some way the generative power of the sexual organs.

[20] Here, too, lack of biological knowledge in the past has tended to reinforce the identification of onanism with contraception, since the distinction between insemination and fertilization has been clear only since the advent of scientific embryology in the nineteenth century.

But the physiological distinction between insemination and fertilization is not the crux of the refutation of this reasoning. The decisive point is that the argument is circular. It says, in effect, that contraception is morally wrong *because* it violates the nature of a human act which by its nature morally requires not merely insemination but also aptness for conception. In other words, contraception is wrong *because* it prevents conception. The logic of *Casti Connubii* is more perspicacious than that of some of the encyclical's defenders. For Pius XI *did* state that the nature of the conjugal act requires unimpeded aptitude for conception. But it would be unjust to the Pope to assert that he offered that statement as an expression of the reason *why* contraception was wrong: that statement *was* his formulation of the teaching that contraception was morally forbidden by divine and natural *moral* law.

To sum up: to solve the problem posed, we must read *Casti Connubii* asking ourselves: what does *it* offer as the basis of the condemnation of contraception? If we read it pre-possessed of the conclusion that it condemned contraception on the ground that the physiological nature of sexual intercourse morally requires aptness for conception, it would not be difficult to find one's presuppositions confirmed by the text. But, obviously, Pius XI was responsible only for what he taught, not for what he may often have been supposed to have taught. We must, therefore, determine the matter from an analysis of the text.

It may be enlightening to commence with the observation that in connection with contraception *Casti Connubii* never referred to "sexual intercourse" or to any of its synonyms, paraphrases or euphemisms such as "the sexual act," "the use of the reproductive or generative powers," and the like. It consistently referred to "the marriage act," (*actus matrimonii*), "the conjugal act" (*actus coniugii*), "the use of matrimony" (*usus matrimonii*) and their derivatives. Could it be said that these expressions are really euphemistic, and formally meant the sexual congress of male and female? This would be hardly tenable. Common sense should suffice to distinguish between the two. The marriage act is a species of sexual intercourse; the latter is a generic term which includes, for instance, fornication and adultery. An act of fornication could not be said to be a marriage act in any meaningful sense of the term: indeed, what makes fornication sinful, as was suggested above, is that it excludes marriage from sexual intercourse.

This distinction is not novel. The classical doctrine of *consent* as the efficient cause of marriage goes back to Roman law. It was adopted by Christianity since earliest times, repeatedly confirmed and, finally, reasserted by *Casti Connubii* itself.[21] It is based upon the fact that sexual intercourse alone, even when so perfect in its own physiological nature that it results in the willful conception of new life, does not of itself constitute marriage. Thus, "the marriage act," a technical expression of long standing in canon law and theology, means an act of sexual intercourse that takes place in virtue of the marriage consent. Of course, there is a very close relationship between marriage and sexual intercourse. This, too, is scarcely a novel suggestion. But theologians do not customarily use the phrase "marriage act" in any but the sense here explained. It must be

[21] AAS 22, 1930, 541.

presumed that this was the sense in which Pius XI intended to use the term.

The context of the encyclical as a whole also supports the view that the Pope's doctrine against contraception was essentially relative to "the conjugal act," not to sexual intercourse generically. The explicit subject treated by the document was, after all, "Christian marriage," and genital coition interested it only under the formality of "the marriage act." The only exceptional instances, in which sexual intercourse was spoken of as such (though even then, only in relation to the doctrine of marriage) are when reference was made to adultery and pre-marital fornication: for instance, when it reaffirmed that "every use of the faculty given by God for the procreation of new life is the right and the privilege of the married state alone . . . and must be confined absolutely within the sacred limits of that state." In *this* context it could not be supposed that the expression "the use of the faculty given by God for the procreation of new life" could be adequately supplanted by "the marriage act" except under pain of tautology. Quite obviously, it meant "sexual intercourse," not "the marriage act."

It follows that the condemnation of artificial contraception in *Casti Connubii* was not based upon the natural moral law which follows from the nature of sexual intercourse (either as a physiological event or as a generic human event). It would be closer to the truth to say that it was based on the natural moral law that flows from the nature of marriage, but even this proposition must be rigorously qualified. For Pius XI could not be construed as having produced, in *Casti Connubii*, a treatise of natural ethics: his concern reached specifically to Christian marriage. However, as the Christian tradition maintains, marriage is both a natural institution as well as a sacramental one. Therefore, the doctrine of Pius XI dealt, in a sense, with a human reality which in virtue of its nature is subject to certain natural moral laws potentially ascertainable by reason. The Christian doctrine of marriage could not but virtually include the natural morality of marriage, as Pius XI himself explained in the encyclical:

[The] conformity of wedlock and moral conduct with divine laws respective of marriage, without which its effective restoration cannot be brought about, supposes, however, that all can discern readily, with real certainty, and without any accompanying error, what those laws are. But everyone can see to how many fallacies an avenue would be opened up and how many errors would become mixed with the truth, if it were left solely to the light of reason of each to find it out, or if it were to be discovered by the private interpretation of the truth which is revealed.[22] And if this is applicable to many other truths of the moral order, we must all the more pay attention to those things, which appertain to marriage where the inordinate desire for pleasure can attack frail human nature and easily deceive it and lead it astray; this is all the more true of the observance of the divine law, which demands sometimes hard and repeated sacrifices, for which, as experience points out, a weak man can find so many excuses for avoiding the fulfillment of the divine law.[23]

The Pope, therefore, could not abstract from natural morality if he wished to deal with the morality of Christian

[22] A likely allusion to the Lambeth Conference which only a few months earlier had approved contraception for the Anglican communion. This event, apparently, was the principal occasion for the issuing of *Casti Connubii.*

[23] The official Latin text of *Casti Connubii* is found in *AAS,* 539-

marriage. This passage alone speaks twice of the "divine law" as the subject of its teaching on marriage, precisely because the sole "light of reason" is not an infallible guide to "the truth that is revealed." Some confusion has been evinced on this point too by those who had previously confused natural law with physiology. There is a correct sense in which *Casti Connubii*'s doctrine against contraception was based upon the natural *moral* law, that is, upon certain moral laws which may or may not have been the direct subject of divine revelation but which in either event bind the human conscience, even of those persons who may lack the supernatural virtue of faith. All the more so in the case of persons who enjoy faith. Thus, a human act is said to be against natural morality rather than revealed morality (and yet bind the Christian conscience) not because human behavior is bound by the laws of physiology or similar natural laws, but because human behavior is to be morally regulated by the humanity of man. Natural moral laws cannot be deduced from natural physical or biological laws. For instance, nothing could be more repugnant to the biological laws of human nature than to will and accept the reality of a violent death. Yet, under certain moral conditions to violate the natural laws that regulate the normal biological functions of man, even to the point of painful death, may be morally required of the natural and even more of the Christian conscience. To choose to preserve

---

592. The English version quoted here is the official English translation published in the United States by the National Catholic Welfare Conference, Washington 1931, henceforth cited as *NC*. But see below, note 24.

one's life may sometimes be a grievous sin against the law of God and nature.

In *Casti Connubii*, then, the Pope's concern was the Christian morality of marriage, that is, not only as elevated to the condition of a sacrament of the new law but, more generally, as a divine institution of the supernatural order in which all nature actually finds itself. For these reasons Pius XI said, in a presumably studied formula, that artificial contraception was "an offense against the law of God and of nature." What the Pope condemned here was clearly of the order of Christian doctrine and morality, and it concerned marriage insofar as it is of divine institution—a doctrine which, in turn, pertains to the Christian faith and is not demonstrable.

Therefore, after this preliminary review of the general context of the doctrine against contraception, it may be initially suggested that the basis of the condemnation was, in a general way, the nature of marriage as a divine institution. Now we must consider the immediate context of the condemnation in more detail.

The Pope's condemnation was the converse of his restatement and defense of the traditional Christian doctrine of marriage. After having shown that for the Christian faith marriage was instituted by God's will, not by man's, Pius XI accepted and repeated the classical doctrine, of Augustinian authority, which explains the nature of marriage as justified by its "goods" or "blessings" (*bona matrimonii*), from which it derives its excellence and character. These goods are, in the well-known formula, *fides, proles* and *sacramentum*—fidelity, offspring and sacrament (or better, perhaps, *consecretion*, since *sacramentum* in this context re-

fers not only to marriage as an efficacious sign of supernatural grace, but also as a *natural* elevation of human
nature). The section against contraception occurs in the
context of the Pope's explanation of "the evils opposed to
each of the benefits of matrimony." It reads as follows:[24]

And now, venerable brethren, we shall explain in detail the
evils opposed to each of the benefits of matrimony. First consideration is due to the offspring, which many have the boldness
to call the disagreeable burden of matrimony and which they say
is to be carefully avoided by the spouses not through virtuous
continence (which Christian law permits in matrimony when

[24] The NC version is seriously defective insofar as it imposes an
interpretation on key passages of the Latin original which is at least
questionable. I present, therefore, basically the NC translation, but
amended wherever needed (with significant NC variants in foot-
notes) to bring it back to agreement with the Latin. The relevant
portions I have restored read in the original (*AAS*, 559-561) as follows:

Sed, ut ad singula iam . . . tractanda accedamus, quae singulis
matrimonii bonis opponuntur, primum de prole sit sermo . . .
quamque a coniugibus, non per honestam continentiam . . . sed
vitiando naturae actum, studiose arcendam praecipiunt. . . .

At nulla profecto ratio, ne gravissima quidem, efficere potest, ut
quod intrinsece est contra naturam, id cum natura congruens et ho-
nestum fiat. Cum autem actus coniugii suapte natura proli gene-
randae sit destinatus, qui, in eo exercendo, naturali hac eum vi atque
virtute de industria destituunt, contra naturam agunt et turpe quid
atque intrinsece inhonestum operantur. . . .

. . . quemlibet matrimonii usum, in quo exercendo, actus, de industria hominum, naturali sua vitae procreandae vi destituatur, Dei
et naturae legem infringere, et eos qui tale quid commiserint gravis
noxae labe commaculari. . . .

Neque contra naturae ordinem agere ii dicendi sunt coniuges, qui
iure suo recta et naturali ratione utuntur, etsi ob naturales sive tem-
poris sive quorundam defectuum causas nova inde vita oriri non
possit. Habentur enim tam in ipso matrimonio quam in coniugalis
iuris usu etiam secundarii fines, ut sunt mutuum adiutorium mutu-
usque fovendus amor et concupiscentiae sedatio, quos intendere
coniuges minime vetantur, dummodo salva semper sit intrinseca
illius actus natura ideoque eius ad primarium finem debita ordinatio.

both parties consent) but by corrupting the natural [marriage] act.[25] Some justify this criminal licentiousness[26] on the ground that they are weary of children and wish to gratify their desires[27] without their consequent burden. Others say that they cannot on the one hand remain continent nor on the other can they have children because of the difficulties whether on the part of the mother or on the part of family circumstances.

But no reason, however grave, may be put forward by which anything intrinsically against nature may be rendered conformable to nature and morally good. Since, therefore, the conjugal act is destined of its very nature for the begetting of children,[28] those who in exercising it deliberately deprive it of its natural

[25] NC: "by frustrating the marriage act."

[26] AAS: *licentiam. NC*: "abuse." *Licentia* is, of course, an abuse of freedom, not *per se* an abuse of marriage.

[27] Evidently, this refers to sexual desires—offspring are spoken of as "the consequent burden." Regardless of the truth of the question whether artificial contraception is to be excluded from the Christian marriage by the good of *proles*, the fact that this curious concept of *sexual nemesis* should be advanced here at all, points to a certain attitude which may be counted among the personal dispositions which tended to determine Pius XI's somewhat infelicitous expression of his doctrine. A person who thinks of the experience of the marriage act as essentially the gratification of cupidity would find it very difficult to imagine the possibility of a marriage act which precisely insofar as it is sexual, and because it is sexual, is an act of mutual love between husband and wife. Granted the relatively undeveloped state of Pius XI's doctrine of marriage, it is most likely that even had he considered the reality of sexual love he would have condemned contraception nevertheless. But the fact that he did not consider that there might be some respects, directly flowing from the nature of marriage (for he did consider extrinsic ones) in which contraception might be desirable, means that he saw no real moral problem in this matter, but simply a question of reasserting what all Christians have always known, namely that no extrinsic reason, however grave, may be advanced by which what is intrinsically immoral may become morally good.

[28] NC: "is destined primarily by nature for the begetting of children."

force[29] and power[30] act [31] against nature and commit a deed which is shameful and intrinsically vicious.

Small wonder, therefore, if Holy Writ bears witness that the divine Majesty regards with greatest detestation this horrible crime and at times has punished it with death. As St. Augustine notes: "Intercourse even with one's legitimate wife is unlawful and wicked where the conception of the offspring is prevented. Onan, the son of Juda, did this and the Lord killed him for it."

Since, therefore, openly departing from the uninterrupted Christian tradition some recently have judged it possible solemnly to declare another doctrine regarding the question,[32] the Catholic Church, to whom God has entrusted the defence of the integrity and purity of morals, standing erect in the midst of the moral ruin which surrounds her, in order that she may preserve the chastity of the nuptial union from being defiled by this foul stain, raises her voice in token of her divine ambassadorship and through our mouth proclaims anew: any use whatsoever of matrimony in which the act, in being exercised, is deliberately deprived of its natural power[33] to procreate life is an offense against the law of God and of nature, and those who commit such are branded with the guilt of a grave sin.

A second passage shortly afterward amplified slightly:

[They are not] considered as acting against the order of nature[34] who in the married state use their right in the correct and natural manner[35] although on account of natural reasons either

---

[29] NC: "frustrate its natural power and purpose."

[30] AAS: *vi atque virtute*. However, arguing *a fortiori*, I have treated this in my analysis below as if it meant "power and aptitude," which is an interpretative rendering slightly stronger than the original. But NC: "power and purpose" would be too great a departure from the text.

[31] NC: "sin."

[32] This is the principal allusion to the Lambeth Conference.

[33] NC: "is deliberately frustrated in its natural power."

[34] NC: "against nature."

[35] NC: "in the proper manner."

of time or of certain defects, new life cannot be brought forth. For in matrimony as well as in the use of the matrimonial rights there are also secondary ends, such as mutual aid, the fostering of mutual love, and the quieting of concupiscence which the spouses are not in the least forbidden to seek[36] so long as the intrinsic nature of this act is always safeguarded and, therefore, so long as [is also safeguarded] the due order of this [act] to the primary end.[37]

We have asked the question: granted that in *Casti Connubii* contraception is held to be against nature, the nature of *what* is it against? The text and the context indicate: the nature of marriage. For the text considers the "conjugal act," which is sexual, but under what formality? The conclusion suggested here is: insofar as it is "conjugal," that is, insofar as it is destined by its nature, which it receives from the marriage consent, for the marriage good of *proles*. It is difficult to read the text as condemning contraception insofar as the conjugal act is an act of sexual coition. Of course, the text is not perfectly lucid. Some misinterpretations may have been unwittingly encouraged by the indirectness and the multiple negativity of the formulations preferred by the Pope.

The use of such terms as "shameful," "vicious," "detestation," "horrible crime," (*nefandum facinus*),[38] "moral ruin," "defiled by this foul stain," is distracting. The subject itself does not tend to disembarrass the intellect; the use of too many tinged and laden words might well facilitate the dispersal of the reader's attention. As we have seen,

---

[36] NC: "are not forbidden to consider."

[37] NC: "so long as they are subordinated to the primary end and so long as the intrinsic nature of the act is preserved."

[38] In contrast, abortion is spoken of (NC) as a "very grave crime," (*gravissimum facinus*).

this appears to have happened to the English translator. Any but a closely attentive reading of the text would take the Pope to have said that artificial contraception was sinful *because* contraceptive intercourse was against the nature of sexual intercourse and, thus, shameful and vicious. But this is a double misinterpretation. First, as we have seen, the reference was to the marriage act as such, not to sexual intercourse as such. But, moreover, the Pope actually indicated the converse causal sequence to that which he has been often attributed. Contraception, he said, is morally wrong because the conjugal act "of its very nature is destined for the generation of *proles*." *Therefore*, he continued, those who in exercising the marriage act "make a deliberate effort" to "deprive it of its natural force and aptitude" (*naturali hac eum vi atque virtute destituunt*)—that is, those who render the marriage act contraceptive—may be said to "act against nature and do something shameful and intrinsically vicious," (that is, they commit a sin, namely that of contraception). In this doctrine, therefore, contraception is condemned as against nature because it deprives marriage of its essential primary good, namely *proles*. The proposition that whoever deprives the marriage act of its natural power and aptitude acts against nature is *not a premise*, but the *conclusion* of the syllogism: it means that contraception, defined as a deliberate act which deprives the marriage act of its natural generative aptitude, is sinful and forbidden. The general principle, the major premise, is that whatever is essentially required by the moral nature of an act cannot be taken away from it without morally corrupting the act. The premise which connects the general principle to the conclusion is: *the conjugal act of its very na-*

ture, *that is, as a* conjugal *sexual act, is directed to the*
marriage good of proles. This is, therefore, the reason why
contraception is wrong.

I have suggested some reasons why this point does not
emerge readily from *Casti Connubii.* We have yet to consider what is, perhaps, the most fundamental one. There
is reason to wonder whether the document's obscurities in
these respects do not stem from insufficient differentiation
of other matters in the minds of the issuer of the encyclical and of the theological advisors who partly or wholly
composed it for the Pope's authorization.

After having expounded the foregoing doctrine against
contraception, the Pope proceeded to show the relation of
his teaching to revelation. To that end he resorted to a scriptural text which, however, was neither unambiguously applicable to the specific problem at hand, nor of easy interpretation in itself: Gn 38:8-10. And, making matters more
difficult for the theologian, the encyclical did not quote
Scripture directly but through St. Augustine's gloss: "Intercourse even with one's legitimate wife is unlawful and
wicked where the conception of offspring is prevented. Onan,
the son of Juda, did this and the Lord killed him for it." [39]

Some biblical exegetes are of the opinion that the sin of
Onan for which the Old Testament expresses such strong
disapproval consisted in violating the laws of levirate and,
thus, doing grave dishonor to his brother and grave in-

---

[39] St. Augustine, *De Coniug. Adult. (De Incompetentibus Nup-
tiis)*, II, 12. Actually, instead of "prevented" the rendering "avoided"
might be considered more faithful to the Latin *divatur*. The point is
not crucial: St. Augustine is not concerned in this text with the
question of means to contraception, but with the contraceptive effect itself.

justice to the latter's widow. This is hardly a strained exegesis, since Gn 38:9 explains Onan's deed not as the general
desire to avoid offspring, but the desire to avoid begetting
children who "should not be his" (e.g. would not bear his
name, would not belong to *his* family). Indeed, some
scholars have searched the fathers before St. Augustine
and have been unable to find any exception to the foregoing
interpretation, so that it appears to have some weight. On
the other hand, to affirm that "none of the Church fathers
before St. Augustine read in this text a condemnation of
contraceptive practices" [40] is somewhat ambiguous and may
be questionable on the following grounds.

If one interprets *contraception* as a physiological event,
then the statement may well be correct. Indeed, one would
have to say, not "before St. Augustine," but rather "none
of the Church fathers, not even St. Augustine." On the
other hand, if contraception refers to a misuse of the marriage act, is there not a somewhat extended sense of the
term which would comprise the violation of levirate laws as
a form of contraceptive practice? The rationale for levirate
and the purposes it serves are several: the honor and service
of the tribe, of the family and of one's own brother, and the
protection of widows. But do they not all hinge upon the
fulfillment of the marriage act as procreative of new life?
Levirate was, after all, an extended form of marriage. It
might be said to be of divine institution not only because it
is legislated positively in Dt 25:5-10, but more fundamen-

[40] A. M. Dubarle O.P., "La Bible et les Pères, ont-ils parlé de la
contraception?," Supplément, *La Vie Spirituelle* 1962, 573-610; as
reported by Louis Dupré, "Toward a re-examination of the Catholic
position on birth-control," *Cross Currents* XIV, 1, Winter 1964, 63-
85: 67.

tally because it harked back to the text of Genesis: "Increase and multiply." Like marriage, levirate was justified by the good of *proles*. There is a real sense, therefore, in which we must say that Onan "was slain" for the sin of contraception —that is, because he prevented the generation of due off-spring.

What is the relation of this to the fact that Onan "spilled his seed upon the ground"? This is another question. Surely the means by which he achieved contraception were sinful, if for no other reason because the end it served was sinful in itself. Yet, at the same time the "spilling of his seed" was also sinful in itself, not because any aspect of the physiological event was sinful, but because the act was against the nature of *human* sexual intercourse, which requires mutuality, reciprocity and interpersonal equality. Therefore, the single physiological event, the "spilling of his seed," contained three different moral components: a) violation of Old Testament revealed laws of levirate (and, therefore, of justice, piety, etc.); b) violation of the natural laws of marriage, insofar as his act excluded the good of *proles* (though some might consider this as virtually contained in his violation of the levirate laws); and c) violation of the nature of human sexual relations between married persons.

The confusion of these three (or two) sins is understandable, since all three (or two) moral effects were achieved together in the one physiological act: "onanism." The natural tendency of the *modern* reader of the Old Testament would be to seize upon the common element, the "spilling of the seed," to describe globally "the sin of

Onan" in the undifferentiated complexity of the moral event.

The global condemnation of onanism by the fathers was, of course, not only legitimate but also sufficient as long as onanism and contraception were, in practice, convertible synonyms. To understand *Casti Connubii* we must understand, however, not only why Pius XI failed to distinguish between the four elements of onanism (i.e. three moral and one physiological) but also between onanistic and artificial contraception. Why did he not do so, when some differences are obvious? Evidently, because he thought that the noticeable differences were irrelevant, and that only their similarity was of moral consequence. Thus, to determine what he assumed as irrelevant to the morality or immorality of artificial contraception, and what he thought was relevant, should help us, not only to confirm under what formality he condemned *all* contraception indiscriminately, but also under what precise formality he condemned *artificial* contraception.

We can surmise without difficulty why Pius XI discarded whatever physiological differences might obtain between onanism and artificial contraception. The "spilling of the seed" is essential to the matter of onanism, but artificial contraception may or may not include it in order to achieve its immoral effect, i.e. avoidance of due conception. At any rate, these considerations pertain to the matter of the act and can be safely put aside: it should matter little whether or not the two acts were bound by this common element.

But what of the moral elements? The reasons why the levirate laws did not enter into Pius XI's consideration are perfectly obvious: they are not in the least involved here except, of course, insofar as the second moral element of onanism, contraception, may be part of the levirate laws— that is why it may have been useful to distinguish between them, as was done above. But what should we say of the third element: does artificial contraception, like onanism, sin against the personal sexual relations of husband and wife? It is not self-evident that it does. At any rate, it is quite clear that Pius XI did not grant the relevance of this point. We can understand why. Since the global condemnation of onanism does not distinguish between this moral defect and the defect concerning the marriage good of *proles*, Pius XI did not find it necessary to distinguish between onanism and artificial contraception simply on the ground that the two have undoubtedly this moral element in common: both sin equally against the marriage good of *proles*. In other words, both onanism and artificial contraception are *contraceptive* acts. Both consist in the use of marriage, in the performance of the marriage act, in such a way as to prevent the marriage good of *proles*, which pertains to the very nature of the marriage act as such. In brief, Pius XI condemned both types of contraception indiscriminately because, in his estimation, the reason why contraception is wrong applied equally to both cases, namely because the exclusion of the good of *proles*, which is immoral since it is against the nature of marriage, was achieved equally and indifferently by both.

This means that Pius XI condemned artificial contraception precisely as *contraceptive*. The suggestion is *not* that if Pius XI had considered the difference within onanism between the infringement of the laws of marriage in respect of *proles* and in respect of the mutual personal relations between husband and wife, he would have condemned onanism only and permitted artificial contraception. (My conjecture is that he would have condemned both anyway.) The point, however, is not what Pius XI might have done but what he did or did not do. *Casti Connubii* indicates the Pope's concern was the marriage good of *proles*, not the relation between the spouses. Onanism clearly infringes on both, but artificial contraception (unless it were independently demonstrated otherwise) must be taken to sin only against the marriage good of *proles*: Pius XI considered only this last moral element in either type of contraceptive act.

Therefore, the indiscriminate condemnation of both types of contraception *cannot* mean that the Pope condemned artificial contraception because it is *artificial* or because, like onanism, it sins against the personal sexual relation of the spouses: the text of *Casti Connubii* cannot reasonably be read in this sense. Pius XI condemned artificial contraception *exclusively* on the grounds that, like onanism, it is *contraceptive*—that is, artificial contraception, like onanism, prevents a marriage good, *proles*, which is essential (at least aptitudinally) to the marriage act as such.

The absence of discrimination between the moral elements of onanism and between onanism and artificial contraception served, however, to obscure somewhat the exact nature of the condemnation. If, moreover, as seems very likely, Pius XI and his advisors shared the culturally conditioned aversion noted earlier concerning the "loss of seed," then we can also understand why although his consistent teaching in *Casti Connubii* placed the moral reason why contraception is wrong exclusively in that it corrupted the nature of marriage, nevertheless his teaching was almost bound to be expressed in formulas which lent themselves to misconstruction—or, in any event, in formulas which did not positively advance in every respect our understanding of the Christian doctrine of marriage.

Casti Connubii's use of St. Augustine's text does not affect the foregoing conclusions, though it further contributed to the possibility of misinterpreting the doctrine of the Pope. In this passage St. Augustine added nothing to the doctrine of Genesis. On the contrary, he stated rather less than Genesis, for the question of the means to the avoidance of offspring is not mentioned by him, either in the passage quoted or elsewhere in the chapter. Of course, there can be little doubt that the means St. Augustine must have had in mind was "onanism," not only because of the actual reference to Onan's case, but also because for all practical purposes "onanism" was the only contraceptive means generally known or used in the Christian world at that time.[41] "Intercourse in which the conception of offspring is avoided" meant to him materially the same as "onanism."

But did it mean so, formally? That is, did he condemn onanism because of "the loss of seed"? It is difficult to imagine a reasonable case for the affirmative. St. Augustine had no interest in the *means* to contraception. Understandably so: the question of means would be highlighted only centuries later, when alternatives became available; at the

[41] See Norman E. Himes, *Medical History of Contraception*, New York 1963; Helène Bergues et al., *La Prévention des Naissances dans la Famille: ses origines dans les temps modernes*, Paris, 1960. Mechanical and chemical contraceptives of varying degrees of effectiveness have been known since Egyptian antiquity, but these methods belonged almost exclusively to the lore of prostitution and libertinage.

time what mattered was that the end itself was held to be wrong. It would be anachronism to read into St. Augustine a distinction which was yet in the very distant future. The point was simply not relevant to the pastoral and theological problems he was dealing with. He, like Genesis, condemned whatever conflicted with the good of *proles*, because "the procreation of children is the primary, natural, legitimate purpose of marriage." [42] Let us remark: marriage, not sexual intercourse. But he, no more than the writer of Genesis, considered the specific moral problem of *artificial* contraception. Thus, the Pope's doctrine gained support from these sources only insofar as artificial contraception might have shared a common moral nature with onanism, i.e. insofar as it conflicted with the essential marriage good of *proles*.

This means that Pius XI may have in fact taught rather less than he might have wished to teach. For it would be difficult to believe that St. Augustine foresaw artificial contraception, but it would be impossible to suppose that Pius XI did not have it most emphatically in mind when he issued *Casti Connubii*. Nevertheless, basing the condemnation of all contraception on what artificial contraception had in common with onanism means that he did not deal with the entire range of the moral problem. A consideration of the differences between the two, even if it sustained the condemnation of artificial contraception, might well have produced further refinements in the doctrine of the nature of the marriage act as such.

Therefore, a hypothetical reformation of the Church's doctrine on artificial contraception should leave much of *Casti Connubii*'s condemnatory doctrine unchanged and

[42] St. Augustine, *De Coniug. Adult.*, II, 12.

even reaffirmed. For such a reformation would have to respect the fact that the condemnation of Pius XI was based upon an indisputable truth, i.e. the doctrine of the good of *proles*. And it would remain true for all time that insofar as this truth does necessitate the rejection of contraception, the teaching of *Casti Connubii* was true.

Pius XI fairly harped on the point: it was the primary end of marriage, *proles*, that required the natural means thereto, the conjugal act, to remain apt "in its very nature" to fulfill its end, that is, to procreate. If periodic continence was permitted the reason was, precisely, that the marriage act was not thereby altered in its nature, and that even if "natural reasons" rendered the act sterile in fact, it still remained aptitudinally fertile while it served other worthy ends.

Conclusion

This first part of our inquiry, then, suggests the following. The teaching of *Casti Connubii* on artificial contraception is somewhat ambiguous, especially in that it failed to discriminate between onanism and artificial contraception—a distinction which may be relevant to the problem of contraception even if Pius XI's condemnation were ratified and upheld in the future. The condemnation was not based upon an analysis of sexual intercourse (either as a physiological event or as a human event), from which it was concluded that artificial contraception was sinful because, vitiating the nature of sexual intercourse (either as a physiological or an interpersonal event), it became an intrinsically evil means to otherwise possibly good moral ends. On the contrary, the condemnation was based upon the nature of the marriage act, which forbids, in order that its natural moral integrity be respected, any use of it which would conflict with the end that its matrimonial nature seeks, i.e. *proles*. Since no distinction needed to be made between onanism and artificial contraception in that respect, Pius XI did not avail himself at all of the distinction. He condemned artificial contraception because it was *contraceptive*, not specifically because it was artificial. Thus, in *Casti Connubii* he failed to consider whether the distinction between the two types of contraception might be relevant to the conjugal act's other essential ends, namely *fides* and *sacramentum*. This aspect of the contraceptive problem was not tackled—or, *a fortiori*, solved. To that extent at least *Casti Connubii* is incomplete and may need further development.

In what direction? To answer this we must first understand why in the teaching of Pius XI the indiscriminate rejection of all contraception is thought to be sufficient, simply because in the Christian doctrine of marriage *proles* is the primary, essential good of matrimony. For this reason we should now analyze *Casti Connubii's* doctrine on the nature of matrimony.

The Doctrine of Casti Connubii *on the Nature of Marriage*

Casti Connubii's teaching "on the nature and dignity of Christian marriage" was not, of course, encyclopedic. Nevertheless, in its brief span it set down the fundamentals of the Christian tradition on the subject. It began by making its own the doctrine of Leo XIII in *Arcanum Divinae Sapientiae*. It wished to

> . . . let it be repeated as an immutable and inviolable fundamental doctrine that matrimony was not instituted or restored by man but by God; not by man were the laws made to strengthen and confirm and elevate it but by God, the Author of nature, and by Christ our Lord by whom nature was redeemed, and hence these laws cannot be subject to any human decrees or to any contrary pact even of the spouses themselves. This is the doctrine of Holy Scripture; this is the constant tradition of the Universal Church; this is the solemn definition of the sacred Council of Trent, which declares and establishes from the words of Holy Writ itself that God is the Author of the perpetual stability of the marriage bond, its unity and its firmness.[43]

Now, it would not be sensible to suppose that the divine institution of marriage implied an arbitrary divine decree which in no way took account of man's free will. As St. Thomas remarked, marriage is "accomplished through the intervention of [man's] free will" [44] (*mediante libero arbitrio completur*). For this reason the Pope added: "Yet

---

[43] The NC version is reproduced throughout in this section except where otherwise noted. The above passage of *Casti Connubii* is annotated to refer to Gn 1:27-28 and 2:22-23, Mt 19:3 sqq., Eph 5:23 sqq. and Council of Trent, sess. XXIV. The latter relies on Scripture. The Matthew text does not add to Genesis except in relation to divorce. Ephesians 5 does teach a specifically Christian doctrine of marriage, but on the point of the divine institution it too grounds itself on Genesis. Thus, Genesis 1 and 2 are the fundamental scriptural texts among those referred to.

[44] *ST, Supp.* 41, 1. However, unlike Pius XI, St. Thomas did not affirm this of the human will as contrasted with the divine will, but as contrasted with necessitation by nature as by a principle. On the whole *Casti Connubii* does not avail itself of St. Thomas' theology of marriage or sexuality, to which it refers exactly once (i.e. to *ST, Supp.* 49, 3). But the quotation is taken out of context and does not actually support the point.

although matrimony is of its very nature of divine institution, the human will, too, enters into it and performs a most noble part." But concretely what role does the human will play in marriage? The document explained that,

> . . . each individual marriage, inasmuch as it is a conjugal union of a particular man and woman, arises only from the free consent of each of the spouses; and this free act of the will, by which each party hands over and accepts those rights proper to the state of marriage, is so necessary to constitute true marriage that it cannot be supplied by any human authority.[45]

Thus, according to the encyclical, human competence in marriage is restricted to what pertains to it as an individual instance of the universal nature whose essential formality is determined by God's will. Can we further specify what pertains to marriage insofar as the human will realizes the divine will *in concreto*? Yes, the Pope explained the precise limits of this freedom of the will in connection with marriage. It extends "only" to two matters, namely, whether to marry and whom to marry:

> This freedom, however, regards only the question whether the contracting parties really wish to enter upon matrimony or to marry this particular person; but the nature of matrimony is entirely independent of the free will of man, so that if one has once contracted matrimony he is thereby subject to its divinely made laws and its essential properties.

Evidently, the metaphysical concepts which structured this doctrine were those of substance-accident and essence-existence. The divine will creates the essence of marriage;

[45] *AAS: humana potestate. NC:* (equivocally) "human power."

the human will brings it into individual existence. The substance of marriage is the result of this cooperation. The accidentals, presumably, might be determined by a variety of wills (e.g. the state might require civil registration, the bride might decide, as is customary, when to marry, the groom where to reside, etc.)

Pius XI seems to mean, therefore, that a certain divine purpose having been conceived by God's Wisdom concerning man and the world, man is allowed to play a cooperative, secondary but free role in the realization of that design. By free obedience we conform meritoriously to the divine will, which has planned, as it were, the *idea* of marriage as a means to its own ends. From this it follows that the moral obligations consequent upon the nature of marriage in no wise depend upon what man may wish, but only on what God has disposed. It also follows, presumably, that the human dignity of chaste Christian marriage is not derived from the human contribution to marriage, precisely as human, but from the divine will's institution of the union. For the specifically human contribution to the institution comes from the human will's mere cooperation with the divine will. The dignity, therefore, comes efficaciously from God, though permissibly from human obedience to the divine will.

In the absence of this obedient and cooperative inclination to the divine will, the union of marriage would be indistinguishable from the mating of animals or from the animal-like union of promiscuity, for marriage would then be governed by the velleities of sensual and affective inclinations:

By matrimony, therefore, the souls of the contracting parties are joined and knit together more primarily and more firmly[46] than are their bodies, and that not by any transitory sensual or emotional inclination[47] but by a deliberate and firm act of the will; and from this union of souls by God's decree, a sacred and inviolable bond arises. Hence the nature of this contract, which is proper and peculiar to it alone, makes it entirely different both from the union of animals entered into by the blind instinct of nature alone in which neither reason nor free will plays a part, and also from the haphazard unions of men, which are far removed from all true and honorable unions of will and enjoy none of the rights of family life.

Consequently, if marriage is rightly understood (i.e. as owing its nature to God's will and not to man's) man's moral duties in its regard are essentially and literally simple: to fulfill God's design, not his own. In marriage as in every other area of human behavior man need have no hesitation or doubt as to what is the correct thing to do, for man's self-realization consists in abiding by God's will and law:

Therefore the sacred partnership of true marriage is constituted both by the will of God and the will of man. From God comes the very institution of marriage, the ends for which it was instituted, the laws that govern it, the blessings that flow from it; while man, through generous surrender of his own person made to another for the whole span of life, becomes, with the help and cooperation of God, the author of each particular marriage, with the duties and blessings annexed thereto from divine institution.

All that remains to be determined is the nature of the divine design for marriage. But Christian tradition is fairly

---

[46] AAS: *prius et arctius.* NC: "more directly and more immutably."
[47] AAS: *nec fluxo sensuum vel animorum affectu.* NC: "not by any passing affection of sense or spirit."

clear on the point. God instituted marriage for the same ultimate reason that he created man and his universe, namely to communicate his love to man. More immediately, he instituted marriage for the propagation of the human race, that is, so that men should come into being in order to receive the blessings of existence. Therefore, God's laws concerning marriage are but an expression of the wise benevolence of God, who designs the ideal pattern of human behavior more wisely (and, thus, more truly benevolently) than man could do for himself. All this Pius XI assumed when he taught, as above, that in the ends for which marriage was designed by God, and in the blessings that flow from its divinely instituted nature, are to be found the principles that rule the morality of matrimony.

In other words, the divine design for marriage is to be sought in the "goods" or "blessings" of marriage (*bona matrimonii*) that make it reasonable and justified, that is, intelligible and of an authoritative nature. The classical Christian formulation in this respect is that the "goods" of marriage are *fides, proles,* and *sacramentum.* Pius XI first adduced St. Augustine's words enumerating them:

"These are all the blessings of matrimony on account of which matrimony itself is a blessing; offspring, conjugal faith and the sacrament." [48]

The Pope immediately quoted again another work of St. Augustine in summary exposition of the meaning of the formula:

[48] St. Augustine, *De Bono Coniugali* XXIV, 32.

And how under these three heads is contained a splendid summary of the whole doctrine of Christian marriage, the holy Doctor himself expressly declares when he said: "By conjugal faith it is provided that there should be no carnal intercourse outside the marriage bond with another man or woman; with regard to offspring, that children should be begotten of love, tenderly cared for and educated in a religious atmosphere; finally, in its sacramental aspect that the marriage bond should not be broken and that a husband or wife, if separated, should not be joined to another even for the sake of offspring. This we regard as the law of marriage by which the fruitfulness of nature is adorned and the evil of incontinence is restrained.[49]

The remainder of *Casti Connubii*'s teaching on the nature of Christian marriage is but a more detailed exposition of what the *bona matrimonii* are, of the duties that they enjoin upon the Christian and of the evils which are opposed to them.

Concerning *proles* Pius XI had remarkably little to say.

---

[49] The quotation is from St. Augustine, *De Genesi ad Litteram* IX, 7, 12. For St. Augustine "incontinence" has a specifically and formally moral meaning. It refers not to sexual activity as such, but to *sinful* sexual activity. St. Augustine assumes in this text that unless a man is undecided about his ultimate station in life, either he marries or he professes virginity: the only other life-state he could embrace would be that of incontinence. If read in context, there is no hint in this doctrine that marriage is reserved for those who, being unable to restrain their baser desires, should marry *rather* than sin. What he teaches is that man should marry—or better still, profess virginity, if he has the aptitudes for the contemplative, intellectual or pastoral Christian life—*instead* of choosing a life of sin. If St. Augustine had taught what he is so commonly thought to have taught, then he could be accused of having condemned matrimony and, in effect, of having conceived it as a legal substitute for the same passions that outside marriage would be sinful. This "legal sex" concept of marriage would be a travesty of the Christian doctrine; it would make of marriage a kind of morally permissible prostitution.

He reproduced the Christian tradition already broached above. Christian belief in the divine institution of marriage for the sake of procreation is founded on the revelation set down in Genesis:

> Thus, among the blessings of marriage, the child holds the first place. And indeed the Creator of the human race himself, who in his goodness wished to use men as his helpers in the propagation of life, taught this when, instituting marriage in paradise, he said to our first parents, and through them to all future spouses: "Increase and multiply, and fill the earth."

Further explanations of the way in which offspring are "a boon of God," and how the begetting of children requires also their proper rearing as its natural complement, were given by the Pope in some detail, but the encyclical did not amplify or elucidate on the nature and meaning of the doctrine that "among the blessings of marriage, the child holds the first place." That is, it explained why according to Scripture *proles* is a marriage good; it did not explain why or in what sense we may speak of the *primacy* of *proles* among the three marriage goods. The cited text of Genesis supports, amply of course, the first point.

For the sake of brevity we shall not consider here the Pope's insistence upon the many reasons why married couples should consider children desirable rather than burdensome, since the point, which is hardly open to doubt, is not quite relevant to the Christian doctrine on the nature of marriage or to the moral problem of contraception. Moreover, the Pope's words in these matters did not expand upon the common secular teaching on the point in any significant respect. It may be pertinent to remark, however, that the

Pope recalled that "the blessing of offspring . . . is not completed by the mere begetting of them, but something else must be added, namely the proper education of the offspring," and he referred to the code of canon law, which states that "the primary end of marriage is the procreation and education of children." [50]

Concerning the sanctifying benefits of marriage, much the same could be said. There is nothing to be found in *Casti Connubii* which had not been taught by the Council of Trent or which was not well-known Christian doctrine. The encyclical taught that marriage is "an efficacious sign of grace" instituted by Christ for our sanctification, but also that it is a sacrament in a natural sense: insofar as the indissolubility and stability of the marriage bond accrue to wedlock "even in the state of nature, and certainly long before it was raised to the dignity of a sacrament [of the new law]," all true marriage is *holy* and bound by the divine law.

Pius XI taught that even in this wider sense the good of *sacramentum* "far surpasses the other two" and is "of outstanding excellence." The sacramental indissolubility of marriage contributes to "the good of the married parties and the offspring [and] to the welfare of human society" for the following reasons: an indissoluble marriage gives to the spouses "a positive guarantee" of the endurance of their marriage," it sets up "a strong bulwark" in "defense of a loyal chastity against incitements to infidelity," and, in brief, precludes "any anxious fear lest in adversity or old age the other spouse would prove unfaithful . . . and in its

[50] *Cod. Iur. Can.*, 1013, 7.

place there reigns a calm sense of security. Moreover, the dignity of both man and wife is maintained and mutual aid is most satisfactorily assured . . ."

But what of the good of *sacramentum* insofar as matrimony is of Christian institution? Since "the valid matrimonial consent among the faithful" is "the sign of grace" instituted by Christ as constituting matrimony,

> By the very fact . . . that the faithful with sincere mind give such consent, they open up for themselves a treasure of sacramental grace from which they draw supernatural power for the fulfilling of their rights and duties faithfully, holily, perseveringly even unto death. Hence this sacrament not only increases sanctifying grace . . . but also adds particular gifts, dispositions, seeds of grace by elevating and perfecting the natural powers. By these gifts the parties are assisted not only in understanding, but in knowing intimately, in adhering to firmly, in willing effectively, and in successfully putting into practice those things which pertain to the marriage state, its aims and duties, giving them in fine right to the actual assistance of grace, whensoever they need it for fulfilling the duties of their state.

Clearly, then, marriage sanctifies. Indeed,

> . . . just as by baptism and holy orders a man is set aside and assisted . . . and is never deprived of their sacramental aid, almost in the same way (although not by a sacramental character), the faithful once joined by marriage ties can never be deprived of the help and the binding force of the sacrament.

The Pope did not treat the question whether or how the sacramental, sanctifying bond of marriage is strengthened, or what relation, if any, the sexual intercourse of the spouses may have to that strengthening or to the sacramental bond. The graces of marriage are credited, as it were, to the spouses upon the public deposit of their consent in the presence of witnesses, but since grace does not fructify unless man cooperates,

> . . . the grace of matrimony will remain for the most part an unused talent hidden in the field unless the parties exercise these supernatural powers and cultivate and develop the seeds of grace they have received. If, however, doing all that lies within their power, they cooperate diligently, they will be able with ease to bear the burdens of their state and to fulfill their duties.

The encyclical's teaching on *fides* is especially pertinent to this essay not only because in this connection *Casti Connubii* deals with the relationship between husband and wife in marriage, but, moreover, because in this respect the document expanded and developed the Christian doctrine of marriage to a point never previously attained by the magisterium. Of course, Pius XI did not diminish or depart from the Christian tradition, according to which one of the goods of marriage is a certain mutual relation called *fides*—a term which in this context is only weakly rendered by *fidelity* or *faithfulness*.

The good of *fides* stems from this: the society produced by marriage is such that it excludes participation by a third person. Adultery, "third party-ness," would breach the good of fidelity, as would polygamy. Indeed, the good of fidelity lies in that exclusion or forsaking of all others and in the mutual cleaving of the spouses in the matrimonial society. The fundamental human relation between the spouses, therefore, most specially requires chastity in this respect:

> . . . that mutual familiar intercourse between the spouses themselves, if the blessing of conjugal faith is to shine with becoming splendor, must be distinguished by chastity so that hus-

band and wife bear themselves in all things with the law of God and of nature, and endeavor always to follow the will of their most wise and holy Creator with the greatest reverence toward the work of God.

But the Pope added that the faithfulness of marriage, the abstention from adultery and polygamy, would be a plain, unadorned, and less valuable good if it sprang simply from the harsh obligation of duty. *Fides* is all the more valuable, beautiful and noble if it grows out of the love of husband and wife for each other. The Pope grounded this teaching upon St. Paul's injunction of charity in marriage:

> This conjugal faith, however, which is most aptly called by St. Augustine the "faith of chastity," blooms more freely, more beautifully and more nobly when it is rooted in that more excellent soil, the love of husband and wife which pervades all the duties of married life and holds pride of place in Christian marriage. For matrimonial faith demands that husband and wife be joined in an especially holy and pure love not as adulterers love each other, but as Christ loved the Church. This precept the Apostle laid down when he said: "Husbands, love your wives as Christ also loved the Church," that Church which of a truth he embraced with a boundless love not for the sake of his own advantage, but seeking only the good of his spouse.

If Jesus' love for the Church is the type of married love, we must find the meaning of married love in what may be characteristic of his love for the Church. This feature, according to *Casti Connubii*, is that his love was not selfish, but wholly directed toward his spouse. It follows that

> The [marital] love, then, of which we are speaking is not that based on the passing lust of the moment nor does it consist in pleasing words only, but in the deep attachment of the heart which is expressed in action, since love is proved by deeds.

Thus, since chaste matrimonial love must, on the one hand, exclude lust and, on the other, be genuine, deep and sincere, it is not difficult to ascertain the criterion by which we can discern it. It is the proverbial *facta, non verba*. And since the most excellent deed Christians can perform for each other is their mutual edification, that is, the mutual perfection of their Christian, spiritual life, the mutual love of the spouses will manifest itself accordingly:

> This outward expression of love in the home demands not only mutual help but must go further; must have as its primary purpose that man and wife help each other day by day in forming and perfecting themselves in the interior life, so that through their partnership in life they may advance ever more and more in virtue, and above all that they may grow in true love toward God and their neighbor, on which indeed "dependeth the whole law and the prophets." For all men of every condition, in whatever honorable walk of life they may be, can and ought to imitate that most perfect example of holiness placed before man by God, namely Christ our Lord, and by God's grace to arrive at the summit of perfection, as is proved by the example set us of many saints.

Evidently, the pure love of husband and wife which beautifies their fidelity and which "holds pride of place in the Christian marriage" is nothing else than charity: naturally, since in the Christian faith charity is the norm for *all* human interpersonal relations. Whether or not there may be any special modality peculiar to the mutual charity of spouses is not discussed by *Casti Connubii*, so that we cannot know with certainty whether or how Pius XI would have characterized it in order to distinguish it from the Christian charity of one man for another, say, or from that of a child for his mother, or that of a brother for his sister.

On the other hand, *Casti Connubii* neither hid nor be-
littled the Christian tradition that this chaste mutual love
which fosters the spouses' growth in the life of Christian
perfection, and which is an integral part of the matrimonial
fidelity, is "in a very real sense" the principal purpose of
Christian marriage. On the contrary, Pius XI emphasized
it to a novel degree:

> This mutual inward molding of husband and wife, this deter-
> mined effort to perfect each other, can in a very real sense, as the
> Roman catechism teaches, be said to be the chief reason and pur-
> pose of matrimony (*etiam primaria matrimonii causa et ratio
> dici potest*), provided matrimony be looked at not in the re-
> stricted sense as instituted for the proper conception and educa-
> tion of the child, but more widely (*sed latius*) as the blending
> of life as a whole and the mutual interchange and sharing
> thereof (*ut totius vitae communio, consuetudo, societas acci-
> piatur*).

But what is the bearing of the sexual relations of the
spouses upon their mutual Christian love and their growth
in the life of Christian perfection? The Pope was not expansive on this point. Nevertheless, he did mention, albeit
somewhat obscurely, that sexual intercourse is in some way
related to the Christian charity of the spouses as such. Since
the terminology used in this connection was that of "rights
and duties" the encyclical failed to make clear why marital
sexual relations could be said to belong to the order of
Christian love. Moreover, the relation of this aspect of
marital love to the "pure" love previously described was
also left undefined—except, perhaps, insofar as charity in
the sexual order is spoken of as "the remainder" (*reliqua*).
But however obscurely and incompletely, *Casti Connubii*
did include a short paragraph to the point:

It is necessary that the remaining conjugal rights and duties (*reliqua conjugii tam iura quam officia*) be ruled by the same love (*caritate*), as the words of the Apostle, "Let the husband render the debt to his wife, and the wife also in like manner to the husband," are not only a law of justice but also a norm of charity.[51]

Finally, under *fides* also falls the question of the order that should obtain within the loving society of husband and wife. The Pope reaffirmed the husband's headship of the family on the authority of Eph 5:22-23. But explicitly referring to Leo XIII's defense of the complementary doctrine of the equality of the sexes in dignity, Pius XI, developing the doctrine more fully, specified:

This subjection, however, does not deny or take away the liberty which fully belongs to the woman both in view of her dignity as a human person and in view of her most noble office as wife and mother and companion; nor does it bid her obey her husband's every request if not in harmony with right reason or with the dignity due to wife; nor, in fine, does it imply that the wife should be put on a level with those persons who in law are called minors, to whom it is not customary to allow free exercise of their rights on account of their lack of mature judgment, or of their ignorance of human affairs.

Such is, in all essential respects, *Casti Connubii*'s doctrine on the nature of marriage. We may be now in a position to understand not only, as in the first section of this study, that Pius XI's teaching on contraception is grounded on his doctrine of marriage, but also that it is an integral

[51] NC: "By this same love it is necessary that all the other rights and duties of the marriage state be regulated as the words of the Apostle: 'Let the husband render the debt to the wife, also in like manner to the husband,' express not only a law of justice but of charity."

part of that doctrine—at least in the sense that it follows
logically and reasonably from that doctrine, a doctrine
which in no essential respect departs from the Christian
tradition.

In the teaching of *Casti Connubii* marriage is, in its
essence, of divine institution. It was willed by God for the
sake of human reproduction. Therefore, man may not without sin contravene God's dispositions in its regard. As in
every other sphere, Christian behavior must be inflexibly
guided not by human caprice but by the objective morality
enshrined in the nature of the institution and, thus, by
God's law. This morality, in its turn, can be ascertained
from the nature of the purposes which are revealed in the
marriage blessings or goods. In a sense, the chief reason
and purpose can be said to be the mutual faith of husband
and wife, especially if this is understood as founded upon
mutual supernatural charity and mutual temporal and
spiritual service. Sexual relations may well fall, in the Pope's
estimation, under the heading of mutual temporal aid, but
the encyclical deals with the topic much too quickly to
allow the exegete to conclude apodictically. The doctrine
means, at very least, that spouses should pay "the debt"
cheerfully and joyfully. It seems very likely it means rather
more. The context seems to hint that it refers both to the
mutual alleviation of concupiscence and to an honorable
mutual pleasing which is in no way to be forbidden as long
as it is not so inordinately sought that it wrongfully dis-
places another essential marriage good, *proles.*

On the other hand, it is perfectly plain that the marriage
act is directly related to the generation of offspring, which
are the primary end of marriage from another viewpoint.

The encyclical did not attempt to differentiate between the two viewpoints, but it seems to imply something of this order: offspring are the primary end of the institution of marriage considered *in itself*, since the population of the world by human procreation is the real purpose behind God's institution of it. Fidelity and the development of Christian love are the primary and chief good *for us*. Moreover, the reproductive powers of man are directly related to generation; whereas it could not be said that they are directly related to Christian love, which can obtain between the spouses quite apart from their use. Thus, the use of the reproductive powers is only incidentally related to the good of *fides* and *sacramentum*. Contraception does not present any true dilemma, it is not a real moral problem, especially since in most instances only the desire to obtain pleasure while avoiding its consequent burdens would recommend it. But even when a less trivial motive, and possibly a worthy one, were to lie behind the contraceptive design, any such motive would be, by definition, extrinsic to marriage. Therefore, it must be discarded. Contraception is forbidden *per se*.

The Pope sincerely sympathized with the cases of genuine hardship which this doctrine may have entailed, but he felt hardly competent to subvert the divine moral order even on their account. All he could do, therefore, was to remind spouses that God shall repay them for their sacrifices:

As regards the evil [i.e. contraceptive] use of matrimony, to pass over the arguments which are shameful, not infrequently others that are false and exaggerated are put forward. Holy Mother Church very well understands and clearly appreciates all that is said regarding the health of the mother and the danger to her life. And who would not grieve to think of these things? Who is not filled with the greatest admiration when he sees a mother risking her life with heroic fortitude, that she may preserve the life of the offspring which she has conceived?

It may be necessary to underline that the context of this paragraph was *not* abortion, but contraception. I cannot account for the evident confusion between the two unless, perhaps, the Pope meant to convey in one single economic sentence his sympathy for a wife who risked conception in full knowledge that the eventual childbirth might be dangerous to her health, as well as for a mother who risked gestation, though the subsequent childbirth might likewise be dangerous to her health. For it would be inadmissible to suppose that Pius XI was not aware that it is one thing to argue for the morality of artificial contraception, and quite another to presume to defend the morality of abortion once conception, for whatever reasons, has taken place. In any event, the paragraph concluded with words of consolation to such a mother—presumably, thus, also to such a wife:

God alone, all bountiful and all merciful as he is, can reward her for the fulfillment of the office allotted to her by nature, and will assuredly repay her in a measure full to overflowing.

Meanwhile, the divine law remains: any use of marriage which through human initiative impeaches the natural generative aptitude of the marriage act must be morally forbidden as a contravention of the divine law.

In sum: *Casti Connubii* was highly consistent. Its teaching on contraception was hypothetically necessary—that is, it followed necessarily once its doctrine of marriage was granted.

Why is it suggested that it followed only with hypothetical and not with absolute necessity? Has it not also been shown here that *Casti Connubii*'s doctrine of marriage is in accordance with the Christian tradition? The reason is that we must not suppose, simply because *Casti Connubii*'s doctrine of marriage was true and in accordance with the Christian tradition, that it was therefore adequate to deal with the moral problems to which it wished to address itself. The ambiguities and ambivalences we have noted may well be rooted in that possible inadequacy. It is conceivable that the traditional doctrine of marriage required further development before it could lead to a doctrine concerning artificial contraception which truly responded to the perplexity which the invention of contraceptive devices had introduced into the Christian world. In other words, it may be that the reaffirmation of the Christian faith was by itself not sufficient to deal with the problem, and that a deeper understanding and appreciation of the Christian doctrine of marriage was required anew by the very novelty of the problem. For the truth of the Christian dogma requires ceaseless perfection and development in an ever changing historical world in order, among other things, to deal with just such cultural novelties at the invention of the vulcanization process and the creation of synthetic latex.

It may be useful, therefore, to investigate in what way *Casti Connubii*'s doctrine of marriage was insufficiently developed and in what way it was not.

Development and Underdevelopment in
Casti Connubii

Since this inquiry's purpose in seeking to establish the place of *Casti Connubii* in the historical development of the Christian dogma on marriage is not to praise the contribution of Pius XI, but to facilitate our understanding of its relation to possible further dogmatic development, a much more pronounced emphasis may be legitimately placed upon those aspects of the Christian doctrine which Pius XI left relatively undeveloped, than upon those which constituted a positive and valuable advance. What Pius XI did *not* do is what requires supplement; what he did accomplish is already an inalterable chapter in the history of the Church.

Therefore, it must not be taken as a reflection upon Pius XI or upon the theological advisors whose opinion he authorized in *Casti Connubii*, when it is said that the encyclical did not, generally speaking, actively consider very many among the real and new problems which the reality and novelty of the modern world posed for Christian marriage. It is scarcely a wonder that *Casti Connubii* had very little to add to the Christian understanding of the faith, when it openly professed an essentially conservative rather than a creative, progressive purpose. Its avowed posture was defensive; it proclaimed the purpose of safeguarding the Church from "pernicious errors and depraved morals" by warning Christians, "as from a watch-tower," of attacks from the enemy. This attitude is understandable. Since the early sixteenth century the possibility that the Church's collective vocation might be more effectively and adequately fulfilled by other than aggressive-defensive procedures has not been in the forefront of the Catholic intellect. Throughout the period our understanding of the Christian task has been usually cast in metaphors deriving from warfare. In 1930 we had not yet regained the idea of an analogical participation in the work of Christ's redemption through the Church's eschatological fulfillment of human history.

It is manifest that Pius XI did not think of himself as leading the Christian collectivity through cultural and temporal history. In *Casti Connubii* he spoke of himself as the voice of a Church that stood, stark and still, "erect in the midst of the moral ruin which surrounds her." Accordingly, in order to reject whatever might endanger Christian morality, *Casti Connubii* confined itself largely to the reiteration of the Christian tradition without a discernible prior development or readjustive effort. Concerning, for example, divorce, it taught nothing that had not been adequately taught before, namely that the unity of marriage forbids it. The document exhibits no sign of having asked of itself why there should be a contemporary divorce problem in the *Christian* society, nor what cultural stresses Christian history itself—I mean, Church history—may put upon the Christian family. The encyclical did not noticeably take account of the possibility that yet another uncompromising, dreary anathematization of divorce might not be as effective towards reducing the divorce rate among Catholics as might be, for example, fostering the cultural conditions in which the *mystique* of romantic love would disappear— and listing certain *fabulae amatoriae* in the Index should scarcely count as a contribution to that end. Is the teaching task of ecclesiastical authority discharged in full once it defines right and wrong and exhorts the Christian conscience *a priori* to be holy and to avoid sin? Or should it not positively illumine the conscience of the world—for *its* benefit—by a diffusion of the Gospel light?

On the other hand, we must also avoid anachronism. We, today, can look back upon *Casti Connubii* with hindsight only because we are a full generation removed from it. But to look back is one thing; to look down is another. He would be either presumptuous or pharisaic who cast a stone in the direction of the writers of *Casti Connubii* unless he were prepared first to submit evidence that as of 1930 his theological advice to Pius XI, had the Pope asked, would have strongly dissented from that which prevailed in the event.

We have seen that the foundation of Pius XI's teaching against contraception is the doctrine of the nature of marriage as a divine institution. When the Pope reasserted this view he stood on solid traditional ground. The first two chapters of Genesis are the starting point of that tradition. Pius XI taught, moreover, that the divine institution of marriage meant: the laws that govern marriage are not subject to man's will, since man's will is not their author. This, too, was neither new nor foreign to tradition. Nevertheless, Pius XI's formulation of this truth seems to have left unconsidered the possibility that the divine will's institution of marriage could have taken place, not by arbitrary *fiat* —least of all a *fiat* subsequent to and distinct from the establishment of human nature—but as implicit in the establishment and creation of human nature.

Casti Connubii used the concepts "nature of marriage" and "natural laws of marriage" negatively and ambiguously. By these terms the Pope designated "what is not subject to man's will respecting marriage" and is, therefore, subject only to the divine will. In his teaching "the nature of marriage" means: what marriage truly is by reason of its divine rather than human foundation. The "laws of marriage" means: the rules that govern marriage because its nature is divinely instituted. Therefore, it is patent that Pius XI's zealous but single-minded intention was to emphasize that right and wrong do not depend upon what man may wish, but only upon what God has disposed. Now, what God has disposed can be described as God's will, of course. But the Pope, apparently, did not give much weight to the possibility that God's will, in marriage as in many other respects, may well be concretized in the objective order of human nature.[52] Could we not understand God's will as the ultimate sufficient reason of the institution of marriage without understanding it also as the immediate reason?

This distinction is not precluded, but it is ignored, by *Casti Connubii*'s predominantly negative assertion: marriage has nothing to do with the human will except insofar as the human will may particularize it in existence. As an expression of the traditional teaching of the so-called

[52] The doctrine of John XXIII in *Pacem in terris* may be of special moment because, as I have suggested elsewhere, its morality of natural law is grounded on the continuity between the moral order and the order of nature. Thus, the natural moral law is derived from the specifically human condition of existing human persons, not from an abstract human nature. See my "Peaceful Coexistence in Soviet-American Diplomacy and in John XXIII's *Pacem in terris*," *Co-existence* I, 1, May 1964, 21-38.

"objectivity" of morality[53] the affirmation could not be doubted. But if it is understood in its literal import it might be less adequate to contemporary marriage problems than is desirable. Thus, it is true, as Pius XI says, that "the nature of marriage is entirely independent of the free will of man." But is it also entirely independent of human nature? Evidently, the question did not arise.

But it is not simply that *Casti Connubii* did not develop the doctrine as much as one might wish or as might have been required. The document did not develop it as much as had earlier teachers who, though of a strictly theological and unofficial authority, nevertheless might have been profitably taken into account at this point. I have in mind specifically St. Thomas, who explains, in answer to the question: "Whether marriage pertains to nature," (*utrum matrimonium sit naturale*):

> . . . something can be said to be natural in two ways. First, as caused by necessity from the principles of nature . . . In this way matrimony is not natural, nor are any of those things which come to pass through the mediation of free will. In a second way, that is said to be natural to which nature inclines . . . In this way matrimony is natural . . . Wherefore nature prompts a certain society of man and woman, in which consists marriage.[54]

The conception that the marriage institution is a *natural* one is not necessarily a *naturalistic* interpretation of marriage, nor does it mean that marriage is not divinely insti-

---

[53] This formula itself could be developed further in order to avoid the difficulties of an object-subject theory of knowledge, and to take advantage of certain epistemological concepts of the phenomenological order.

[54] *ST, Supp.* 41, 1.

tuted. Why, then, did Pius XI find it inexpedient to take advantage of this distinction? There are indications supplied by the text of the encyclical. Apparently, Pius XI assumed that the supernatural character of marriage is dependent upon a certain exegesis of the text of Genesis: "Increase and multiply," which would place much reliance on God having actually uttered the words. Today we understand, perhaps rather better than we did in 1930, when biblical scholarship was suffering from certain reverses, that it is not necessary for Christians to choose between a rationalistic and a quasi-fundamentalist interpretation of Scripture. The more that Catholic biblical research has learned that Scripture is, in general, less than accurate and perfect *historiography*, the more it has learned to appreciate the *historicity* of divine revelation.[55] Conversely, to the same extent that one takes, say, Genesis, literally and in abstraction from its cultural form, one must fail to appreciate the historical nature of the revelation it communicates. If one reads Genesis in the first way, the divine institution of marriage must be conceived as an early episode in a series of concatenated *tableaux*. This episode would remain relevant to us today in virtue of God's utterance having set, as it were, an inalterable jurisprudential precedent. Alternatively, we could consider the divine institution of marriage as a divine event in history. In this case marriage remains today, as it shall forever, a divine institution, but not because God's voice resounding through the ages is to be understood either as a physical fact or as a mystical

[55] This is better expressed, perhaps, in the distinction proposed by some German theologians between *das Historische* and *das Geschichtliche*.

figure. For no metaphor is involved: marriage is a divine institution because God's presence to human history is a matter of historical fact.

Thus, if it is *not* literally true that God walked paradise "at the afternoon air" and commanded the human race through our first parents to undertake marriage, then it may be *literally* true that every marriage takes place in the presence of God, and that the human decision to marry is *literally* a free, obedient, personal undertaking in response to God's call. In the Christian tradition marriage is not an excusable whim, permissible as long as it does not infringe upon the limits of morality. It is a true vocation to which the Christian faith responds.

In this conception, therefore, marriage depends upon God's will because it depends upon human nature—a human nature which is itself created in a certain historical situation the most fundamental factor of which is God's historical decision to enter into personal relations with men. The divine institution of marriage is discernible in Gn 1:28 only because it is first evident in Gn 1:27. For when "God blessed them, saying: Increase and multiply, and fill the earth," this was but an extension of the fact that when he created man, "to the image of God he created him: male and female he created them." Therefore, it is true, as Pius XI taught, that the moral obligations of marriage in no wise depend upon what man may wish, but upon what God has disposed. But this should not gainsay the possibility that what God has disposed in connection with marriage is to be found, in part, in the fact that the institution of marriage is related to human sexuality—that is, to human male-and-femaleness. This side of the Christian doctrine of marriage was not developed in *Casti Con-nubii* as much as the contemporary Christian world may require.

Against the background of this relative underdevelopment of the role of human nature in marriage, we can rightly understand *Casti Connubii*'s doctrine on the nature of the union of marriage. According to Pius XI, as we have seen, "the souls of the contracting parties are joined and knit together more primarily and more firmly than are their bodies." The reason why he contrasted the priority and firmness of the union of souls with the union of bodies is evident from the context: he wished to distinguish the marriage union, which is specifically human, from the promiscuous, casual unions of animals, and from the animal-like unions into which human beings can sinfully enter. In opposition to these, he taught, the union of marriage is firm and indissoluble. This could not be, he seems to have assumed, if the union did not derive its stability from a "firm act of the will." The sense, therefore, is clear: marriage is to be distinguished from animal or animal-like unions because it is a stable bond between male and female.

It cannot be doubted that this is an authentic, ancient element of the Christian doctrine of marriage. On the other hand, the anthropological reason advanced, that the bond is created by the will and that, therefore, the bond of marriage joins the souls more closely than the bodies, is not the most exact among the imaginable formulations of the matter, nor the one which would most easily lend itself to further development. The issue involved here is, in fact, a question that has agitated theology since earliest

Christian times: what does efficiently constitute the marriage bond? The complexity of the problem can scarcely be accorded justice in a few lines, but the following points should be brought to mind.[56]

The root of the problem is that although marriage is a human sexual union, not every sexual union of man and woman can be said to be a marriage. A man seduces a woman and impregnates her: are they married therefore? Or a married woman abandons her husband and lives in concubinage with another: is she married to the other? In order to deal with the obvious civil problems which stem from the distinction between sex and marriage, Roman law had formulated the principle: *nuptias non concubitus sed consensus facit.* This principle was generally followed by the fathers. As St. John Chrysostom declared, in a sentence which can be said to be in the direct line of Pius XI: *"Matrimonium non facit coitus, sed voluntate."* [57] On the other hand, not every legal or moral problem can be easily settled in the light of this principle alone; for instance, what should we think of seduction with promise (or promissory oath) of marriage, especially in conjunction with betrothal? Are the parties married or not? In 1040 Gratian, the father of systematic canon law, concluded that marriage is effectively constituted by consent, but that this union is only a *matrimonium initiatum*. Marriage is ratified (*ratum*) only when it is consummated (*consummatum*). This solution became generally accepted. It was indispu-

[56] See the comprehensive study by G. H. Joyce S.J., *Christian Marriage: A Historical and Doctrinal Study*, London 1948.
[57] *Patrologia Graeca*, 56, 802.

tably prudent, and remained a cornerstone of marriage law thereafter—even if it did not solve other problems concerning the nature of the consent. For example, what constituted *free* consent? what degree of coercion invalidated consent? Moreover, this principle allowed by implication that both the consensus and the consummation were essentially private affairs, so that clandestine marriages remained a distinct possibility under its provisions. The difficulties—indeed, the practical impossibility—of trying to determine, in case of litigation between the parties, whether a given clandestine marriage was valid or not, can be readily surmised. Hence further development of the doctrine took place during the next four centuries and culminated in the Council of Trent's decision declaring all clandestine marriages totally invalid. This decision was incorporated in the new code of 1917.

The Tridentine decision can hardly be called unwise. It served to increase the socialization of marriage. It was an obviously progressive and healthy development—we can scarcely imagine doing without it today. On the other hand, this development also meant that the marriage consent has tended to become more and more exclusively a *public*, external, verifiable event. Therefore, it has facilitated the theological neglect of the question of the relation of *concubitus* to *consensus:* it has tended to divorce sexuality from marriage. Of course, the fundamentally sexual nature of the *consensus* has never been in doubt. But since it is possible—and under certain admittedly *abnormal* conditions perhaps even virtuous—for the matrimonial parties to abstain from sexual intercourse, even permanently, the doctrine was developed that the object of the marriage consent was the *right* to sexual relations[58] rather than *actual* sexual intercourse. Again, it would be difficult to deny that from the point of view of the good order of society as a whole, as regulated by civil or canon law, this development has filled a genuine social need. Nevertheless, the *exercise* of the "right" has never been wholly foreign to the moral questions involved, since it is the exercise of the right that constitutes the *consummation* of marriage. But here, too, the development of Christian dogma has tended to be largely implicit in the jurisprudence of ecclesiastical marriage courts rather than on strictly dogmatic or moral grounds.

In Pius XI we can glimpse an attempt to deal in principle with the *total* moral problems of contemporary Christian marriage. But in the absence of unmistakably relevant and adequate speculative contributions to the subject by dogmatic and moral theology, *Casti Connubii* relied heavily on the contributions of canonical developments. This is quite evident in the Pope's placing on the naked will all the efficiency for the creation of the marriage bond. This is clearly traditional—but so is the doctrine that a non-consummated marriage can be dissolved as to the bond. Therefore, does the doctrine that the will is the sole efficient cause of the bond remain sufficiently adequate as a basis for the definition of the specifically human character of marriage? Is this doctrine sufficient to enable us, today, to refine and develop, for purposes of contemporary moral guidance, our understanding of the relation of *coitus* to *voluntas?* For it is one thing to assert that the bond is cre-

[58] *Cod. Iur. Can.*, 1081, 2.

ated by the will. It is another to convey the impression that the firm union and coalescence of the souls is *not* produced in and through a specifically *sexual* union willed by husband and wife.

Casti Connubii properly and correctly reminded us, in line with tradition, that it is possible for man sinfully to engage in animal-like sexual behavior. But the animal-like sexual behavior of man is animal-like not because it is sexual: it is animal-like only because human sexuality is debased by the human will. A sexual sin is not sinful because the body perverts the soul; it is the soul that perverts the body, and the more bestial the sin, the more animal-like the soul becomes. Pius XI, presumably, would not have denied this. On the other hand, it seems he did not consider it relevant to the doctrine of marriage.

Moreover, as we have become increasingly aware in our individual and collective historical experience of the substantial unity of man, it has become decreasingly useful to depend too much upon the distinction between soul and body; instead, we have found it ever more necessary, establishing a much more radical distinction between man and beast than was ever possible on the basis of a specific difference alone, to think of man's humanity in terms of the factual, historical condition of a person. Man's increasing awareness of his personality suggests a direction in which we might proceed in the future in order to realize more adequately the most basic intentions of *Casti Connubii*. For instance, the distinction between truly human and Christian marriage, and animal-like unions, would not be well-formulated, if we adopted a non-Aristotelian anthropology, by contrasting "the coupling of beasts" (*coniunc-*

tionibus pecudum), as *Casti Connubii* puts it, and the "contract" (*contractus*) willed by man and woman. For the coupling of beasts is infinitely below the dignity of human marriage, since it is entered into by beasts, whereas the most insidious act of human fornication retains the perfection of its having been consciously willed.

Pius XI was not mistaken in distinguishing between man and beast; it is possible, however, that he did not distinguish between them radically enough. The dignity of marriage, thus, is perhaps not well expressed by removing the act of the will from the bodily and sexual nature of the object of the will; that dignity might be better expressed by recalling the personal nature of the human sexual society to which the marriage consent is directed. The spirituality of Christian marriage, which Pius XI eagerly wished to preserve, should not be in the least impaired if we realized that in a very real sense the marriage contract is a bodily and sexual contract. Sexual intercourse, in the less common connotation of the word "intercourse"—namely society— means a sexually grounded society between man and woman. Human sexual intercourse, therefore, is not merely sexual copulation: precisely as intercourse it is a spiritual achievement of man.

Of course, *Casti Connubii's* ascription of efficient causality in marriage to a "firm act of the will" rather than to the "transitory sensual or emotional inclination" is undoubtedly sound in what pertains to the reasonableness and rationality which must guide a person's marriage choice. No marriage counselor, however irreligious, is likely to disagree that infatuation is a very unstable and unfortunate foundation for a marriage. More important, perhaps, the doctrine of Pius XI could be further developed in order to take account of the fact that the will or rational appetite is not identifiable with the power of deciding between alternatives. *Liberum arbitrium* is a function of the will. But the will *is* an appetite, that is, a power by which we incline to an end and cleave to a good. In the matter of marriage the will is not essentially the power to choose between matrimonial candidates A and B, but above all the power of loving a person with a love that makes the two become one flesh.

The marriage liturgy reminds us that love is relevant to the marriage contract. From the point of view of morality, then, the contractual nature of marriage would not mean so much and principally a commitment (in the juridical sense of the term) as it would a promise and an undertaking. At law, marriage is consummated only once: in real life it is consummated only throughout life: a common sexual life binds the spouses ever more strictly and closely. Is this not a possible development of Pius XI's doctrine that marriage is "the blending of life as a whole and the mutual interchange and sharing thereof" (*ut totius vitae communio, consuetudo, societas accipiatur*)? Matrimony is a life-long undertaking, a per-durable, pluperfectible commitment through time toward a common human man-woman life. And if it is a *unique* society for mutual perfection at all levels of existence and experience, the reason is that it is a man-woman, that is, a sexual, society: the family life can obtain only in marriage. The sexual union is, thus, not accidental to the perfection of matrimony's nature.

Do these views conflict with *Casti Connubii*? I believe

they do not. But they are certainly not affirmed by Pius XI, and it would be impossible to derive them from that document alone. At any rate, the Pope's doctrine of the divine institution of marriage and on the nature of the marriage union, dictated certain consequences in his teaching on the marriage goods. The stage of relative historical development or underdevelopment of the doctrine on the first two, the institution of marriage and the nature of the union, was reflected in his treatment of the third, the marriage goods.

There can be no doubt but that the common life of man and woman is ordered to the propagation of the race. This, too, is part of the bi-sexual nature of man, and it is equally well founded in the Christian tradition. Therefore, in this respect also Pius XI rightly—indeed, inevitably—taught that "among the blessings of marriage, the child holds the first place." It is inconceivable that he should not have stressed this. What is striking, on the contrary, is that he taught so little on the subject. He might well have considered why and in what sense *proles* is the first of the marriage goods: in a sense this is one of the most serious problems that the contemporary Christian marriage faces. As we have seen, *Casti Connubii* did little more than to reiterate the fact without elaboration or theological explanation.

Indeed, *Casti Connubii* not only failed to consider the nature of the primacy of *proles* but, in a sense, created an additional problem. When the document dealt, after *proles*, with the other marriage goods, it indicated (directly and unequivocally in the case of *fides*, indirectly only in respect of *sacramentum*) that these, too, were primary in their own order. Nevertheless, the question of the order of the marriage goods in relation to each other was not explicitly considered. To determine, therefore, what the document may implicitly contain in this respect and, thus, to extricate the meaning of Pius XI's doctrine on the nature of the primacy of *proles*, it is necessary first to consider in what way his doctrine on *fides* and *sacramentum* was developed and in what way it remained underdeveloped.

The Pope's teaching of the good of *sacramentum* can be dealt with briefly. In *Casti Connubii* we find a good summary of the essentials of the Christian tradition concerning indissolubility and stability as developed up to Tridentine times. As is well known, the Christian dogma had developed these points considerably, especially since the twelfth century. But given the cultural context of western Europe between the age of Gratian and the days of Bellarmine, it is perfectly understandable that the Christian faith had considered much more intensively the doctrinal problems which arise, for instance, out of Mt 19:6[59] and Lk 16:18[60] than with those which have to do, say, with Eph 5:25.[61] Very specially during the early Christian centuries, to expound the negative aspects of the marriage union (that is, what it excluded) was perhaps more pressing

[59] "Therefore now they are not two, but one flesh. What therefore God hath joined together, let no man put asunder."

[60] "Every one that putteth away his wife, and marrieth another, committeth adultery: and he that marrieth her that is put away from her husband, committeth adultery."

[61] "Husbands, love your wives, as Christ also loved the church and delivered himself up for it."

than to develop those which had to do with the positively
Christian sacramental nature of the union.[62]

We cannot enter now into the many historical and cultural factors which account for the fact that the theology
of the matrimonial union has not in the past made much
use of the implications of the Pauline doctrine. The analogy of Christ's gracious and sanctifying love for the Church
which is his bride and spouse has tended to mean, as with
Pius XI, that marital love should be "pure" rather than
"lustful." The truth of this proposition is not open to
doubt. But since it is easy to construe all sexuality as selfish, "pure" or unselfish love hastened to become asexual by
definition. Moreover, it is doubtlessly correct to interpret
Eph 5:25 to mean that Jesus Christ's *deed* for the sake of
the universality of man, namely laying down his life, *manifested* his sanctifying love. But does the deed also *define*
the nature of his union with the Church? Jesus died once,
but his union through the Spirit with his body is enduring
and living. It is ever more perfect as we, his people, realize
in history the kingdom of God. Thus, there may be some
ground in St. Paul's doctrine for wondering whether the
marital union is not part of the sacramental economy, just
as Christ's love for the Church *is* the grace and the gift
that makes the Church holy. The idea that "the marriage
act is meritorious" is not, of course, new.[63] But usually the
problem has been posed in the terms whether it is sinful or

---

[62] The theology of those separated Christians who do not count
matrimony a sacrament is based in part upon the scarcity of early
documentary evidence to the point.

[63] See *ST, Supp.* 41, 4, where St. Thomas affirms that it is meritorious in one who is in the state of grace if the motive for the act is
virtuous.

meritorious in one who is in the state of grace, not whether its merit is related to the sacramental grace of marriage.

One historical reason for these emphases is that the doctrine of Christian love of friendship between husband and wife, which has always been an integral part of Christianity, has awakened a torpid Christian conscience much too leisurely and slowly. Cultural factors which put woman in an inferior light, especially in sexual matters,[64] have made it very difficult for a "pure" marital love to be sexual and conversely, for the marital sexual society to be one of love. The specifically sexual love of husband and wife has become a real possibility only as the equality of the sexes in every other respect has become recognized and practiced. A long memory is not indispensable to recall the status of woman in western society as little as thirty years ago, or to remark upon its extensive transformation since.

Thus, we should not find altogether anomalous that Pius XI remained satisfied with repeating that "since the valid matrimonial consent among the faithful was constituted by Christ as a sign of grace, the sacramental nature is so intimately bound up with Christian wedlock that there can be no true marriage between baptized persons without it being by that very fact a sacrament." But if consent is, more than an aseptic "firm act of the will," the beginning of sexual union, that is, a decision, a promise, and an under-

---

[64] The long-held biological theory that the male seed is the "active principle" of generation, which the female passively receives and nurtures, is partly responsible for this. For instance, it implies that a child is more truly his father's offspring than his mother's. The existence of female ova in mammals was established only in 1827 by von Baer; only then was finally overthrown the theory of the embryo's pre-formation in the seed; William C. Dampier, *A History of Science*, Cambridge 1949, 260.

taking related not merely to "the right to each other's body" but to the creation of a common life through sexual society, then the marriage consent could be said to produce grace in its very sexuality. The question, in short, is not merely whether the marriage act can be meritorious, but whether it is not, in the sacramental sense of the term, also *holy*.

This question was not raised by Pius XI—one should not realistically have expected him to have raised it. But it must be raised by us today if we are to understand the marriage act in its very sexuality and corporeity, not simply as a physiological event involving the congress of two genital systems, but as a supernatural event which solicits and demands an interpersonal relation of the order of the purest and holiest Christian love. For it may be true that in special callings a virginal marriage may be permissible and holy—that is another question. But this would be, *ex hypothesi*, an exception to the rule that it proves.

Moreover, the "deep attachment of the heart," which Pius XI mentioned in one of the most eloquent pages of *Casti Connubii*, is fittingly distinguished in the document from the vice of lust. But it might be at least as important to stipulate that lust does not exhaust the species of sexual behavior, and that it is only a vice, not a synonym of sexuality—for most Christians already know quite well what lust is, but not all of us are aware what Christian marriage in its contemporary historical situation means. Most Christian couples, indeed, are probably so ill-prepared for marriage, in the absence of a positive, relevant, constructive, non-romantic Christian teaching on married sex-

uality, that normally it takes them years of marriage to un-
learn all they must, and to discover—if ever they do—the
horizons of Christian sexual love. Wastefully, it takes them
a good part of their married lifetime to reach the truth that
the "deep attachment of the heart" between husband and
wife is in no way more powerfully generated or more abundantly fostered than by their common sexual life. The mutual love by which "man and wife help each other day by
day in forming and perfecting themselves in the interior
life" need not exclude common prayers at mealtime; but it
should not in the normal course of events substitute common prayers for sexual intercourse.

But to *Casti Connubii*'s credit, though it developed the
doctrine of the divine institution of marriage much less
than the theology of St. Thomas had already done, and the
doctrine of *sacramentum* to a roughly comparable degree,
in what pertains to *fides* Pius XI's encyclical constituted a
genuine contribution to the growth of the Christian faith
in a way and to a degree which St. Thomas would have
found difficult to imagine. We have seen what the Pope's
doctrine was. Now let us observe in what way it constituted a dogmatic development.

To appreciate this, it may be helpful to explain why in
the Christian tradition *fides* has been thought of as a marriage good. The etymology of the noun usually translated
as "fidelity" would be more illustrative if the word were
translated as "trust" or "confidence." Why do we give to
the abstention from adultery a name which means trustworthiness rather than chastity? The reason is that the
institution of marriage confers upon its contractors a cer-

tain *security* concerning "the mutual services which married persons render one another," [65] in a wide range of respects, from the sexual to the economic. But the society of marriage is mutually beneficent only if it is exclusive. Therefore, marriage gives its partners security in respect of those benefits on condition that they abide by the promise to "forsake all others." Thus, all the ordinary mutual benefits of marriage hinge upon mutual trustworthiness. To break the pledge to exclude all others is, of course, to break the marital loyalty or faith. This would be not simply sexually immoral but, above all, a sin against the justice due to the plighted troth. Our civil courts to this day recognize the admissibility of suit for "loss of services," sexual, economic and of companionship, on account of "alienation of affection" or of adultery.

Now, in the same measure that the marital society had been understood as taking place between matrimonial unequals (i.e. in the same measure as the wife has been held as property, or as quasi-property, or as a servant, or as a ward, or as a natural or social inferior, or as reproductively passive) the benefit of the marriage covenant tended to be conceived as: first, of a basically negative character, and, second, as imposing mutual but disproportionate duties of fidelity upon husband and wife. As to the latter, we may note that from Christian antiquity until very recent times the duty to exclude third parties has been held to be mutual—but as weighing more heavily upon the wife. This is

[65] *ST, Supp.* 41, 4. We may also recall how according to Pius XI the sacramental indissolubility of marriage gives the spouses a "positive guarantee" of stability and banishes "any anxious fears lest in adversity or old age the other spouse would prove unfaithful," and thus provides "a calm sense of security."

the origin of the so-called "double standard," a principle
of legal validity in British courts until late in the nineteenth century.[66]

As to the first, it should be sufficient to remark that if
the term "marital *fidelity*" has not been superseded by
another with more positive connotations—such as *love*—
the reason may have to do with an inherent tendency in
Christian history to think of this good as the reciprocal
exclusion of others rather than as the mutual inclusion of
each spouse into the other's total personal life. Conversely,
to the same degree that the equality of man and woman has
become a fact of life—the process is far from complete—
we have permitted ourselves a more positive understanding
of this marriage good. In the Church's acceptance of the
emancipation of women we find the principal antecedent
of Pius XI's doctrine on *fides* as well as the reason why this
should be understood as a development of a doctrine which,
in principle, the Church has always held.

For St. Thomas *fides* meant no more than this: that "a
man goes into his own [woman], not into another one" [67]
(*ad suam accedit et non ad aliam*). He would not in the
least deny of course that spouses should love one another
—or even that they should do so within their sexual inter-

[66] St. Thomas reflected the mores of thirteenth century western
Christendom in a harsher, more primitive version of the double
standard. Condemning uxoricide on the grounds that not even a
cuckolded husband should take the law into his own hands, he explained: if he is "moved by zeal for justice and not by vindictive
spite or hatred, a man can, without sin, bring a criminal accusation
of adultery upon his adulterous wife before a secular court and demand the capital punishment established by the law." *ST, Supp.*
60, 1.

[67] *ST, Supp.* 49, 2.

course. But it would not be typical of him or of his time to think of love as part of *fides* or, therefore, of *fides* as a positive good.

For Pius XI, however, there can be little doubt that "the love of husband and wife . . . pervades all the duties of husband and wife and holds pride of place in Christian marriage." We have noted the unhesitating manner in which he goes so far as to assert that the mutual Christian love of the spouses "can in a very real sense . . . be said to be the chief reason and purpose of matrimony," and that it is in a "restricted sense" that matrimony can be said to have been instituted for procreation. What is the exact meaning of "restricted"? It is difficult to say from the text. We have seen that there is some obscurity in *Casti Connubii* whenever it deals with the possibility of sexual love. But the implicit reasoning of the Pope seems to run like this: whether or not there may be a true sexual love, we can be sure that the purest love of husband and wife is not sexual but "spiritual." On the other hand, there can be no doubt as to whether procreation is a sexual *or* a spiritual act. Since the truest love of husband and wife is not essentially sexual—or, conversely, since sexual intercourse at its highest moral pitch is devoid of lust, but is not in itself and as sexual an act of Christian love—then sexual society has more strictly to do with procreation than with mutual love.

If this is the meaning of the Pope's distinction, then, it seems, *fides* is (perhaps after *sacramentum*) the most essential good of marriage *for us*, but *proles* is the most essential good of marriage *in itself*. If so, then Pius XI came rather close to the position that *proles* is essential to marriage insofar as marriage is of divine institution, but that *fides* is essential to it insofar as marriage stems from the human will. This, of course, would be untenable. Could we believe, in accordance with the Christian tradition, that it is more essential that offspring be born of sexual inter-course than that sexual intercourse be undertaken only as constitutive of marriage? We can well understand why *Casti Connubii*—perhaps instinctively—shied away from discussing the relative order of the goods. Granted its un-derstanding of *fides* and *proles*, to do so would have proved a very difficult exercise.

At any rate, whatever his reasoning, Pius XI experienced no overt need to explain how his two statements, on the primacy of *proles* and on the primacy of positive *fides* or love, could be reconciled. For him there was, probably, no conflict to reconcile. Pure love may admit of honorable, chaste mutual sexual service (the honor and chastity of which may be fairly easily tested by whether the pleasures of sex are subordinated to the duties of marriage), but this love pertains to the "wider" compass of marriage. Sexual congress, however (which need in no way exclude the pleasure of the body, the alleviation of concupiscence and even the "fostering of mutual love"), does not simply foster the good of *proles:* it creates *proles*. Therefore, no more need be said. Sex may be good in itself, but its es-sential purpose is *proles*. Mutual love may be, in a way, even more important than *proles*. But mutual love *may* include sex, it is not sexual in itself.

And yet, if there were a sense in which the vulgar tongue in its crude expression, "to make love," unconsciously ex-pressed a profound truth of contemporary matrimonial experience, it follows that there would be a real unresolved problem in the relation between *fides* and *proles*. The doctrine of *Casti Connubii*, however, cannot be mistaken for a solution to a problem of whose existence Pius XI was not noticeably aware—or at any rate, a problem which the encyclical did not actually consider. It was a problem, in any event (if it is true that *Casti Connubii* lacked a sufficiently developed doctrine of marriage), which this document was not ready to take up.

This brings us to the Pope's doctrine of *proles*. Perhaps the most curious feature of *Casti Connubii* is the paradox that it has earned the fame of stoutly defending the primacy of *proles*, whereas in reality, as has been noted above, this encyclical offers a weaker exposition of the Christian doctrine than could be found in the theological tradition. The vagueness of the Pope's expression: "the child holds the first place" (*primum locum tenet proles*), contrasts markedly, for example, with St. Thomas' precise and technical formula: "offspring is the most essential thing in marriage," [68] (*proles est essentialissimum in matrimonio*). One marvels that Pius XI did not quote St. Thomas in addition to St. Augustine on this point.

Not only was the Pope's formula weaker, since *Casti Connubii* nowhere stated that *proles* was either the most essential of the marriage goods, or even more essential than any other—that is, it abstains from comparisons—but the substance of the matter is not supported as firmly as it might be. In fact, it is not at all clear exactly what support is claimed for the statement that *proles* "holds the first place."

Some support is hinted at, in view of the adverb that in-

[68] *ST, Supp.* 49, 3.

troduces the assertion: "thus (*itaque*) among the blessings of marriage, the child holds the first place." Yet the immediately preceding quotation from St. Augustine in no way indicates the order of the goods, nor does it illustrate the primacy of *proles*, or supply a reason therefor which Pius XI could take advantage of. It is possible, therefore, that the Pope's statement is related to the *first* quotation, also from St. Augustine, which preceded the quotation just considered. But if so, then the only support adduced by the Pope in *Casti Connubii* (which is not to say that no other support could have been adduced) stems merely from the order in which the three goods are enumerated by St. Augustine in the quoted passage. In this sense, that is, in St. Augustine's enumeration in this passage, *proles* "holds the first place." Evidently, it could not be seriously maintained that Pius XI took this as a sufficient ground for his statement about the primacy of *proles*, especially if we remember that the more common order of enumeration places *fides* in the first place. On the other hand, it would be equally vain to draw any conclusion from the more common order, for it is highly variable. Even the same author is often inconsistent—as witness the two Augustinian passages quoted by the Pope. Sometimes variations in the order of enumeration are found within a few lines of a single text.[69] Traditionally, then, the order of enumeration is not significant.

As for the scriptural texts cited, their relevance is to the question whether *proles* is a marriage good, not to what relation *proles* has to the other goods. The Pope aptly recalled Gn 1:28 in this connection. Indeed, this passage in-

[69] E.g. *ST, Supp.* 49, 2.

dicates the divine institution of marriage *only* because it
is concerned with procreation. The verse does not directly
state anything about the marriage society. But its direct
reference to procreation is enough to reveal the divine institution of marriage on the reasonable and common sense
assumption that marriage is directly related to *human* procreation. The other text quoted by the Pope, 1 Tim 5:14
(again, not directly, but in St. Augustine's interpretation)
adds nothing to Genesis regarding the primacy of *proles*.
For it cannot be doubted that in the Christian tradition it
is desirable that "the younger [women] should marry, bear
children, be mistresses of families." But this is scarcely to
say that to bear children is the primary essential good of
marriage—unless, once again, we were to draw this from
the fact that the Apostle's wish that young women should
"bear children" is listed ahead of the wish that they should
be "mistresses of families." [70]

[70] This would have been much clearer if *Casti Connubii* had
quoted Scripture directly. The English translation reproduced above
is Douay's literal rendering of the Vulgate: "*Volo iuniores nubere,
filios procreare, matresfamilias esse.*" But St. Augustine's exposition
is a little more complex: "*Generationis itaque causa fieri nuptias.
Apostolus ita testis est: 'Volo,' inquit, 'iuniores nubere.' Et quasi ei
diceretur: 'Ut quid?' continuo subjecit: 'Filios procreare, matresfamilias esse'.*" Thus, St. Augustine clearly explained that generation is causally related to matrimony; this is a perfectly legitimate
exegesis precisely because it did not take up the question of the
priority of *proles* or the relation of *proles* to the other goods, for
these questions are not dealt with in the scriptural text. In other
words, in this passage St. Augustine pointed out, more explicitly and
clearly than the scriptural text did, that *proles* is a marriage good for
the sake of which marriage exists. But unlike the scriptural text, St.
Augustine could be misread as signifying that *proles* is *the* cause of
marriage—in fact, it was so misread by the NCWC translator. But
apart from the fact that St. Augustine's text establishes causality not
determinately, but indeterminately, the substance of the matter

Both Scripture and St. Augustine, therefore, substantiate the opinion that *proles* is a marriage good, but they cannot be construed as dealing with the relation of this to the other goods. Pius XI quite rightly elaborated the point "how great a boon of God this is, and how great a blessing of matrimony." For even if to stress the desirability of the good of *proles* is not the same as to establish its primacy, the matter is not irrelevant to the problem of contraception. It is probable that some persons would seek to practice it for predominantly selfish reasons, and as if children were neither desirable nor a great marriage blessing. Thus, the Pope taught that the avoidance of *proles* in Christian marriage cannot be admitted insofar as such avoidance would imply the denial of *proles* as a marriage good. He did not consider the possibilities that contraception might be undertaken without prejudice to the truth that *proles* is a marriage blessing, or that it might serve honorable and Christian purposes having to do with the other marriage goods, both *fides* and *sacramentum*. But the teaching of *Casti Connubii* on this point would remain valid even if the magisterium of the Church taught in the future that under certain conditions contraception is justified by the goods of *fides* and *sacramentum*. For such a teaching would not deny the truth that *proles* is a marriage good or, indeed, the truth that in a certain order *proles* is the marriage good that "holds the first place."

We need not concern ourselves, in connection with *Casti Connubii's* doctrine of the primacy of *proles*, with that

---

would forbid such an interpretation. For there can be no possible doubt that in the Christian tradition *proles* is not the only marriage good, or the only good for the sake of which marriage exists. Therefore, it could not be said to be *the* cause of marriage.

part of the encyclical which, forbidding contraception, speaks of the conjugal act as "destined of its very nature for the begetting of children," for no question of either primacy or exclusiveness of proles is involved here, explicitly or implicitly. But we must consider that part which permits periodic continence with the object of avoiding *proles:* here the doctrine does refer to the question of primacy. Unfortunately, on this precise point the teaching is slightly obscure, predominantly negative and somewhat vague. The passage should be reproduced again:

> For in matrimony as well as in the use of matrimonial rights there are also secondary ends, such as mutual aid, the fostering of mutual love, and the quieting of concupiscence which the spouses are not in the least forbidden to seek so long at the intrinsic nature of this act is safeguarded and, therefore, so long as [is also safeguarded] the due order of this [act] to the primary end.

It is quite clear, therefore, that there are primary and secondary ends. But *what* are they the ends of? The text answers: they are the primary and secondary ends of marriage and of the use of the matrimonial rights. The secondary ends of marriage and of the conjugal act may be sought as long as the nature of the conjugal act retains all that its nature requires of it insofar as the primary end of marriage is concerned. Thus, the primary and secondary ends mentioned are essentially the primary and secondary ends of marriage. Being the primary and secondary ends of marriage they also are, *therefore,* the primary and secondary ends of the conjugal act, for this act derives its moral nature from its matrimonial formality. For this reason it is morally necessary to safeguard "the due order of this [conjugal act] to the primary end [of marriage]." This is but another way in which we find confirmed the thesis proposed earlier: that *Casti Connubii* condemned contraception on the ground that contraception violated the nature of the conjugal act *as such*, that is, insofar as the nature of the act is determined by the nature of marriage.

So much is clear. The principal difficulty in the interpretation of this passage results from the fact that the priority and posteriority of the ends of the marriage act are explicitly made to depend on the nature of marriage (not of sexual intercourse). For if the distinction between the primary and secondary ends of the marriage act results from the nature of marriage, then that distinction depends on the doctrine of the order of the marriage goods. This passage, therefore, has exactly the same meaning and force as has the Pope's doctrine on the primacy of *proles* —which, as we have seen, is less well developed in the encyclical than might be required by the problem of contraception. Thus, to the same degree that the doctrine of *proles* is subject to further development and the order of the marriage goods made more explicit, the doctrine of the order of ends in the marriage act may be correspondingly developed and, if need be, modified.

But this is a relatively minor point. A more fundamental consideration is that this text does not condemn contraception *because* contraception would subvert the due order of the ends of marriage and the conjugal act. Notice, first, that it forbids contraception by negative implication: it explains what use of matrimony is *allowed* even though it "cannot" (*non possit*) bring forth new life. Thus, the implied prohibition (there cannot be any doubt that it is intentionally implied) forbids contraception hypothetically: that is, the prohibition would depend on whether or not contraception would safeguard the nature of the act of marriage as such. (For instance, the "rhythm method" is permitted, under certain conditions, because it safeguards the nature of the marriage act—and is, therefore, not *truly* contraceptive.) From this also follows, *"therefore"* (*ideoque*), that contraception is forbidden if it subverted the due order of the marriage act to the primary end of the act and of matrimony.

Thus, the text condemns contraception. But what would be the relation between a hypothetical future teaching permitting contraception and this teaching of *Casti Connubii?* In this text,[71] *Casti Connubii* condemned contraception on such grounds that no later teaching could contradict. For no future teaching allowing the morality of artificial contraception could violate the condition that contraception, however justifiable and desirable on other grounds, may in no event pervert the nature of the marriage act (nor, therefore, the nature of marriage), nor subvert the order of ends in the marriage act (nor, therefore, the order of the marriage goods). The problem of contraception, thus, rests fundamentally upon this issue: what order and mutual relation among the marriage goods is implied by the nature of marriage? *Casti Connubii* asserted, albeit weakly, the primacy of *proles*. But what did it teach concerning the relation among the marriage goods?

The document, as we have seen, did not take up this

---

[71] A *fortiori*, the same is true of the earlier text which, as we have seen, is weaker. For it condemns contraception on the same grounds as this, but does not mention the priority and posteriority of ends.

question directly. That is, it did mention, as has been noted, the "first place" of *proles* (and the "primary end" of marriage) but it did not explain what is the place of the other marriage goods in relation to it. For that matter, it also spoke of the primacy of *fides,* but did not explain clearly its relation to *proles* or to *sacramentum.* As to the relation of the latter to the others it says nothing. However, *Casti Connubii* included a possible indication of how it would deal with the relation of *proles* and *fides* when it stated that *fides* was the primary marriage good in the wider (*latius*) sense of marriage, but *proles* was primary in the stricter sense of the term. What does this mean? What is the difference between the strict and the wide sense of marriage? The text does not enable us to answer categorically. We can but repeat the conjecture offered above as the only hypothesis which could bring into order the various aspects of the doctrine: the distinction is based between the sexual and the non-sexual aspects of the marriage society. Strictly considered, the society is sexual and, thus, *proles* is prior. More widely considered, it is non-sexual and, in this respect, *fides* is prior. If this is correct, then *Casti Connubii* did not answer the question of the relation of *fides* and *proles* insofar as *fides* may be a positive good of the marriage society precisely as sexual.

In any event, it is apparent that *Casti Connubii* assumed a relatively primitive stage of doctrinal development on the nature of marriage and that a more developed dogma could have been assumed had it taken advantage of certain aspects of St. Thomas' theology of marriage. It should go without saying that it was not necessary for Pius XI to have taken advantage of St. Thomas. We can only judge whether or not it would have profited the development of the Christian faith if he had done so.[72]

For the absence of a clear doctrine on the order of the marriage goods in *Casti Connubii* is especially disappointing when we remember that St. Thomas explicitly dealt with the question. He asked: "Whether *sacramentum* is more important (*principalius*) than the other goods of marriage." His reply should be reproduced in full:

Something is said to be more important in a certain matter in one of two ways: either because it is more essential than another, or because it is more worthy. If [we consider the reason] that it is more worthy, then sacrament is, in every respect, the chief among the three marriage goods. For it belongs to marriage insofar as marriage is a mystery of grace (*sacramentum gratiae*), whereas the other two goods belong to marriage insofar as marriage is, so to speak, a work of nature—and the perfection of grace is more worthy than a natural perfection.

But if we say more important, meaning more essential, we must distinguish as follows. Faith and offspring can be considered in two ways. First, in themselves. In this sense faith and offspring pertain to the use of marriage, by which [use] children are begotten and the marriage covenant is observed. But inseparability, which is brought about by the sacrament, pertains to matrimony itself by its very nature (*ad ipsum matrimonium secundum se*): for it follows, from the very fact that by the marriage pact the spouses give each other authority over each other in perpetuity, that they cannot be put asunder. Hence matrimony never obtains without inseparability; yet it can be found without fidelity or offspring, for the existence of a thing does not depend upon its use. In this way, sacrament is more essential to matrimony than faith and offspring.

[72] It should also go without saying that to have taken advantage of the thirteenth century's theology of marriage would have been hardly sufficient to deal with a twentieth century problem. The weight of my affirmation is that the thirteenth century's theology was an advance over the fifth's.

Second, faith and offspring may be considered as what they are in principle (*secundum quod sunt in suis principiis*). In this sense offspring means the intention of begetting children, and faith means the duty to observe fidelity. And without these there cannot be matrimony, for they are caused in a given marriage (*in hoc matrimonio*) by the conjugal pact itself—so that if anything contrary to them were expressed in the consent that makes a marriage, there would be no true marriage. Taking faith and offspring in this sense, offspring is the most essential thing in marriage, faith is second, and sacrament is third: just as it is more essential for man to have a nature than to have grace, even if to have grace is more worthy.[73]

An extensive gloss on this text would be superfluous, given its clarity. *Proles* is the most essential good of marriage, in the sense that there could be no valid *marriage* without the intention of begetting children, at least in principle. The procreation of *proles* is the chief good of marriage insofar as this good is considered in principle, that is, as determining the nature of marriage. It is absolutely essential in principle: without it as a principle there would be no marriage institution. But it is not essential to the use of marriage: in this respect what is most essential is *sacramentum*. This doctrine is not unreasonable: especially for the Christian, it is more essential that an individual, concrete marriage be holy and sanctify than that it procreate.

This does not mean that from the theology of marriage of St. Thomas we could deduce or justify the morality of artificial contraception. It may mean, however, if this doc-

[73] *ST, Supp.* 49, 3. Interestingly, this was the only article of St. Thomas on marriage or related questions to which *Casti Connubii* referred. But the encyclical quoted from it in a different context, namely, regarding whether the nature of marriage is determined by man's will or God's.

trine of St. Thomas is in accordance with the Christian faith, and if it constitutes a legitimate development over the more primitive doctrine of the order of the marriage goods reproduced in *Casti Connubii*, that it enables us to understand why this encyclical, despite its clear prohibition of artificial contraception, should not be considered as having definitely solved the problem of artificial contraception. *Casti Connubii*'s prohibition was extended to each and every conjugal act when, on the basis which it itself supplied—the primacy of *proles* as required by the nature of marriage—a generic prohibition alone would have been justified. There can be little doubt that the good of *proles* requires the human race to reproduce and expand. But the question whether the marriage good of *proles* requires that each and every conjugal act be apt to procreate is perhaps more doubtful and a more complex issue than Pius XI seems to have assumed.

Conclusions

If the foregoing is correct, there seem to be some dogmatic ground for considering that the doctrine against contraception is reformable. More to this study's purpose, a hypothetical reformation of the doctrine should not be construed as a direct contradiction of the teaching of Pius XI in every respect; instead, it should be principally considered as a different, more refined conclusion, drawn in the light of a fuller elaboration and a more thorough development of the same Christian dogma on marriage on the basis of which, and for the sake of the preservation of which, Pius XI issued the condemnation. It also means, finally, that in the doctrine of St. Thomas we may find a valuable indication of the direction in which we should seek for the justification of contraception in Christian marriage, namely in a further development of the doctrine of the good of *sacramentum*.

But the most basic reorientation required before the magisterium could begin to entertain a fundamental reconsideration of the matter—regardless of outcome—would be that it became aware of what the problem of today's Christian marriage really is. From *Casti Connubii* to our own day the magisterium sometimes has been unable to grasp the fact that the Christian conscience faces a genuine dilemma. The problem has been persistently conceived as if at bottom it were little more than an attempt to gain religious sanction for sexual self-indulgence. Mistaking the chastity of celibacy for the chastity of marriage, the magisterium, not illogically, has sometimes pointed to its own self-denial as the principle of solution:

> We know that sometimes there can be an agonizing choice between natural instincts and the law of God. Our hearts are full of sympathy, but we cannot change God's law. We must all— married and unmarried, priest and layman—realize that following Christ calls for sacrifice and self-denial. Holy Scripture, ecumenical councils, and the popes are at one in declaring, aided by divine grace, all God's children are capable of chaste living.[74]

If the moral problem is well put above, there can be no doubt that the remainder of the statement is wise and morally sound. It is difficult to imagine that the magiste-

[74] Statement of Archbishop Heenan of Westminster, on behalf of the hierarchy of England and Wales, May 7, 1964, *Herder Correspondence* I, 7, July 1964, 217.

rium would ever opt against the law of God. Cross purposes have not always been absent in the hierarchy-laity
dialogue.

It is not impossible, however, that these communication
blocks will be dismantled and that the Church will come
to know its true mind. Perhaps the most significant
aspect of Pope Paul VI's recent statement—that the problem of "population growth on the one hand and of family
morality on the other," was under study "in the light of
scientific, social and psychological truths which in recent
times have had new and very extensive study and documentation" [75]—was the frank recognition that the question
of birth control presented a true problem of conscience for
both the magisterium and the faithful of the Catholic
Church.

If it should turn out, after all, that the Church's true
mind sees in artificial contraception an ornament of Christian marriage, what should we think of *Casti Connubii?*
The conclusion reached by this study is that the doctrine
of *Casti Connubii* was and should remain valid in relation
to the moral problem to which *in fact* it addressed itself,
namely the possible dangers to the traditional Christian
doctrine of marriage. But the encyclical, which in the
wishes of its author was surely intended to serve more concrete needs as well, did not in fact manage to envisage adequately the *new* problem of contraception under the *new*
cultural conditions in which Christian marriage now ex-
isted. The token of this indistinctness is the *indiscriminate*
condemnation of artificial contraception under the same
title as the "natural" contraception of onanism. As indis-

[75] *The Canadian Register*, July 4, 1964.

criminate, the doctrine was and remains valid. Greater discrimination in the future teaching of the Church may well respect (and possibly enhance) the truth of the earlier position, even if a different practical conclusion might be reached in respect of one of the discriminate parts, namely artificial contraception.

But since it has been granted that *Casti Connubii* dealt globally with *all* contraception, must we not also grant—precisely because it did not discriminate between onanism and artificial contraception—that it *did* implicitly and in fact address itself to the *new* problem of contraception? Here again, we must distinguish. For the question is, indeed, whether or not the encyclical's failure to discriminate did not *ipso facto* restrict the applicability of its doctrine; in other words, whether or not the nature of the actual problem demanded that such discrimination be made as a *sine qua non* of the adequacy of the solution.

Pius XI and his theologians were doubtlessly aware of the existence of artificial contraceptive devices. In this sense they intended to deal and, moreover, did actually deal—adequately or not—with the problem of contraception: that is, with the problem posed by the industrial-economic processes that made cheap and efficient contraceptive devices available to all. But the new moral problem was not in reality created by this development alone, which furnished merely the matter of the problem, as it were. The formality of the moral problem was given by the generally experienced desirability of their use on *new* sociological grounds, that is, not merely for the strictly negative end of avoiding in principle or altogether the procreation of children, but for the sake of positive ends, principally the welfare of children already procreated and the possibility of new dimensions of Christian love between husband and wife. Therefore, the new problem of contraception was more truly due to the sociological changes in the social status of women than to the technological processes developed by Goodyear and Hancock in 1943-44. This means: the real problem to which *Casti Connubii* had to address itself, before it could hand down a stable decision on the problem of contraception, was the question of the role of sexual relations in marriage under the new cultural conditions of the modern world. But to attack that problem, let alone solve it, the magisterium would have had to develop the Christian doctrine of marriage considerably beyond the point to which *Casti Connubii* took it. Precisely as undeveloped, the doctrine of Pius XI may not have communicated, as it wished, the will of God in this respect. The magisterium might yet, even after reconsideration, reaffirm the teaching of *Casti Connubii*—but this time in relation to the real and specifically contemporary problem of Christian marriage. To do so, however, it would have to base itself upon a developed doctrine of marriage which considered the relations of sexual intercourse to Christian marriage under contemporary conditions. To the date of this writing the magisterium has done neither.

If, on the other hand, the magisterium ever teaches that artificial contraception is morally permissible—and, indeed, a positive benefit, in view of the sacramental character of marriage—it should be possible to affirm that such a development harks back, not only to such aspects of marriage as *Casti Connubii* may have neglected, but also in a very real sense to at least one aspect that the encyclical did develop—the doctrine of *fides*. Why?

St. Thomas taught that *proles* is essential, not to the use of marriage, but as an intention from which marriage generically proceeds as from a principle. On the other hand, though this theology makes clear that *sacramentum* is the least essential (while remaining nevertheless the most valuable) good of marriage, curiously, St. Thomas did not at all explain why *fides* is second to *proles* as a principle of marriage. Throughout his argument he dealt with *proles* and *fides* together and on the same footing, until it was time to conclude when, seemingly gratuitously, he asserted that both are essential, but *proles* is most essential and *fides* is second. It is not difficult to surmise why St. Thomas should naturally have assumed this. He thought of *proles*, naturally, as a positive good. But, as we have noted, the cultural conditions of his time precluded the concept of *fides* except as a negative mutual good and, in several respects, a unilateral benefit for the man. The concept of a positive, mutual, reciprocal good of *fides* had to wait until the days of feminine equality. Only in our time, therefore, have we arrived at a position from which we might realize that both goods are essential, and that there may be no legitimate question to be asked as to which is more essential than the other, since both are equally indispensable as principles of marriage—and that, therefore, the problem of their mutual order should be posed a) in terms of the direct or indirect contribution of each of these principles to the sacramental good; and b) in terms of the generic or individual requirements that they impose either upon the

Christian society generally or upon each concrete Christian marriage, and upon each and every conjugal act.

Thus, St. Thomas' doctrine of the order of the goods is well complemented by that of Pius XI on the good of *fides*. If we combined the two we would arrive very close to the following position.

The divine institution of marriage imposes upon mankind a generic obligation to reproduce and preserve itself. Therefore *proles* is the most essential good of matrimony, insofar as it is the generic principle of matrimony. For this reason individual married couples may not avoid offspring without good and sufficient reasons, or without safeguarding the duties which are imposed on the use of matrimony by the goods of *fides* and *sacramentum*. The mutual sanctification of the spouses is the most essential use of marriage and, therefore, is the principal good which individual couples are to seek in every action of their married life, but very particularly in the conjugal act *par excellence*, that is, in their sexual relations. For the good of *fides* more directly serves and fosters the good of *sacramentum* than does the good of *proles*, if *fides* is positively understood as the mutual love of man and woman, proper and exclusive to marriage, which marriage generates and which, reciprocally, fulfills and perfects wedlock.

CAN THE CHURCH CHANGE HER POSITION ON BIRTH CONTROL?

GREGORY BAUM, O.S.A.

There are contemporary Catholic theologians who suggest that a deeper understanding of the human person and, consequently, of the natural order of human values may lead to a new appreciation of sexuality in married life and eventually modify the Catholic position on birth control. They say that the morality of an individual act must not simply be measured by the perfection of its physical execution, but also and more especially by its context in the total life of man, and therefore, if a marriage is orientated toward selfless love, fruitfulness, and the service of the community, frustrating the fertility of an individual act of intercourse need not constitute a sin at all.

Quite apart from the validity of these arguments on birth control, the question arises whether the official teaching of the Holy See condemning contraception as "intrinsically evil" and hence never permissible, is irreformable and definitive. Is the infallibility of the Church involved in this position?

The Authority of the Official Position

Catholics believe that the Church has received the Holy Spirit enabling her to believe and announce, without fear of error, the message and events of universal salvation. The Spirit in the Church guarantees the Gospel. The ultimate criteria for the infallible testimony of the Spirit are the solemn definitions of the Church and the ordinary magisterium of all the bishops in union with the pope. According to the First Vatican Council: "By divine and Catholic faith must be believed all those things which are contained in the word of God written or handed on by tradition, and proposed by the Church, either in a solemn pronouncement or through her universal ordinary magisterium, to be believed as divinely revealed" (*Denz.* 1792).

This declaration is founded upon the Church's commission to teach with authority what is contained in the word of God. Divine revelation is the primary and central area of the Church's teaching office. Yet the teaching authority of the Church does not end here. It has always been taken for granted in the life of the Church that her teaching authority extends beyond the proclamation and explanation of the Gospel to all matters necessary to protect and defend this Gospel in the world. In particular, since the Gospel has been revealed to communicate to man his true identity, the Church is appointed as guardian of humanity and has the authority to protect with her teaching the dignity of man and the natural order of human values.

There are times when the Church must make courageous declarations, in the name of the Gospel, on matters such as slavery, discrimination, atomic warfare, the abuse of sex and other forms of injustice, in order to safeguard the natural values of human life. The Church has undoubtedly the right and authority to condemn errors regarding the meaning of sexual life. At the same time, since the natural order of values is only partially revealed in the Scriptures, the Church's understanding of this reality (often called the natural law of human life) has undergone a considerable evolution and is still subject to further refinements.

Catholics believe that the Spirit assists the Church in her teaching. Yet, in addition to the central area of Christian teaching, where the Spirit supplies the unfailing assistance which is called, inadequately perhaps, "infallibility," there are areas of teaching where the assistance of the Spirit enables the Church to teach with authority without, however, claiming to speak infallibly. How can we detect the limit between these two areas of teaching? Are we always able to tell whether a doctrine of the Church belongs to the central area where the assistance of the Spirit supplies infallibility, or whether it belongs to the area where the divine guidance granted to the Church does not necessarily produce definitive and irreformable statements?

The above quotation from the First Vatican Council tells us that the infallible expression of Christian teaching is given to Catholics a) through the solemn definitions (the extra-ordinary magisterium) of councils and popes speaking *ex cathedra* and b) through the ordinary magisterium of the universal Church. The latter category, the universal ordinary magisterium, consists of the unanimous Christian teaching of all the Catholic bishops as expressed in pastoral letters, sermons, catechisms, decrees, etc. In order to speak of universal magisterium and seek in it the infallible guidance of the Spirit we must presuppose that the consensus of the bishops is not the result of external conformity nor the effect of the authority of the pope on the bishops subject to him, but rather that the unanimous conviction regarding the meaning of the Gospel is one to which all the bishops have made their contribution, by listening to God's word, wrestling with the exigencies of truth, probing into the meaning of the Gospel for our day, and reflecting on the Christian convictions of their own people.

The doctrine of collegiality which emerged at the Second Vatican Council has recalled very forcefully that the bishops in the Church do not derive their teaching mission from the pope, and hence do not fulfill their task by simply repeating the papal teachings in their dioceses. As members of the episcopal college, the bishops have a teaching mission of their own and hence have their proper responsibility in giving expression to the faith of the Church. To have a clear expression of the universal magisterium bishops must act as true *judices fidei*, as judges or discerners of the Christian convictions which are held in the Churches entrusted to them. While we firmly believe that God provides the infallible guidance through the universal magisterium of the Church, we realize that the formation and formulation of this teaching may be a long and drawn out process.

Of highest authority in the Catholic Church, though not claiming to be acts of solemn teaching or an expression of the universal magisterium, is the ordinary teaching of the Holy See, as found in papal encyclicals and the decrees of the Roman congregations. In the last hundred years this teaching has exercised an ever growing normative function in the Catholic Church, though no claim has ever been made that the ordinary teaching of the popes is infallible.

The condemnation of contraception as "intrinsically evil" was clearly contained in the ordinary teaching of the Holy See during the nineteenth century, long before the encyclical *Casti Connubii* of Pius XI forcefully reiterated it. The latest edition of *Denzinger*, prepared by Schönmetzer, lists a series of such condemnations beginning with the year 1822 (see *Index Systematicus* K4eb).

For the purpose of our article it is of greatest importance to know what kind of assent the Catholic must give to the ordinary teaching of the popes. Realizing that in the exercise of its ordinary magisterium the Holy See, while insisting on obedient submission, lays no claim to infallibility, the traditional manuals of theology have created a special category to describe the required intellectual assent. The assent demanded is not one of faith. What is demanded is an *assensus internus et religiosus,* an internal religious assent to the decrees of legitimate ecclesiastical authority, i.e. an act of intellectual submission from religious motives of loyalty to the Holy See and from trust that God will supply the best available guidance through the visible head of the Church. This assent must be whole-hearted and sincere: respectful silence is not deemed sufficient.

This special category of internal religious assent is in harmony with the claims made by the popes themselves in their ordinary teaching. Pius IX, in a letter to the Archbishop of Munich in 1863 and Pius X, in the motu proprio *Praestantia* of 1907, insist that Catholics are in conscience bound to submit to the doctrinal decisions of the Holy See

(see *Denz.* 1684, 2113). In *Casti Connubii*, the encyclical condemning contraception as intrinsically evil, Pius XI writes: "The faithful must be obedient not only to the solemn definitions of the Church but also, in proper proportion, to other constitutions and decrees in which certain opinions are proscribed and condemned as dangerous or evil" (*AAS*, 1930, 580). The same thought is expressed in a paragraph of Pius XII's encyclical *Humani Generis*. Here it is stated quite clearly that the decrees of the Holy See are binding in conscience and that the teaching of the popes in encyclicals intending to settle theological controversies is authoritative and must be obeyed (*Denz.* 2313). At the same time the claim has never been made that this ordinary teaching of the popes is equivalent to acts of solemn teaching or to the universal ordinary magisterium: in other words, the claim has never been made that this teaching is an infallible testimony to divine truth.

The internal religious assent to authoritative teaching is a concept which poses considerable theological difficulties. The manuals agree that an unconditional surrender of the mind is permissible only before the word of God, especially as it is proposed to us by the infallible magisterium of the Church. Then we speak of an act of divine faith. On the other hand, the manuals agree that the internal religious assent to the ordinary teaching of the Holy See cannot be absolute: it is conditional and prudential. The teaching of the Holy See has an obligatory character, not because it is necessarily a definitive statement of Christian truth, but, rather, because it is a pastoral measure in proposing the safest solution for grave and urgent problems, overcoming dangerous controversy in the Church and steering the energy of theologians along a more unified path. The assistance of the Holy Spirit granted to this teaching body belongs to the prudential order. The obedience of Catholics to these decrees, therefore, belongs properly not to the virtue of faith but to the moral virtues by which we submit to legitimate religious authority. Explaining this situation, Pesch writes: "The obedience of the intellect extends much farther than the sphere of divine faith and infallible certitude" (*Inst. Propaed. S. Theol.* 1903, 327).

It is not surprising, therefore, that the manuals, even the stricter ones, readily admit that the sincere obedience to the non-infallible decrees of the Holy See does not exclude the possibility that a scholar in his theological investigations may arrive at different conclusions and that he may humbly submit his arguments to the ecclesiastical authority, asking that the matter be taken up again and the original decision be modified (see Hervé, *Manuale Theol. Dogm.* vol. 1, 1952, 514, and Tanquerey, *Synopsis Theol. Dogm.* vol. 1, 1921, 561).

That the ordinary teaching of the Holy See is susceptible to modification and has in fact been modified, we see from the celebrated example of religious liberty. Many authoritative declarations of the popes of the last century condemned as dangerous the doctrine which asserted that every man had the natural right to religious liberty. In *Quanta Cura* of Pius IX we read: "From this completely false conception of social rule (naturalism) they did not hesitate to foster that erroneous opinion which is especially injurious to the Catholic Church and the salvation of souls, called by our predecessor Gregory XVI *deliramentum* (insane raving), namely that freedom of conscience and of worship is the

proper right of each man, and this should be proclaimed and
asserted in every rightly constituted society" (*Denz.* 1690;
see 1613). Through a deeper understanding of what the
human person is as well as through many changes in the
social order, this condemnation of freedom, at one time
taught with authority demanding obedience, has on the
whole been abandoned.

For this brief treatment of the question we conclude
that the Catholic theologian is bound in conscience to submit to the decision of the Holy See condemning contraception as intrinsically evil, and that he may, at the same
time, provide arguments and insights based on theology and
Christian experience which will eventually call for a re-
examination of the question by the ecclesiastical magisterium. Since the problem first arose in the last century,
many new insights have been gained into the role of sexuality in human life and many new social factors have
modified the framework in which we must discover what
is "natural" for a family. Since the Holy Spirit has not provided the Church with an infallible verdict it would be
irresponsible, at the present time, to say that the whole
matter needed no new investigation.

The Catholic theologian must help the ecclesiastical
magisterium in this examination. But it takes courage for
the Catholic theologian of our day to reflect on the meaning of sexual life and the morality of contraception. Some
theologians find it difficult to transcend the categories in
which they have been brought up. Others, wishing to be
faithful to the teaching of the Holy See, hesitate to study
marriage problems with perfect honesty, fearing that they
might come up with solutions contrary to the official posi-

tion. Since most Catholic theologians are priests, and hence
unmarried, they feel somewhat incompetent to examine
the role of sexuality in marriage and hence are particularly
grateful for an authoritative teaching on the subject dispens-
ing them from forming their own convictions.

On the other hand, many cherished positions held by
"traditional" theology and ecclesiastical authority have been
challenged in the last few years. It is perhaps for this reason
that recently more theologians have dared to reflect on the
Christian meaning of sexuality. Theologians have not simply sought new arguments to defend the official position;
they have taken a fresh look at the subject in the context
of man's total life and begun to question a number of
principles which had been taken for granted for some time.
Because of the obedience due to the teachings of the Holy
See, priests have been unable to publish their studies on
this matter. But priests among themselves talk about it a
great deal. In connection with the Second Vatican Council
and lectures on ecumenical subjects, I have done much
traveling during these last few years in North America and
Europe, and wherever I went, at every college and at every
gathering, I have always spoken to priests who seriously questioned the official position on contraception and were convinced that a deeper understanding of sexuality was required to be able to distinguish between sin and holiness in
this area.

Priests have always known how much misery is caused
in some families when husband and wife are unable to limit
the number of their children. They have been made more
aware of this in recent times when Christian men and
women have the courage to testify to their situation in

religious publications. There comes the point in the life of a priest theologian when the arguments given to prove the Church's official position no longer convinced him, and he lies awake at night in anguish because he is unable to speak out in public on a crucial moral issue according to the requirements of his own conscience. Why do we insist on the official position? Is it because we have grasped the meaning of sexual life and really understand what is natural in Christian marriage? Or is it because we think that this insistance is demanded by our loyalty to the ecclesiastical teachers of the past? The awful thought comes to mind that we may be pushing millions of people into conditions of misery just because we don't want to admit that we were wrong! Could a man be saved and live with Christ if he did this? The Catholic priest may reach a point where he must speak out to save his own integrity and be faithful to the conscience the Church has created in him.

Since the official position of the Catholic Church does not involve her infallibility and is therefore subject to re-examination by the ecclesiastical magisterium, the Catholic theologian must help the bishops in their re-examination of this question by stating, with honesty and courage, the conclusions of his own investigations. Normally such statements would not be submitted to the public. At the time of the council, however, when the whole Church is involved in a process of renewal and reform, the right moment has come to submit the dimensions of the problem to the public in order to invite discussion and further research.

The Gospel of Holiness

People sometimes have the impression that the new movements in the Catholic Church (liturgical, biblical, catechetical, etc.) try to make the Christian life "easier." These people regard the attempts of the Church to adapt her life to the exigencies of the modern world as a way of compromise, as a search for a soft and comfortable Gospel. Certain conservative spokesmen keep on voicing the suspicion that the driving force behind the new approaches is the desire to come to terms with the world. They complain that Catholics of this generation begin "to give in," that they are willing to modify strict doctrine and discipline to please the world, and that they do not take their religion as seriously as former generations.

These suspicions are not well founded. The movements of renewal in the Church are inspired by the desire to be more faithful to the Gospel of Jesus. This is obviously true of the liturgical and biblical movements. It is equally true of the renewal of moral theology. The concern of contemporary theologians is not how to find loopholes in the fabric of moral demands to get away with something one might desire but ought not to do; on the contrary they are trying to express the true moral imperative implied in the Gospel so that the Christian people may become more obedient to the will of the Father and hence more conformed to the image of Christ.

It would be quite unjust to attribute a desire for a lax Christianity to the theological schools fostering the renewal movements. At the same time it may well be that certain people who are tired of the Christian life, who never taste the sweetness of God and hence find the call to discipleship too frustrating, become enthusiastic about the renewal movements, speculating that a modernized, streamlined Christianity will be easier on them, less demanding, capable of coexistence with the spirit of the world. These people may well exist; but unless we have definite proof, we have no right to suspect that the enthusiasm of the faithful for the reform movements and the renewal of moral theology is the result of mediocrity or waning faith.

Catholic writers often misunderstand, and sometimes misjudge, Protestant theologians and moral philosophers in this fashion. If a Protestant writer is opposed to the natural law or, more generally, to any laws of universal validity, we often try to refute him, showing that he wishes to reduce man's moral responsibility and that his ideal of justice and holiness is lower than our own. But such a supposition may be quite groundless. We have no reason to suppose that a Protestant theologian reflecting and writing on the moral life has an ideal of holiness which is below that of the imitation of Jesus. The Protestant theologian too conceives of the Christian life as a way of obedience to the will of the Father. Such an author may well be wrong in his theological position, but in order to refute his doctrine we have no right to assume that his desire to follow Jesus is less than our own.

This observation may also be applied to the authors of this book. Because they disagree with the official position on contraception, do they therefore intend to advocate a moral ideal which is less than doing the will of the Father?

Some reviewers of this book wishing to defend the official position will perhaps boldly assert that here the spirit of the world is at work, that here ways are being justified allowing people to give in to their sexual drives, that here legal loopholes are being devised enabling men to create for themselves a comfortable exemption from the commandments of Christ. "Look at the world!" some writers will perhaps say in reply to this book. "See the sexual excesses to which men are going these days. You encourage all this, you justify sensuality, you destroy the basis of morality by undermining the law." Yet such arguments are groundless accusations. One must take for granted that responsible Christians reflecting on man's moral life are concerned with obedience to the Gospel. If the position taken by the writers of this book is to be refuted, the arguments must be taken from the objective order!

In this section I wish to discuss the meaning of the Gospel for sexual life in marriage. In the Gospel, God reveals himself as Father, as merciful Father, offering us forgiveness through the death and resurrection of his Son and making us new according to an ever growing likeness to Jesus crucified and risen. In this Gospel, which we encounter in the Church, we not only come to know who God is but also who we are. God tells us who we are. We learn that we are his children. We are told again and again, every Sunday at Mass, that we are sinners and that we are redeemed. Every time God speaks to us in the liturgy, in his word and sacrament, he calls us to be converted to him anew. He shows us where selfishness still dominates our lives, and he moves us that we turn to him with contrition and hope, to be forgiven, restored and healed—at least partially healed. This kind of conversion is a constant dimension of the Christian life.

This is what it means to say that the word of God at one and the same time accuses and pardons us, judges and restores us, condemns and heals us. "The word of God is living and active, sharper than any two-edged sword, piercing to the division of soul and spirit, of joints and marrow, and discerning the thoughts and intentions of the heart" (Heb 4:12). The word of God revealing to us what the eternal Father has done for us in Jesus Christ, teaches us the dimensions of our own failure and makes us realize that salvation is by faith in divine mercy. This turning to the Lord in faith is a way of salvation, since in it we find forgiveness of sins and enter upon new life. Faith is the beginning of healing. In faith we find a source of holiness and a way of obedience which was not open to us while unbelieving.

Sometimes certain priests acquainted with the biblical and catechetical movements complain that the aspect of sin and punishment is often avoided in modern teaching. "You only talk of love," they say, "you are silent about the judgment of God and the choice between heaven and hell." It is perhaps well to be reminded of this. Yet if contemporary Catholic teaching tends to center upon the Gospel of salvation, then it will not fail to declare that divine grace is also God's judgment on our sins. On the cross of Jesus both the love of God and the extent of our transgressions are revealed. We discover that God is our Father and loves us, precisely to the extent that he makes us aware of our sins, of our dependence on him and our

need for conversion. Quietism under any form is not biblical. Faith and obedience are never separated in the Scriptures. The kingdom of God is not for those who say yes to
the Son and resist the will of the Father, but for those who
listen to the word of God and act upon it. "Blessed are
those who hear the word of God and keep it" (Lk 11:28).

At the same time the judging and comforting action of
God's word as announced by the Church must not be
equated with the preaching of precepts or the imposition
of legal obligations. The Christian's call to holiness is not
founded upon any set of laws. It is not true to say that
God gives us a series of commandments, then waits whether
we shall observe them, and finally rewards or punishes us
in accordance with our achievements. The whole point of
the Gospel is that in one and the same redeeming gesture
God offers us the knowledge that we are sinners and the
gift of forgiveness and new life. God demands our obedience to his redeeming will and asks for our total dedication
to him in our lives, but he does so not by imposing upon
us a set of laws, be this the Mosaic law or any other code,
but by meeting us in the person of Jesus Christ crucified
and risen, whom the living Church, especially in her liturgy,
mediates to us. Christ is the truth, the way and the life: in
other words, Christ is our "law."

This emancipation from the law, taught in the New
Testament with special emphasis by St. Paul, does not
imply that the Christian is dispensed from observing the
content of holy laws and commandments. Laws and precepts will be useful to him as guides to know what is the
will of the Father. But laws and precepts might also make
him forget that his call as a Christian is to be a disciple of

Jesus and that this discipleship cannot be reduced to the observance of a series of precepts however well formulated. Morality for the Christian is constituted not by conformity to any law, but by conformity to the new life he has received.

The Gospel of Jesus is a dividing line passing through all the areas of human life, distinguishing our action, showing us the dimensions of heaven and hell. In the light of this Gospel we discover the sins in which we are involved, how we are still dominated by self-love, and where we collaborate with the cause of the devil. We come to realize the moral ambiguity in which we live and the mixture of our motives in doing good. However, the very same Gospel which accuses us also saves us from this ambiguity: not totally and completely, but really and truly. We believe that holiness is possible in this world. With Christ, as we meet him in so many ways in the Church, we are able to do the will of the Father. This we hold, especially after the controversies of the sixteenth century and the clarification of the Council of Trent. Grace transforms the heart of man.

The Gospel which draws a dividing line through all the areas of the life of the Christian will also draw this line through his sexual existence. There too, in sexuality, we find the ambiguity connatural to man (fallen man), from which Jesus willed to save us. Sexuality is not more than, but just as ambiguous as other areas of human existence. The Gospel contains a discerning and redeeming message on sexual love in married life.

In the Scriptures marriage is described as a lasting creative union between man and woman for the sake of fruitfulness, mutual love, and common service, so holy that it is regarded as an image and sacrament of God's free covenant with humanity. Sexuality is a power for the creation of a family in love. Sexuality is so deeply personal that two persons reveal themselves to one another in the act of love, and true communion, or family, becomes possible. Sexuality gives concrete expression to the mind and heart of two persons and hence renders possible the deep communication between man and woman by which the two accept one another and become one flesh, or one person, in the creation of a family.

The Church must announce this message. By formulating laws about what is allowed and what is not allowed between married people, the Church really intends to draw the line of the Gospel across man's sexual existence in marriage. These rules are for her the most efficient way of separating in man's married life the holy from the unholy, and hence of applying the Gospel to human life on this level. For this reason the Church attaches so much importance to these rules. She repels all attempts to weaken them, conscious that they are the means through which the Gospel is to be effective in the lives of Christians.

At the same time we may seriously ask ourselves if Catholic preaching has really announced the full demands of the Gospel in regard to sexuality. Have we clearly taught the permanent need of purifying the marriage act from self-seeking? Have we dared to declare that to seek sexual union without wishing to love one's partner in marriage is against the natural law of human life, and hence sinful? There is a tendency in our teaching, sometimes called legalistic, suggesting that provided husband and wife do not use certain specified instruments or abstain from certain specified actions, everything is permitted in marriage. We speak of "the marriage debt" which one partner owes to the other, as if the sexual act were a payment in fulfillment of a legal contract. Have we really tried to help Christians to face the demands of God's word in this area and to find the line drawn by the Gospel across their sexual existence in marriage?

The goodness of sexuality in marriage, as that of other human activities, cannot be taken for granted. It shares in the ambiguity of human life. Being so highly personal, the sexual life of a man may reveal his selfishness, his possessiveness, his egoism; or it may reveal his tenderness, his concern, his desire to give and to protect. Sexual life in marriage may be a wrestling between two egoists, each one seeking his own satisfaction, or it may be a school of self-giving, each one learning to think of and belong to the other. The unity created by sexual love may turn out to be a closed and padded room of pleasure, or it may open out upon a garden of fruitfulness and creativity. There are married couples whose sexual life leaves them as small, egoistical, calculating as they were, while others aspire to become more united through their love, more generous, more sensitive to the moods and feelings of their partner. Through their sexual love they become joyful as a family, courageous in facing life together, and ready to give warmth and love to their children. In order to fulfill the demands of the Gospel, married couples must continually purify their sexual love from self-seeking.

If we want to announce the meaning of the Gospel for the sexual life of married people, then we must courageously declare that the quest for sexual joy without love is sinful.

It simply will not do to say that if couples do not use certain instruments or refrain from certain actions that then everything is permitted. This is not the Christian message. A man may observe all these rules and yet reach out for his partner in the egoism of his heart. Though he follows the rules, a married person may yet regard his partner as an object to be used, rather than a person to be loved. Christian couples who seek to form their conscience by their life in the Church—by the celebration of the liturgy, listening to the word of God and sharing in the sacraments—will discover for themselves the dividing line of the Gospel cutting across their sexual existence.

Unmarried men (like priests) sometimes believe that sexuality is easy. They tend to think that sexual love in married life is natural and almost automatic—all one has to do is to get undressed—just as other bodily functions are almost automatic. However the story told by married people is quite different. Sexual love is difficult. It demands self-control, concern for another, waiting and helping, prolonged tenderness, searching to discover and respect the feelings of the other. There is a whole asceticism of the sexual life in marriage of which unmarried men (among whom I belong) know nothing at all. The dying to self is a requirement in every area of human life. There is no happy sexual love in married life without the pain of purification.

We now come to the special concern of this article. If married people who seek to live as Christians and try to be faithful to the demands of the Gospel, tell us that the dividing line which the Gospel cuts across their sexual existence does not always exclude the use of contraceptives, we must take their conviction very seriously. We have no right

immediately to reply that they have been misled into subjectivism. The Christian conscience, constantly formed
through Christ in the Church (through Scriptures, preaching, liturgy, sacramental life) is a sure guide to holiness.
There are some difficult situations where the decisions of
such a conscience formed through living contact with Christ
may be questionable, but on the whole we would have to
assert that a living Christian conscience in touch with
Christ's teaching will be led into a holiness which is *objective*. In other words, the obedience to Christian conscience
constantly formed does not only prevent us from sinning in
the subjective order; it is also the most certain guide to a
life conformed to the will of God (in the objective order)
as expressed in his creation and redemption. If we call
"natural law" the profound inclination of historical man
toward his fulfillment, then surely the Christian following
his living conscience will discover it.

Theology is of greatest importance to the life of the
Church. But we must clearly understand that theology does
not create what we believe: it simply reflects on it. In the
same way, moral theology does not create the Christian
life, but reflects on it. The Christian who follows the
Gospel will discover the will of the eternal Father thanks to
the "new life" he has received, in other words, thanks to a
connaturality with Jesus which "divine grace" produces in
him. His reason guided by faith must reflect on his decisions, constantly check them and sometimes discard
them (and here we have the place for theology), but his
reason guided by faith does not create the convictions in
the first place. This is a basic fact which we learn when
reading the account of holiness in the Scriptures, when

reflecting on the lives of saints and other great Christians, and when considering the curious fact that the great moral advance in human society (abolition of slavery, social reform, racial integration) have by no means been initiated by specialists in moral theology, but by men (Christian and non-Christian) with deep moral convictions who were able to discover the objective structure of God's creation by a connaturality the Lord had imprinted on their hearts.

If therefore Christian couples who wish to subject themselves to the Gospel and form their conscience daily from their life with Christ in the Church, tell us that the demands of holiness in married life do not always exclude the use of contraceptives, the theologian must reflect on their conviction very seriously, and unless he can prove, by a rational reflection guided by faith, that this conviction is wrong, against the order of God and nature, the presumption of truth is on the side of the married people.

Are our arguments that contraception is "intrinsically evil" and hence never, under no circumstances, permissible, really so conclusive? Or can we foresee a change in the official position of the Church?

Development of Doctrine

Can a Catholic reflect on the possibility that the official position on contraception is wrong and continue, as a Catholic, to hold that the Church is "the pillar and mainstay of the truth" (1 Tim 3:15) in the world? Can the Church be wrong? We firmly believe that the Catholic Church is the faithful people of Christ guided by his Spirit into all truth and that the universal magisterium of Catholic bishops teaching with the pope is the ultimate test for the meaning of God's word. At the same time one may envisage the possibility that in certain areas of teaching, areas not central to the Gospel, there occurs real growth of insight, so that the positions held by the Church in different ages are part of a gradual evolution. Behind this development of teaching there stands the perpetual intention of the Church to announce the unchanging Gospel for its time. In the area of moral teaching, in particular, the Church has tried to apply unchanging moral values in various ways, as best as was known at the time, to the varying conditions of each age.

The most obvious case which comes to mind here, is one to which I already referred above: in the last century the Holy See repeatedly condemned the idea that every man has the right to religious liberty. The Holy See regarded it as absurd and untrue to assert that a just constitution of a state should include a paragraph guaranteeing religious liberty to its citizens. Yet today we teach that according to the Gospel and to "natural law" a human person has the right to choose his religion according to the dictates of his conscience and be free to worship God with his fellow-believers.

Bishop de Smedt, reporting to the Second Vatican Council on the chapter on religious liberty, tried to find an explanation, in harmony with Catholic ecclesiology, for the apparent change of position that had taken place in this area. He suggested that the Church has always announced and defended the same unchanging value of human liberty. In the last century, according to the report of Bishop de Smedt, the ideal of religious liberty was proposed by men who had a rationalistic misconception of the jurisdictional omnipotence of the state and who regarded the individual conscience to be subject to no law or no divinely given norm. In this context the Church condemned religious liberty. In our own century, however, according to Bishop de Smedt's report, the ideal of religious liberty has been severed from the political context in which it arose, and it is for the sake of the same human freedom that the Catholic bishops are now ready to teach that religious liberty is a natural right of man. Bishop de Smedt said: "This doctrine must be understood as the contemporary terminus of a process of evolution both in the doctrine on the dignity of the human person and in the Church's pastoral solicitude for man's freedom" (*Council Speeches of Vatican II*, New York 1964, 245).

Bishop de Smedt showed that this doctrinal development is governed by two principles, a principle of continuity expressed in the abiding concern of the Church for human liberty, and a principle of progress expressed in the growing insight into the meaning of this value and the change of policy in its political application. According to the Belgian bishop, this progress took place because of a change in the structure of modern society and, more profoundly, because of a deeper understanding of who man is.

It seems to me that a similar evolution of doctrine has already taken place in the Church's attitude toward sexuality in married life! Theologians have been driven to a deeper reflection on what is really natural in man, partially because of the changed social conditions in which we live, and partially because of the growing concern with Christian anthropology. Who is man? Who are we? These are the

questions which, under various aspects, have been the preoccupation of Christian theologians and secular thinkers in
our generation. It is not surprising that this has led to a
change of outlook on one of the principle aspects of human
existence: sexual life in marriage.

I wish to indicate how the Catholic attitude toward sexuality in marriage has evolved in our generation in regard
to two distinct points.

First, the Church's teaching in the past regarded procreation as the primary end of marriage, yet never spelled
out in clear terms that the number of children in marriage
must be determined by a responsible choice on the part of
the parents. We created the impression, either expressly or
by our silence, that the number of children in a marriage is
simply a matter of divine providence. To be reminded of
this we only have to examine sermon books of a few
years ago. Responsible parenthood was a word which Catholics did not use. It was often suggested that the desire to
limit the number of children was due to a lack of faith
and trust in the Lord. We made people feel guilty because
they desired to limit their families.

This position has been abandoned. Not only certain
contemporary theologians but the ecclesiastical magisterium itself today is teaching the contrary position, namely
that the number of children in a marriage must be determined by an intelligent choice on the part of the parents.
Procreation, according to present Catholic teaching, is not
without, but within the sphere of personal responsibility.
We have begun to speak of responsible parenthood. We
teach now that the act of procreation is a fully human act:

man's personal responsibility is involved in the generation of a child.

What is the kind of reasoning which has led Catholic teachers to this new position? Since Catholics hold that the first end of marriage is procreation (a position which is difficult to prove) and that the *finis* determines the *form* of an institution, a change of outlook on human responsibility in procreation touches the very nature of married life.

Catholic theologians have become deeply aware of the fact that procreation in the human family is not something biological, but human. Human procreation is not just a matter of conception, pregnancy, and birth; it includes the longer and more difficult process of the children's education. Education in this context refers to the formation of that fundamental relationship between parents and children which is necessary for children to come to the use of reason and the free possession of their personalities. The home, in this spiritual sense, is the matrix of personhood. We are what we are through our dialogical relationship to others. We could never speak a single word without that. We would have no language, no emotional life, no deep thought, no meaning or purpose in life. Catholic theologians have come to see that the primary purpose of marriage (in terms of their hypothesis) is the procreation-and-education of children and that the obedience to this end must find expression in a total orientation of married life. Reflecting on a set of factors, psychological, economic, personal, etc., the parents must responsibly and generously decide for how many children their home can be the matrix of personhood. There are many situations where precisely in obedience to the primary end of marriage, husband and wife are morally obliged to prevent a new pregnancy.

What are in this "development of doctrine" (in the terms of Bishop de Smedt) the principles of continuity and of progress? The principle of continuity is the abiding concern of the Church for the fruitfulness of married life. Fruitfulness in some form belongs to the essence of marriage, and the Church proclaiming the Gospel of charity will always condemn the attempts of selfishness to curtail and damage this fruitfulness of marriage. The principle of progress, on the other hand, has to do with the deeper understanding of the very nature of married life. By reflecting on the care and concern required for the education of children, it became clearer to Catholic teachers that what they regarded as the primary end of marriage determined not a biological but a spiritual fact in married life. Marriage is a bond between two people capable of supplying the human context in which the children born to them may be joined to their parents in love. A proper notion of procreation demands that we understand marriage in terms of interpersonal relationship. Catholic theologians concluded that the morality of an act in married life cannot be evaluated by a standard lower than that of love.

Second, the second change in the traditional position of the Church occurred when the rhythm method of preventing conception was approved by the ecclesiastical magisterium. At first permission was granted for certain special cases, and it was often said that the approval of a confessor was required; but today it is generally taught that all couples who regard themselves entitled to it may utilize this method.

Why was this permission so remarkable? Before that time Catholic theologians had regarded the sexual act in married life to be justified and holy by its ordination to procreation. They had permitted married couples to have sexual intercourse even when they could not hope to have any children. But they did not conceive of any sexual activity in married life carried on with the positive intention of excluding conception. This was regarded as unnatural, against the very nature of the sexual act, and hence gravely sinful.

When the Catholic Church officially approved the rhythm method, it acknowledged for the first time that sexuality in married life was a value as such. Sexual love could be meaningful, good and holy without being directly related to the generation of a child. By permitting the rhythm method, the Catholic Church taught that it was licit and sometimes of obligation for Christian couples to seek the joy and mutual encouragement in sexual union while not desiring another child. This was new.

Despite this rapid evolution, the principle of continuity in this development is evident. It is the abiding concern of the Church to protect the fruitfulness of marriage and to prevent the exploitation of sex for selfish purposes. The principle of progress is verified in a deeper insight into the role of sexuality in married life. It was discovered, first of all, that the biology of human sex did not foresee the perpetual fertility of the woman. If parenthood is truly responsible, therefore, the question arose whether a couple who are morally obliged to prevent a new pregnancy should abstain from sexual intercourse or seek sexual union during the periods of the woman's temporary sterility. To answer this question, the moralists had to reflect on the role of sexuality in married life. Is it better to abstain from sexual activity as much as possible, or does sexual joy have a place in the marriage union between two people? This question could not be answered by an *a priori* consideration. The answer must be given, and was given, *a posteriori*, on the basis of the witness of married people who explained that sexual activity was a means of expressing their mutual love and a source of encouragement, making them into better fathers and mothers, enabling them to show more affection to their children, etc. The moralists listened to married people. They concluded that if a marriage is orientated toward fruitfulness, mutual love and selfless service, it is licit and good for married people to plan their sexual intercourse for the sake of love with the intention of preventing conception. In other words, in a well-ordered marriage sexuality in itself is a positive value.

Seeing this extraordinary doctrinal development in regard to sexuality in so short a time, we may wonder if this will not continue and eventually lead to a limited approval of contraception. Would it not be in harmony with the total development just described to expect that the ecclesiastical magisterium will eventually acknowledge that in a well-ordered marriage (i.e. a marriage orientated toward children, mutual love and selfless service) sexual love as such is a good and that therefore married couples may regulate conception by any means agreeable to the conscience of the two partners?

According to the present position of the Church, contraception is regarded as intrinsically evil and hence never permissible. This verdict was made for the first time in the last century, at a time when the ecclesiastical magisterium had not yet acknowledged responsible parenthood nor the positive value of sexuality in marriage as such. The arguments against the use of artificial contraception then belonged to a wider refutation, denying the need to limit the family conscientiously and opposing a tendency to justify sexuality by something intrinsic to itself beyond its ordination to the child. But after the official position changed on these two points, our arguments against contraception are no longer as good as they seemed to Catholic theologians of a previous generation. At that time, moreover, the common conscience of mankind agreed with the position of the Catholic Church. But today, after a development of moral thought in the Church and in other moral institutions (particularly other Christian Churches), the common conscience of those who seek to be guides of morality no longer confirms the official Catholic interpretation of "natural law" in this area.

No theologian will deny that the Catholic position on contraception is difficult to prove rationally from the natural inclination of man as understood by human reason. This becomes painfully evident when Catholics, be they theologians or ordinary intelligent laymen, try to explain (not defend) the Catholic position to their non-Catholic friends. As we produce our arguments we feel strangely uncomfortable. They sound unreal, theoretical, not based on the substance of life, but on a formula. We find ourselves bound to a technical vocabulary; we cannot explain in ordinary words, in our own words, why contraception should be intrinsically evil, for the simple reason that we have not really understood the position. This, alas, is a common experience of Catholics in dialogue with other men, Christian or non-Christian, who are concerned with moral issues. Can we then really be so sure that our position adequately formulates what is "natural" in family life?

Everyone agrees that contraceptive means can be a great danger to married life. It could encourage the tendency innate to fallen man to exploit love, to regard pleasure as the highest value in marriage, and to shirk the responsibility of growing in Christian selflessness. Contraception could lead to hedonism. But this is no reason for calling it "intrinsically evil." To call an act intrinsically evil is to make a judgment which means, in the practical order, that no situation can be imagined in which it would be good and licit to perform such an act. Dropping atomic bombs on large cities, for instance, is so dreadful an activity that we cannot think of it without shuddering, yet the Church has never called it intrinsically evil. No weapon of human destruction has ever been called this by the Church. (One might add here that many Catholics strongly hold that nuclear warfare is intrinsically evil and hence never permissible!) The question arises why the Church hesitates to make universal judgments when it comes to the conflicts between men and men in wars, exploitation, oppression, etc. and yet speaks in categorical terms about sexuality in married life. The presupposition on the part of Catholic theologians here is the idea that the individual human nature is more easily understood by human reason than man's social nature. Is this really true? Do we really understand what is "natural" in the human person?

A number of recently published essays by Catholic thinkers have raised grave objections to the customary arguments attempting to prove that contraception is intrinsically evil. These authors claim that the arguments which try to show that contraception is essentially different from the use of rhythm and that the former is against the very nature of the marriage act, either descend to the level of biology or move over into the area of esthetics, i.e. they leave the sphere of the specifically moral. In the first set of arguments, these authors claim, the official Catholic position is defended by stating that contraception frustrates the sexual act in its natural (i.e. biological) coherence and finality. We discover what this natural (i.e. biological) finality is from studying the nature of genital organs and hence may conclude that to use these organs and at the same time to frustrate the end which is connatural to them is an act of inner contradiction and hence intrinsically evil. The objection to this kind of reasoning is that sexuality is here regarded as a biological, and not a human reality. The authors mentioned above reject any attempt to measure the morality of a human act by the inner coherence of its biological structure.

According to the same authors, there is a second kind of argument proving that contraception is intrinsically evil and the use of rhythm permissible. It is derived from the esthetic consideration that the sexual act in marriage must always be a sign of perfect surrender and that the use of contraception, in contradistinction to the use of rhythm, prevents the sexual act from being such a sign. The use of mechanical or chemical means makes the marriage act a symbol of calculation and reserve, and hence creates an inner contradiction in it, considered as sign, and thus must be called intrinsically evil. The objection to this kind of

reasoning is that the sexual act is a *means* of total surrender in marriage in the context of the entire family responsibility, and that a consideration of the act as *sign* is
indeed meaningful but belongs to the sphere of esthetics
which, important in its own order, does not constitute morality. There is no reason, then, why the total surrender
between husband and wife, mindful of the complexity of
their moral obligations, may not be embodied in an act
which, in the order of signs, expresses this surrender im-
perfectly.

These grave objections urgently demand that we study
anew our traditional proofs that contraception is essentially
different from the rhythm method. A Catholic theologian
has recently suggested that, in fact, the use of contraceptives and the use of rhythm are strictly analogous. Both
practices seek to erect a barrier between the living sperm of
the male and the fertile egg of the female: the rhythm
method erects a barrier of time, contraception a barrier of
space between them.

These are strong arguments against the traditional proofs
that contraception is intrinsically evil. I find them convincing. If, therefore, Christian couples seeking to follow
the Gospel and constantly forming their conscience from
the eucharistic life of the Church, come to the conviction
that the demands of fruitfulness and love which the nature
of marriage makes on them, do not always exclude and
sometimes counsel the use of contraceptives, we have no
strong rational argument proving to them that they are
being misled into subjectivism. The presumption of truth
is on their side, since Christian conscience guided by Christ

in the Church leads into objective holiness. The burden of proof is on the side of the Church's official position.

The reader will have noticed that I have based my argument on the Christian conviction of married people aspiring to follow the Gospel. This method is theologically justified. Christian witness fulfills a prophetic function in the Church. Theologians and the ecclesiastical magisterium must take it very seriously.

If, following such witness, the official position of the Church were to change on this issue and admit that in a marriage which is orientated toward fruitfulness, mutual love and selfless service, the conception of children may be regulated by any means agreeable to the conscience of husband and wife, then—theologically speaking—the change would be less than the changes that have already taken place in this area: introducing the notion of responsible parenthood and acknowledging sexuality in a well-ordered marriage as a value in itself.

The principle of continuity in such a change of position would be the abiding concern of the Church that marriage be fruitful with children and always remain a school of selflessness and love. The principle of progress in such a change would be seen in the growing appreciation of the sexual act as a human value in a well-ordered marriage, the morality of which is not determined by the biological coherence of its performance, but by its meaning in terms of interpersonal relationship between husband, wife and the existing children.

Conclusion

The present position of the Catholic Church on birth control does not involve her infallibility. Because of the emergence of new insights into human nature and new facts in man's social life, the question should be re-examined. The first and most important inquiry is to seek out the Christian witness of married people. They must tell us what the demands of the Gospel are for their sexual life in marriage. Examining their witness theologically, the theologian must take account of the ecclesiological fact that large numbers of Catholics are no longer convinced by the old arguments used to prove that contraception is intrinsically evil. If the magisterium were to change its position and teach that contraception, while dangerous and not generally commendable, is not *intrinsically* evil and hence permissible on certain occasions, this would be in harmony with a general development of doctrine that has *already* taken place in the Church. The Catholic Church would then continue to proclaim the unchanging value of fruitfulness and selfless love in marriage, but favor an application of this value in a way which leaves more room for human planning. Changing her position on birth control, the Catholic Church would not be unfaithful to her own self-understanding.

Notes on Contributors

E. R. Baltazar, Assistant Professor of Philosophy at the University of Dayton, received his theological training at Woodstock College, and his doctorate in philosophy from Georgetown University.

Gregory Baum O.S.A., Consultant to the Secretariat for Promoting Christian Unity and author of a number of studies on inter-church relations, is editor of *The Ecumenist*.

Kieran Conley O.S.B. received his doctorate from the University of Fribourg, and is presently Professor of Dogmatic Theology at St. Meinrad Seminary.

William V. D'Antonio has a doctorate in sociology and anthropology from Michigan State University, and is presently Associate Professor of Sociology at Notre Dame University.

Elizabeth A. Daugherty, a graduate of Mills College, was formerly with the Division of Biological Research, Alaska Department of Fish and Game, and had previously been engaged in research in micro-paleontology.

Leslie Dewart, Associate Professor of Philosophy at St. Michael's College, Toronto, is the author of *Christianity and Revolution: The Lesson of Cuba*.

Stanley Kutz C.S.B., Professor of Moral Theology at St.

Michael's College, Toronto, received his doctorate in theology from the University of Munich.

Justus George Lawler, Professor of the Humanities in the St. Xavier College, Chicago, is editor of *Continuum.*

Julian Pleasants, Research Associate in the Lobund Laboratory of Notre Dame University, has graduate degrees in theology and chemistry.

Most Rev. Thomas D. Roberts S.J., former Archbishop of Bombay, has lectured widely in the United States and England on the questions of nuclear war and contraception.

Rosemary Ruether has a doctorate in classics and Christian archeology from the Claremont Graduate School; she is currently preparing for publication a work on St. Gregory Nazianzus.